GLOBAL ETHICS AND CIVIL SOCIETY

Ethics and Global Politics

Series Editors: Tom Lansford and Patrick Hayden

Since the end of the Cold War, explorations of ethical considerations within global politics and on the development of foreign policy have assumed a growing importance in the fields of politics and international studies. New theories, policies, institutions, and actors are called for to address difficult normative questions arising from the conduct of international affairs in a rapidly changing world. This series provides an exciting new forum for creative research that engages both the theory and practice of contemporary world politics, in light of the challenges and dilemmas of the evolving international order.

Also in the series

Cosmopolitan Global Politics
Patrick Hayden
ISBN 0 7546 4276 3

Understanding Human Rights Violations
New Systematic Studies
Edited by Sabine C. Carey and Steven C. Poe
ISBN 0 7546 4026 4

International Environmental Justice
A North-South Dimension
Ruchi Anand
ISBN 0 7546 3824 3

Global Ethics and Civil Society

Edited by
JOHN EADE
Roehampton University
DARREN O'BYRNE
Roehampton University

ASHGATE

Published by
Ashgate Publishing Limited
Gower House
Croft Road
Aldershot
Hampshire GU11 3HR
England

Ashgate Publishing Company
Suite 420
101 Cherry Street
Burlington, VT 05401-4405
USA

Ashgate website: http://www.ashgate.com

British Library Cataloguing in Publication Data
Global ethics and civil society. - (Ethics and global
    politics)
    1.Civil society 2.Ethics 3.Globalization
    I.Eade, John, 1946- II.O'Byrne, Darren J.
    170

QM LIBRARY
(MILE END)

Library of Congress Cataloging-in-Publication Data
Global ethics and civil society / [edited] by John Eade and Darren O'Byrne.
        p. cm. -- (Ethics and global politics)
    Includes index.
    ISBN 0-7546-4214-3
    1. Civil society. 2. Ethics. 3. Globalization. I. Eade, John, 1946- II. O'Byrne,
Darren J. III. Series.

    JC337.G557 2004
    170--dc22

                                                                        2004025167

ISBN 0 7546 4214 3

Printed and bound in Great Britain by MPG Books Ltd, Bodmin, Cornwall

Contents

List of Contributors

Nigel Dower is Honorary Senior Lecturer in Philosophy, University of Aberdeen, with a continuing interest in teaching and research in cosmopolitan issues. His publications include *World Poverty: Challenge and Response* (1983), *World Ethics: The New Agenda* (1998) and *An Introduction to Global Citizenship* (2003).

John Eade is Professor of Sociology and Anthropology at Roehampton University and Executive Director of the Centre for Research on Nationalism, Ethnicity and Multiculturalism. His main interests are globalisation, urban ethnicity and pilgrimage. His recent publications include the single authored *Placing London* (2000) and the co-edited volumes *Understanding the City* (2002) and *Reframing Pilgrimage* (2004).

Luigi Esposito is Assistant Professor of Sociology at Barry University, Miami Shores, Florida. His main areas of interest are sociological theory, race relations, and globalization. His work has appeared in various professional journals.

Paul Kennedy is Reader in Sociology and Global Studies at Manchester Metropolitan University. His current research interests are transnational professionals and social networks, the socio-cultural foundations of the global economy and the making of an emergent global society. His recent publications include the co-authored volumes *Global Sociology* (2000), *Globalization and National Identities* (2001) and *Communities Across Borders* (2002).

Ray Kiely is Senior Lecturer in Development Studies at the School of Oriental and African Studies. Books include *Sociology and Development: The Impasse and Beyond* (1995) and *Industrialisation and Development: A Comparative Analysis* (1998). He is currently completing a book on 'The Clash of Globalizations'.

Douglas Lewis is Director of the Centre for Socio-Legal Studies and Professor of Law at Sheffield University. He is also a qualified barrister and one of the country's leading public lawyers. He has vast experience of funded and theoretical research over many aspects of public law, including the effect of corporatism, the use of Ombudsmen and human rights. He is the sole or joint author of many leading books, including *The Noble Lie* and, more recently, *Choice and the Legal Order: Rising Above Politics*. His current research is in the field of Law and Globalization.

Sorcha MacLeod is a Lecturer in Law within the Faculty of Law at the University of Sheffield. She teaches, researches and writes in the fields of human rights, public international law, globalization and public law. Her current research primarily relates to the regulation of transnational corporations. She holds an LLM in International Natural Resources Law from the University of Dundee and is currently completing a PhD at the University of Glasgow on the regulation of transnational corporations in international law. Publications include 'Maria Aguinda v. Texaco Inc.: Defining Liability for Human Rights Violations Resulting from Environmental Degradation', *Contemporary Issues in Law* 4, pp. 188-209.

Raffaele Marchetti is CNR scholar at the Department of Philosophical and Epistemological Studies, Università La Sapienza, Rome, and a Ph.D. student and part-time teacher at the LSE's Department of Government. His current research concerns international justice, particularly cosmopolitanism, citizenship and migration. In 1998 he was a Socrates visiting student at the University of Nottingham, and in 2002 a Research Fellow at the Centre for the Study of Human Rights-CERSDU, LUISS University, Rome.

John W. Murphy is Professor of Sociology at the University of Miami. His areas of specialization are sociological theory and social philosophy. For the past few years he has been writing on topics related to globalization, particularly in Latin America. His most recent book (with Manuel Caro) is *The World of Quantum Culture* (2002).

Kate Nash is Senior Lecturer in Sociology at Goldsmiths College, University of London. She is the author of *Contemporary Political Sociology: Globalization, Politics and Power* (2000) and *Universal Difference: Feminism and the Liberal Undecidability of 'Women'* (Macmillan 1998) and co-editor of *The Blackwell Companion to Political Sociology* (2001).

Darren J. O'Byrne is Senior Lecturer in Sociology and Human Rights at Roehampton University, where he teaches human rights, globalization and social theory. He is the author of *Human Rights: An Introduction* (2002) and *The Dimensions of Global Citizenship* (2003). He is also Chair of the Global Studies Association and was responsible for convening the 2002 conference from which this volume derives.

Bhikhu Parekh is Emeritus Professor of Political Theory at the University of Hull and a member of the House of Lords. He was Deputy Chairman of the Commission for Racial Equality in the United Kingdom, 1985-90 and chaired the Runnymede Trust's report on multiculturalism in Britain. He was Vice-Chancellor, University of Baroda, India, 1981-84 and Visiting Professor at several North American Universities, including Harvard. He is the author of several acclaimed books in political philosophy and on India. His recent publications include *Rethinking Multiculturalism* (2000) and *Gandhi: A Very Short Introduction* (2001).

Lisa Whitehouse is a Senior Lecturer in Law at the University of Hull. Her research interests include corporate social responsibility, globalization and regulation. She has recently completed a comparative study of corporate social responsibility in the UK and the US. Publications arising from that project include 'Railtrack is Dead – Long Live Network Rail? Nationalization under the Third Way', *Journal of Law and Society* **30**, pp. 217-35 (2003), 'Network Rail: A Missed Opportunity?', Web Journal of Current Legal Issues (http://webjcli.ncl.ac.uk) (2003), 'Corporate Social Responsibility as Citizenship and Compliance: Initiatives on the Domestic, European and Global Level', *Journal of Corporate Citizenship* **11**, pp. 85-98 (2003) and 'The Company as Property – Implications for the Regulation of Corporate Behaviour' in A. Hudson (ed.), *New Perspectives on Property Law: Obligations and Restitution* (2004).

Heather Widdows is a Lecturer at the Centre for the Study of Global Ethics at the University of Birmingham. Her background is Systematic Theology, Moral Philosophy and Bioethics. Her current research focuses are the nature and status of moral value, communication across value frameworks and belief-systems and practical ethical issues (particularly bioethical issues) in the global context. Her recent publications include the single authored book, *The Moral Vision of Iris Murdoch: A New Ethics?* (forthcoming) and 'Disparities in Parenting Criteria: An Exploration of the Issues, focusing on Adoption and Embryo Donation' (with Fiona McCallum) in *Journal of Medical Ethics* **28**, pp. 139-42 (2002).

Chapter 1

Globalization, Cosmopolitanism and the Problem of Civil Society: Some Introductory Remarks

Darren J. O'Byrne

The Global Civil Society Debate

At present, the concept of global civil society is very much in vogue. For many commentators – academics and activists alike – it provides a framework within which to locate a diverse range of contemporary public concerns, from the much publicized 'anti-globalization' (or more accurately, 'anti-capitalism') protests, through the worldwide expressions of concern over American and British involvement in Afghanistan and Iraq, to on-going political and ideological struggles in the areas of human rights, the environment, development, labour standards, anti-racism and anti-sexism. The idea of global civil society is thus presented as an alternative to the three apparently unsatisfactory frameworks for understanding the global condition – namely, the *global marketplace* model which celebrates unregulated capitalist expansion in a borderless world; the *nation-state* model which accepts that it is the duty of the militarily and economically powerful states to oversee world affairs; and the *world federal* model which demands more centralized political administration at the supranational level.

In recent years, there has been no shortage of academic literature outlining the structures of this emerging global civil society. Possibly the leading theorist working within this tradition is Richard Falk. In a series of important publications, Falk and his colleagues have sketched out a defence of what they call 'globalization-from-below', which emerges from the struggles of grass roots movements and the concerns and actions of 'global citizens' (Falk, 1999, 2000a, 2000b, see also Brecher, Brown Childs and Cutler, 1993; Brecher, Costello and Smith, 2000). Falk's work belongs to a 'cosmopolitan' tradition which has its roots in Kant's famous essay on perpetual peace (for a slightly different version of cosmopolitanism, see Archibugi and Held, 1995).

The contributors to this volume are by no means unsympathetic to the writings or the intentions of Falk, or of the cosmopolitan tradition in general. The purpose of this volume is not to provide an ideologically cohesive critique of cosmopolitan thinking. Rather, it is to advance those debates *from within*, by drawing on ideas and literature outside the cosmopolitan tradition in order to highlight and overcome some of its weaknesses. Three general weaknesses can be summarized here:

1. The cosmopolitan tradition tends to rely on an overly simplistic, polarized view of the world, reducible to a few dichotomies ('cosmopolitanism *versus* the nation state' or 'global civil society *versus* global capitalism').
2. The cosmopolitan tradition accepts rather too quickly and uncritically the role of new social movements (and more recently, the global anti-capitalist movement) as the agents responsible for building the new civil society.
3. The cosmopolitan tradition reifies concepts such as capitalism, and thus fails to provide a critical analysis of the structures and dynamics of these concepts, and ignores the important distinction between *institutions* and *logics*.

Concerned that such weaknesses in cosmopolitan theory might also weaken the noble wider project undertaken by cosmopolitans in practice, we seek in this volume to extend the cosmopolitan perspective by introducing into it a range of diverse theoretical tools, which can provide a clearer understanding of global processes. To this end, we draw on such unlikely but useful concepts as sentiment, embodiment, consequentialism, friendship and many others.

In order to develop an academic understanding of global civil society as it is defined here, and thus to develop a sympathetic critique and expansion of the cosmopolitan tradition, we want to ask two distinct but inter-related questions:

1. *How is such a society constituted?* Clearly, the idea of global civil society evolves largely from the Kantian concern with 'cosmopolitanism'. However, located as it is within the ethical sphere, it cannot and should not refer solely to a global political community administered via a 'world-state' (by which one could mean either a futuristic 'world government' or, in a more moderate sense, a re-empowered United Nations). The separation of ethical and political dimensions remains at the heart of this project. It is important, then, to provide a clear theoretical framework within which to understand the emerging global civil society.
2. *What are its dynamics?* In particular, who are the agents operating within the global civil society, and what form does their agency take? Global civil society is a broader category than global citizenship, and while such citizens clearly do operate as agents within the civil society, so, surely, do corporations, networks and social movements.

Each of the contributors to this volume addresses one of these questions. The earlier chapters deal with the constitution of global civil society, the later ones with its dynamics. Before we turn to the various contributions in more detail, we need to explore two frequently used but by no means uncontested concepts, which are central to the themes in this book, namely, *civil society* and *globalization*.

The Problem of Civil Society

Jeffrey Alexander, the American sociologist, has defined 'civil society' as 'the realm of interaction, institutions, and solidarity that sustains the public life of societies outside the worlds of economy and state' (1993: 797; see also Alexander, 1998; Cohen, 1995). Note that, for Alexander, civil society exists *outside* both the market and the state. The complexities surrounding the definition of civil society are most evident in the contributions of its greatest theorist, Hegel, for whom civil society was alternately the realm of social and individual relations mediating between the private realm and the political society (the state), or a realm either synonymous or dialectically related to the state as the ultimate suppression of pre-state ('natural') society (Bobbio, 1979). In fact, Alexander is the latest in a line of social theorists, who have undertaken the task of providing a clear and distinct definition of civil society. In another recent publication, a field of distinguished scholars sought to grapple with this problem, and typically reached no consensus (Walzer, 1995a). As the editor bluntly states in his introduction to that volume, there is considerable disagreement over the meaning of civil society, and it sits in a peculiar position *vis-à-vis* the state, the market, and the nation (Walzer, 1995b: 1).

The common interpretation of Hegel's theory of civil society is that he saw it as containing not just economic relations but also legal and juridical ones: in other words, the public institutions through which the state manifests itself to private individuals. This tendency to equate civil society with the economy influenced the young Marx; needless to say. As Marx further refined his base-superstructure model, this became a source of tension in his writings, in so far as it became problematic to equate the entirety of civil society with the economic base. This tension reached its pinnacle in later Marxist thought in Gramsci's writings, where the celebrated Italian revolutionary clearly relocated the realm of civil society from the base to the superstructure (Bobbio, 1979). Civil society is, for Gramsci, 'the political and cultural hegemony of a social group on the whole of society, as ethical content of the State' (Gramsci, 1966: 164, cited in Bobbio, 1979: 31).

That civil society stands in opposition to the market is largely uncontested by most contemporary scholars (although see Kai Nielsen's contribution, which in orthodox Hegelian fashion posits civil society between the state and the private domain, thus incorporating the economy within its boundaries {Nielsen, 1995}). To separate civil society from the state is a more controversial proposition, at least in so far as the state is traditionally viewed as the site of all *political* action. Surely, if the concept of civil society is to have any currency at all, it must involve a politics of sorts (Cohen, 1995) – a politics which is both ethical and democratic, and which is grounded in identities and differences without being hampered by postmodern relativism. Thus, to best understand the concept of civil society, one should first seek to understand the complex and contested concept of *ethics*. In this volume, the chapters by Parekh, Esposito and Murphy, and Widdows, all contain useful summaries of the major historical contributors to the philosophy of ethics.

Of course, the assertion that political action is not confined to the realm of the state is hardly new, and has been made most forcefully by Foucault. The state is the institutionalization of political action, the agency responsible for administering the centralized means of violence. The relocation of political action away from the individual consciousness and into the hands of the state machinery exemplifies the increasing dominance of systemic forces which, according to Habermas, has been a core characteristic of modernity.

Civil society, then, can be understood as the space in which political action takes place *outside* the formal, institutionalized structures of the state; the residue of political action left within the consciousness, the *lifeworld*, untainted by the colonizing, systemic machinery of administration and governmentality. Furthermore, it is an inherently *ethical* space – a claim consistent with the classical formulations of civil society provided by Hegel and Gramsci. It serves to provide the necessary checks and balances on the powers of the state and its institutions. As an example of the relationship between civil society (in the sense advocated here) and the state, consider the idea of human rights. This idea was invented to serve as an ethical framework within which to condemn the atrocities committed against individuals and groups; that is, a *legitimation* of that condemnation. Thus, to reduce human rights to a purely legal positivist framework – rights are whatever the law says they are – is to deny their purpose (Freeman, 2002: 10). If the institutionalization of rights occurs when they are embedded in positive law, the law still remains a state institution, and it is the state which, more often than not, commits these atrocities, often utilizing its institutions, including the law, for this purpose. Where, then, is the condemnation of such atrocities legitimized? Not within the law, for sure, but within an ethics which exist outside of the formal institutional system, in the realm of the lifeworld, where the discourse on human rights still resides, regardless of its formalization within the legal framework. Civil society thus serves to connect the political sphere to the realm of public opinion and, in doing so, acts as an important check on government activity (Cohen, 1995; Nielsen, 1995).

If civil society represents the possibility for de-colonized, emancipatory political action, is it not reasonable to assume that it also represents the possibility for economic action free from the dictates of the capitalist market economy? After all, the concern for contemporary critical theorists is not that the political and economic realms are necessarily oppressive, but that the logic which drives them – an instrumental, purposive-rationality – *is* restrictive to human freedom. If a trace of civil society remains within the economic sphere, perhaps it can be found in economies held together not by the desire for profit for profit's sake, but by networks of friendship and trust, or in transnational corporations exhibiting corporate social responsibility, topics covered in this volume.

Civil society, then, reflects the politicized core of the lifeworld, sustained through social interaction and through a normative engagement with values, which generates the struggle within the personality for emancipation. It is related to, but broader than, the concept of citizenship. Indeed, as Walzer (1995b) points out, the concept of civil society, unlike that of citizenship, allows us to understand better the complex ways in which actors are involved in participatory decision-making through associational networks of interest groups, social movements, cultural allegiances, and so on. Citizens might ideally act out their political and ethical commitments within the realm of civil society, but so might (and do) social movements, networks, and even corporations. The contributors to this volume share many of the concerns of, and ask similar questions to, communitarians such as Walzer and neofunctionalists such as Alexander. However, they seek to answer them equipped with a commitment to a new democratic politics, which has, in social theory at least, manifested itself in two distinct but related forms: the 'radical democracy' of Laclau and Mouffe (1985), with its roots in Foucauldian discourse theory, and the Habermasian-inspired projects of 'discursive' or 'reasonable' democracy (Chambers, 1996; Dryzek, 1990).

The Challenge of Globalization

The classical positions on civil society – Hegel, Marx and Gramsci – were clearly formulated within the paradigm of the nation-state. The task of this volume is to explore the impact of processes, which have commonly come to be called 'globalization', upon this concept of an ethical civil society. Contributors discuss a variety of different actors in what we can loosely, but not without controversy, call the 'global civil society', and a diverse range of forms which participation in this sphere can take.

In fact, the possibility of global civil society is implicitly presupposed in the major work on globalization by Roland Robertson, possibly the foremost scholar in the field. In outlining four images of world order, Robertson presents us with at least two that correspond with some image of global civil society: a cultural-ethical image of world order which he calls *global gemeinschaft 2*, and an image of world order as a network of socio-cultural and economic exchange relations which he calls *global gesellschaft 1* (Robertson, 1992: 78-79). Other writers are more explicit in their advocacy of global civil society based on human rights and a 'cosmopolitan' democracy (Archibugi and Held, 1995; Falk, 1999), or on the active realization of 'global citizenship' (O'Byrne, 2003). Falk – whose contributions to this debate have already been summarized and are subjected to more detailed critical examination in this volume by Kiely – makes his position clear when he defines global civil society as 'the field of action and thought occupied by individual and collective citizen initiatives of a voluntary, non-profit character both within states and transnationally' (Falk, 2000a: 163). Even contributors more sceptical towards the possibility of global restructuring on political and ethical grounds concede that the *ideal* of global civil society is important. As Sklair (2002: 45) points out, 'now that humankind is vulnerable to destruction through nuclear and toxic catastrophes, a democratic and just human society on the global level, however utopian, seems to be the best long-term guarantee of the continued survival of humanity'.

The discourse on globalization is as complex and contested as that on civil society, particularly in those cases where it throws up peculiar intellectual alliances which transcend traditional ideological divides. For example, Robertson's historical and non-Marxist account of globalization, which suggests that, despite recent changes in form and intensity, the process is largely a continuation of a much more long-term transformation, shares a number of similarities with Hirst and Thompson's robust refusal to concede that globalization is anything other than the continuation of the long-term project of capitalist internationalism, which purports to be more sympathetic to traditional left-wing ideology (Robertson, 1992; Hirst and Thompson, 1996). Arguing from a neo-Marxist (indeed, Gramscian) perspective, Leslie Sklair maintains that globalization signals a new phase in capitalism (and at the same time for alternatives to capitalism), a position not overly dissimilar to that of neo-liberals such as Ohmae (1990).

It needs pointing out that the contributors to this volume are not seeking to engage directly with the theoretical literature on globalization, nor is this volume intended to serve as a contribution to globalization theory. At this theoretical level, where the meaning, nature and constitution of 'globalization' is discussed, three dominant approaches can be outlined. The first, which is associated primarily with Robertson (1992), sees globalization as a long-term historical process which runs concurrently with modernity and modernization. Opposing this is the belief that globalization signals less of a process than a disjuncture, which disrupts the flow of modernity, either signalling its demise or transforming it radically. An extreme version of this approach is Albrow's 'global age hypothesis' (Albrow, 1996). A third approach, favoured by many contributors to this volume, looks instead at the multiple possible applications of globalization, and contrasts a dominant, 'top down' model (usually synonymous with global capitalism) with an alternative 'bottom up' model in which individuals, NGOs and even corporations are seen as actors involved in bringing about global change, and thus as agents in the creation of alternative globalizations. Such an approach, as has already been outlined in this Introduction, is primarily associated with Falk (2000b; see also Falk, 1999, 2000a; Brecher, Brown Childs and Cutler, 1993; Sklair, 2002; O'Byrne, 2003). This third paradigm is favoured here because the argument made throughout this volume – in the empirical as well as theoretical chapters – defends the vitality of such actors, and advocates global civil society as an ethical sphere which stands in opposition to the marketplace as the arena in which processes of globalization are administered.

Theorizing Global Ethics and Civil Society

The volume opens with a contribution from Bhikhu Parekh which sets the scene for subsequent chapters. Parekh has enjoyed a distinguished career as a political theorist and as the Acting Chair of the UK Commission for Racial Equality. The report he chaired – *The Future of Multi-Ethnic Britain* (2000b) – was a well-publicized, if largely unsuccessful attempt to challenge complacent views about British toleration of difference. In this paper he develops his approach to multiculturalism as set out in *Rethinking Multiculturalism: Cultural Diversity and Political Theory* (2000a) in the context of globalization and the possibilities for a global civil society.

His approach places at centre stage the dialectical interplay between shared humanity and its cultural mediation. Cultural diversity is given a positive value and a multicultural society has to be politically structured around the concept of collective rights *and* a shared multi-culture to which all citizens contribute. Equality in such a society would be based on equality of difference, equal treatment and a contextualized view of equality which prevents discrimination. As he states in *Rethinking Multiculturalism:*

> When we take legitimate cultural differences into account, as we should, equal treatment is likely to involve different or differential treatment, raising the question as to how we can ensure that the latter does not amount to discrimination or privilege. There is no easy answer to this. As a general rule it would seem that different treatments of individuals or groups are equal if they represent different ways of realizing the same right, opportunity or in whatever other respect they are intended to be treated equally, and if as a result none of the participants is better-off or worse-off. (2000a: 261)

Parekh begins with questions about the nature of ethics and civil society and applies his thinking to the problem of globalization. He questions the usefulness of those frameworks most frequently used in the development of a global ethics: Kant's universalisability thesis, Rawls's 'veil of ignorance', Habermas's 'ideal speech situation', and arguments from theology associated with Hans Küng and others. A global ethic, he contends, can only be arrived at by means of a dialogue within and between societies. Such a dialogue has, in fact, been taking place throughout the second half of the Twentieth Century, and has provided us with a general set of principles which make up international law. There is, he argues, a current consensus – comprised of 'respect for human dignity, equal human worth, civil and political liberties, democratic freedoms, the rights to life, personal autonomy and collective self-determination and so on' – which should serve as the foundation for a global ethic, but this consensus remains flawed, limited and incomplete, and a more fully developed global ethic must build on this.

In her chapter, Kate Nash also attempts to engage with the theoretical models, which have been proposed to serve as frameworks for the emerging global civil society. Nash is committed to moving beyond certain false dichotomies, which stifle any deep intellectual engagement with globalising transformations. In particular, Nash is concerned with differing interpretations of cosmopolitanism. While the dominant interpretation remains the rationalist neo-Kantian one, Nash proposes instead a 'popular cosmopolitanism' based on *sentiments*. The neo-Kantian view, Nash argues, is based on an overly simple dichotomy: cosmopolitanism, which is rational and 'cool', is placed in direct opposition to nationalism, which is emotional and 'hot'. Such a dichotomy, claims Nash, tends to reify nationalism and idealize cosmopolitanism, and ultimately misunderstands the dynamics involved in both. Indeed, the apparent absence of a recognition of emotion in the literature on cosmopolitanism can be attributed to its origins within the liberal-democratic framework of human rights rather than the communitarian framework of political community – there can be no cosmopolitan political community because, quite clearly, there is no global state. So, the question posed by Nash is: 'In the absence of a global state … how might a cosmopolitan community be imagined that could compete with nationalist particularisms?' To answer this, she turns to the concept of human rights. 'For human rights to be democratic', she states, 'it is necessary that members of national political communities learn to think and feel beyond the limits of national interests, otherwise governments will continue to address voters on this basis and the gross inequalities of the New World (Dis)Order will remain, both within national borders and beyond'. Thus, echoing a point made earlier in this Introduction, the concept of human rights has to exist within a cosmopolitan political community not reducible to the institutions of particular nation-states. She quotes Habermas (2001: 112): '(T)he crucial question is whether, in the civil societies and political public spheres of increasingly inter-connected regimes ... a cosmopolitan consciousness – the consciousness of a compulsory cosmopolitan solidarity, so to speak – will arise.'

Nash's answer is drawn from the sociology of emotions. She adopts a social constructionist approach to nationalistic sentiment which, rather than locate nationalism and cosmopolitanism as polar opposites, presupposes the possibility of the latter in the former, and allows for the 'conversion' from nationalism to 'popular cosmopolitanism'. For example, while sentiments expressed by Americans following the World Trade Center attacks on September 11th 2001 certainly reflected a sense of nationalism (always heightened during times of war or national tragedy), it was a nationalism deeply rooted in humanism – a kind of collective grief – which need not and, in fact, did not exclude a more cosmopolitan sense of solidarity. Nash thus identifies a different form of cosmopolitanism, which, while clearly linked to the Western project of extending 'human rights' through force, nonetheless provides a useful alternative to the rational, altruistic cosmopolitanism of Kant, and perhaps provides the basis for an understanding of global civil society as an ethical sphere without the extension of the machinery of political administration on a global scale.

Like Nash, Esposito and Murphy take issue with overly rationalistic versions of cosmopolitanism. The 'rational' New World Order, they point out, promotes on the one hand a myth of progress and, on the other, the perpetuation of global inequality. Why might this be? The popular answer, they claim, is that the world order is devoid of an appropriate global ethic. To fully understand what this might mean, they proceed to investigate the concept of ethics as it has been used in Western philosophy. This history has been dominated by two competing interpretations of ethics: on the one hand, conformity to some objective universal truth, be it God or 'natural law', and on the other, passive obedience to 'moral instincts'. 'As a result', they conclude, 'morality becomes disassociated easily from social conditions and human concerns and transformed into a fetish that may promote oppression, extreme inequality, and exclusion.' This is further perpetuated by the logic of global capitalism, in which 'a moral order is one where people are allowed to exercise their innate (and rational) desire for pleasure/profit without facing external restraints'. In the logic of the market, human life is commodified, divorced from ethical principles and from real social conditions.

What is to be done about this? One solution, argue Esposito and Murphy, is, following Hans Küng (1991), to develop a new global ethic grounded on inter-cultural dialogue and dedicated to tolerance and understanding. But the constitution of such an ethic would itself be contentious, because there is no clear consensus on crucial ethical issues. 'As a result', they warn, 'an ethics based on consensus runs the risk of constraining dialogue in such a way that subverts cultural or social differences.' Instead, Esposito and Murphy turn to Karl Marx, Emmanuel Levinas, Alejandro Serrano and liberation philosophy to construct an 'embodied' ethic, which is dynamic and historical, and based on interaction and intersubjectivity.

Nash locates the source of the cosmopolitan ethic in sentiment, Esposito and Murphy in embodiment. The two approaches are not incompatible – Bryan Turner has provided a sociological theory of human rights based on sympathy and embodiment (Turner, 1993). In seeking to develop an ethical theory of international relations, Marchetti defends an alternative perspective, which prioritizes instead the individual need for self-fulfilment. Rejecting Kantian deontological ethics (and other rights-based approaches), he turns instead to impartial consequentialism, with its roots in utilitarian philosophy, to provide a basis for cosmopolitan ethics. The ultimate goal of a cosmopolitan ethics must be, he argues, the maximization of the world's welfare, which can also be treated as the ultimate utilitarian rule. Consequentialist cosmopolitanism, according to Marchetti, consists of three special features: pluralism, multilevel dimensionality, and moral agency, each of which makes it preferable to right-based approaches with their universalistic, normative biases. Marchetti summarizes his own argument as follows. First, the well-being of human beings is synonymous with the moral good, so 'the best moral code ... would produce the best consequences in terms of the world welfare conditions. Since the latter refers to the average utility functions of every person, the morally ideal world is, in conclusion, identified as that which maximizes, through a scheme of public rules, the citizen's capacity to choose.' Second, 'the current world system does not maximize the world's welfare'. Thus, thirdly, a new consequentialist cosmopolitan code is needed to re-interpret the world system and propose 'new normative principles ... able to improve world welfare conditions'. According to Marchetti, these principles would interweave between individual, state and world levels, and provide the framework for global civil society, wherein not just individuals but states, NGOs, multinational corporations, and supranational organizations all share a responsibility towards vulnerable people as long as they can influence the welfare of those people, who lack access to the basic interests.

If, at first glance, is appears that Marchetti's stance is not at all in line with those of Nash, and Esposito and Murphy, then closer inspection reveals this not to be the case. Like them, Marchetti accepts that sweeping global changes have transformed the relationship between the individual and the globe: the 'common sense' attitude towards the domain of international relations has been radically altered as citizens become increasingly aware of the influence of global factors upon their lives. The political realm needs to reflect these changes, but Marchetti is not calling for a world government in the Kantian sense, but for more accountable forms of cosmopolitan governance of global issues.

Similar concerns resurface in Widdows's contribution. She begins by asking two key questions: '(F)irst, why has ethics become prominent; and second, what constitutes – and what should constitute – (global) ethics?' She then provides a historical account of developments within the discourse on ethics, with particular emphasis on how 'traditional sources of moral authority' – which had provided the grounding for ethical systems – had been marginalized by the increasing dominance of liberal democratic ideology. In this respect, her argument echoes concerns made by Esposito and Murphy about the relationship between ethics and the capitalist market economy. Drawing heavily on Parekh's writings on this subject (especially Parekh, 2000a), many of which are reproduced in his contribution to this volume, she suggests that liberal democracies, rather than embracing cultural difference which would be in keeping with an inclusivist ideology, run the risk of coming into conflict not only with minority groups within their borders, 'but also with those who hold different value frameworks in the global context'. Widdows then considers the constitution of a possible global ethics, which must be more than merely a language of debate, more than a sphere of communication and understanding, and more than a respect for difference. Widdows rejects relativism as a source for a global ethics, but is cautious about a return to universalism. Global ethics 'must consciously take account of values and beliefs that affect and substantiate local ethics ... and yet insist that the local must be understood in the global context. Not to recognize the importance of differences ... and to attempt to impose a single ethic for all people at all times, is at best naïve, resulting in a vague and therefore inapplicable and meaningless moral framework, and at worst arrogant, resulting in reductionism and oppression of other substantive and potentially enriching moral frameworks.' Widdows concludes with a brisk and appropriate response to the question which might be addressed of this entire volume, 'why global ethics?' – 'Ethics provides (or could provide) a means of moral communication in the public sphere across value frameworks and belief systems; something which is urgently needed in the current pluralistic context.'

Agents and Institutions of Global Civil Society

So far, the chapters have dealt with the constitution of global civil society at a rather abstract level, necessary to provide the foundations for subsequent debates. The chapters that follow focus not on the philosophical issues which underpin this new cosmopolitan ethic, but on the practices of the agents who act out the dynamics of global civil society. An excellent example of this is Paul Kennedy's study of friendship networks among transnational professionals. While Kennedy is interested in analyzing these networks at the empirical level, he carefully locates their practices within wider debates over cosmopolitanism and the ethical engagement with civil society. Kennedy is interested not only in the extent to which these professionals are celebrating the plurality of local cultures, but also how far they actively demonstrate a sense of belonging to the world as a whole, including a sense of ethical responsibility to become involved in helping to overcome shared global problems. He is thus engaging directly and critically with Hannerz's (1990) idea of the culturally engaged cosmopolitan and also with Tomlinson's notion of 'ethical glocalism' (Tomlinson, 1999). Kennedy's study is significant because it does not merely seek to identify these professionals as 'citizens of the world', but also explores the dynamics which underpin and make possible such an identification. Furthermore, it is grounded in a critique of much existing literature on cosmopolitanism – particularly that of Hannerz (1990) – as elitist, and a demand for 'a theory which allows us to think in terms of different degrees and types of cosmopolitanism'.

The chapters by Whitehouse and MacLeod and Lewis focus not on networks as agents in global civil society, but on corporations. Whitehouse is concerned with the necessary development of 'corporate citizenship' as a complement to corporate social responsibility. However, a narrow understanding of corporate citizenship is insufficient, as evidenced by the apparent failure of the United Nations 'global compact' to meaningfully reform corporate behaviour. In particular, this relates to the accountability and responsibility of corporations in respect of the consequences of their practices. Whitehouse's contribution to this volume is crucial in two key respects. First, the sphere of global civil society necessarily incorporates (or should incorporate) *all* agents whose actions have some impact upon the safe stewardship of the world. It is a widely held belief that under conditions of globalization, corporations exert greater power in the global arena than most nation-states. They are *by definition* global actors, and thus cannot – empirically or ethically – be excluded from the sphere of global civil society. Second, as has already been said in this Introduction, and restated using slightly different terminology by Espinosa and Murphy, it is the systemic *logic* which drives the corporate capitalist economy, and not the economy *per se*, which dictates modern rationality; an increasing sense of corporate citizenship and social responsibility re-introduces into this picture an ethical dimension which is not reducible to the logic of capitalism, and which duly establishes the realm of civil society as an alternative space to that of the market economy for corporations to inhabit.

Lewis and MacLeod's concern with the behaviour of corporations echoes that of Whitehouse, but they concentrate on the more conventional 'transnational corporations' (TNCs) which remain key players within the global economy. TNCs influence the policies of governments and supranational bodies alike, and the relationship between the practices of such corporations and concerns around development, human rights and the environment has been well documented. Lewis and MacLeod endeavour to investigate the values and mechanisms for ensuring that these corporations do not stand outside the framework of cosmopolitan democracy. They accept that some advances have been made in the area of corporate social responsibility, but maintain that such regulations cannot and should not be delimited by the corporations themselves. Corporations must be encouraged to accept that they have responsibilities not only to their shareholders but also to numerous other stakeholders at the global, regional and domestic levels. The United Nations 'global compact', discussed in the previous chapter, is seen as a positive step and one which needs protection from colonization from the TNCs themselves. Lewis and MacLeod conclude that greater regulation is required at global, regional and domestic levels to 'ensure economic development without sacrificing common values'.

Kennedy's chapter looked at transnational friendship networks as agents of global civil society. The chapters by Whitehouse and Lewis and MacLeod focused instead on corporations. The following two chapters introduce different, but equally important, agents. Ray Kiely concentrates on the role of social movements (and, in particular, the growing 'anti-capitalist' movement), while Nigel Dower turns his attention to the role of individual citizens. Kiely not only examines the role of social movements in challenging economic globalization, he also returns to the theoretical discourse on global civil society in the earlier chapters of this volume, challenging the claim that global civil society must be clearly separate from state and market, arguing instead that it should be seen in the context of changing state-market relations. Kiely begins by discussing the claim made primarily by Falk (2000b) that 'globalization-from-above' has made possible an alternative 'globalization-from-below' reflected in part in the membership growths experienced by international non-governmental organizations in recent years. While not unsympathetic to this approach, Kiely warns that is does not paint a wholly accurate picture of competing globalizing processes. Put simply, the tendency to set the idea of global civil society (Kiely refers to such approaches as 'postmodern') as the polar opposite to the (modernist) defence of the nation-state, is misleading. In rejecting such simplistic categorizations, Kiely echoes the concerns made in an earlier chapter by Nash. He is adamant that, rather than losing their privileged position in the international arena in the light of globalizing processes (as Albrow, 1996 and others contend), nation-states have been integral to these processes. In place of this crude dichotomy, Kiely suggests that we are witnessing 'a reconfiguration of the relationship between nation states and global – or perhaps more accurately, still international – civil society'.

To illustrate his claim, Kiely turns his attention to the global 'anti-capitalist' movement which, he suggests, undermines such false dichotomies. The movement – if indeed it can be described in the singular – defies conventional labelling. Instead, it is a federation of interests, which includes diverse opinions and ideologies in respect of the role of the state and the emergence of a 'global civil society'. The cosmopolitan views of commentators, such as Falk, often evade these complexities in the name of their progressive ideologies, but in doing so, Kiely argues, they misunderstand the way in which many social movements, and indeed nation-states, actually engage with processes of globalization.

In the final main chapter, Dower provides a critical assessment of one of the most fashionable ideas in contemporary social theory – global citizenship (on which, see also Dower, 2000; O'Byrne, 2003). No volume on global ethics and civil society would be complete without some reference to the role played by active citizens in constituting this global ethical domain. Dower's approach to this subject is interesting and informative – he looks at the various tensions which might exist between three inter-related terms: 'global citizenship', 'globalization' and 'citizenship'. 'Global citizenship' conflicts with 'globalization', he suggests, in so far as the latter is primarily an economic process which undermines the normative basis of the idea of global citizenship and which marginalizes the influence of globally concerned individuals. 'Global citizenship' also conflicts with 'citizenship' because the cosmopolitan ethic implied by the former challenges the foundations of the latter and undermines the role of nation-state citizenship. Finally, 'globalization' conflicts with 'citizenship' because the former undermines the capacity for individual citizens to control their own destinies within borders and weakens national identities and loyalties, which are fundamental to the concept of nation-state citizenship. Dower then proceeds to explore these tensions in greater depth, and concludes that more positive relations can be found between them. In advocating the strengthening of the realm of global civil society – which like other authors in this volume Dower does not necessarily see as undermining the role of nation-states – he returns us to the themes and issues discussed by Parekh in the opening chapter.

Conclusion

This volume serves as a contribution to an important debate. For a long time, the academic literature on globalization remained somewhat abstract and theoretical. With growing interest in the anti-capitalist movement as an agency of resistance, these debates have taken a more empirical turn. Social scientists are therefore beginning to take seriously issues and concepts raised by activists some ten year previously. This volume brings together a critique of cosmopolitan theory and an analysis of the actors involved in building the emerging global civil society. Although each contributor is indebted to a different set of intellectual influences, they share a cautious belief in the possibilities of the cosmopolitan project, a desire to overcome the weaknesses in cosmopolitan theory, and a commitment to the dialectical relationship between theory and practice.

References

Albrow, M. (1996), *The Global Age: State and Society beyond Modernity*, Cambridge, Polity Press.
Alexander, J. (1993), 'The Return of Civil Society', in *Contemporary Sociology*, **22**, pp. 797-803.
Alexander, J. (1998), *Real Civil Societies: Dilemmas of Institutionalization*, London, Sage.
Archibugi, D. and Held, D. (eds) (1995), *Cosmopolitan Democracy*, Cambridge, Polity Press.
Bobbio, N. (1979), 'Gramsci and the Conception of Civil Society', in C. Mouffe (ed.), *Gramsci and Marxist Theory*, London, Routledge & Kegan Paul.
Brecher, J., Brown Childs, J. and Cutler, J. (eds) (1993), *Global Visions: Beyond the New World Order*, Boston, South End Press.
Brecher, Costello, T. and Smith, B. (2000), *Globalization from Below: The Power of Solidarity*, Cambridge, Mass., South End Press.
Chambers, S. (1996), *Reasonable Democracy: Jürgen Habermas and the Politics of Discourse*, Ithaca, Cornell University Press.
Cohen, J. (1995), 'Interpreting the Notion of Civil Society', in M. Walzer (ed.), *Toward a Global Civil Society*, Oxford, Berghahn.

Dryzek, J.S. (1990), *Discursive Democracy: Politics, Policy, and Political Science*, Cambridge, Cambridge University Press.

Falk, R. (1999), *Predatory Globalization: A Critique*, Cambridge, Polity Press.

Falk, R. (2000a), 'Global Civil Society and the Democratic Prospect', in B. Holden (ed.), *Global Democracy: Key Debates*, London, Routledge.

Falk, R. (2000b), 'Resisting "Globalization from Above" through "Globalization from Below"', in B.K. Gills (ed.), *Globalization and the Politics of Resistance*, London, Macmillan.

Freeman, M. (2002), *Human Rights: An Interdisciplinary Approach*, Cambridge, Polity Press.

Gramsci, A. (1966), *Passato e Presente*, Turin: Einaudi.

Habermas, J. (2001), *The Postnational Constellation: Political Essays*, Cambridge, Polity Press.

Hannerz, U. (1990), 'Cosmopolitans and Locals in World Culture', *Theory, Culture and Society*, 7, pp. 237-51.

Hirst, P. and Thompson, G. (1996), *Globalization in Question*, Cambridge, Polity Press.

Küng, H. (1991), *Global Responsibility: In Search of a New World Ethic*, New York, Crossroad Publishing Co.

Laclau, E. and Mouffe, C. (1985), *Hegemony and Socialist Strategy: Towards a Radical Democratic Politics*, London, Verso.

Nielsen, K. (1995), 'Reconceptualizing Civil Society for Now: Some Somewhat Gramscian Turnings', in M. Walzer (ed.), *Toward a Global Civil Society*, Oxford, Berghahn.

O'Byrne, D.J. (2003), *The Dimensions of Global Citizenship: Political Identity beyond the Nation-State*, London, Frank Cass.

Ohmae, K. (1990), *The Borderless World*, London, Collins.

Parekh, B. (2000a), *Rethinking Multiculturalism: Cultural Diversity and Political Theory*, Basingstoke, Palgrave.

Parekh, B. *et al.* (2000b), *The Future of Multi-Ethnic Britain*, London, Profile Books.

Robertson, R. (1992), *Globalization: Social Theory and Global Culture*, London, Sage.

Sklair, L. (2002), *Globalization: Capitalism and Its Alternatives*, Oxford, Oxford University Press.

Tomlinson, J. (1999), *Globalization and Culture*, Cambridge, Polity Press.

Turner, B.S. (1993), 'Outline of a Theory of Human Rights', in B.S. Turner (ed.), *Citizenship and Social Theory*, London, Sage.

Walzer, M. (ed.) (1995a), *Toward a Global Civil Society*, Oxford, Berghahn.

Walzer, M. (1995b), 'Introduction', in M. Walzer (ed.), *Toward a Global Civil Society*, Oxford, Berghahn.

Acknowledgements

Thanks to John Eade for comments on and contributions to this introductory chapter.

Chapter 2

Principles of a Global Ethic

Bhikhu Parekh

Introduction

In recent years concern with a global ethic has come to occupy an important place on our philosophical and political agenda. It raises several questions, such as whether it is new or another name for the old idea of universal morality that goes back to the Stoics, why it is necessary, how it can be arrived at, and what its contents are. This chapter addresses these and related questions.

The Need for a Global Ethic

Human beings stand in a variety of relationships with each other, such as parents, children, spouses, friends, brothers, sisters, colleagues, neighbours, business partners, fellow citizens, and fellow-religionists. Whether they are inherited, voluntarily entered into, grow half-consciously, or are of some other kind, all relationships are regulated by norms and involve mutual claims and duties. Moral conduct broadly consists in recognizing and respecting these norms and discharging the relevant duties. A difficult question arises concerning outsiders with whom one does not stand in any recognizable form of relationship. No norms regulate our encounters with them, and there are not even common interests from which one can derive mutual claims and duties, leaving one wondering how to respond to them and even whether one may treat them as one pleases including kill or harm them. Societies can easily live with this moral vacuum as long as they are relatively self-contained and lack regular contacts with outsiders. Once these contacts become regular and extensive, they need general norms to structure and guide their relations and establish a reasonably clear system of claims and duties. Not surprisingly the search for such norms first began in the West with the rise of the Roman Empire, which brought different societies under a common rule and encouraged an extensive movement of goods and people across social and territorial boundaries.

The Stoics were among the first to address the question in a systematic manner. They argued that as long as human beings mistakenly defined themselves only as members of a particular society and structured their moral life in terms of the roles they occupied within it, outsiders meant nothing to them and were like an alien species. If they rose to a higher level of understanding, they would see that outsiders were human beings like them, sharing distinctively human capacities especially reason, and forming a universal moral community. For the Stoics social, cultural, linguistic and other differences were contingent, arbitrary, and devoid of moral significance. What really mattered was humanity, which all human beings shared in equal measure and represented their true nature or essence. All human beings were members of a universal *polis*, and hence fellow-citizens. Unlike the *polis* which was a contingent human creation, the cosmopolis was a natural community, and just as civil laws governed the relations between the members of a political community, the natural law or the principle of natural justice governed those between human beings. These principles were not derived from human agreement or consensus but from human nature itself, and were inherently binding. To act according to them was to express and realize one's human nature or common humanity. Despite their differences, all Stoic thinkers maintained that the natural law included such principles as equality of all human beings, refraining from harming and deceiving them, keeping one's promises to and contacts with them, and respecting their property.

Christianity radically transformed the Stoic natural law tradition and represents a second stage in the development of universal morality. For it the universe was an ordered whole, as it was for the Stoics but for a very different reason. It was divinely created and governed, and was a cosmopolis in the full sense of having a ruler in the shape of God, who issued commands backed by a system of rewards and punishment. All human beings were not only equal but brothers, created by the same God and members of a common human family. While agreeing with the Stoics that human reason could discover the principles of natural law, Christian theologians argued that it was liable to error and needed the guidance of an explicitly revealed divine law. In the Christian view the natural law had a substantive and positive content and, unlike the Stoic, involved the duty of mutual help, care, benevolence, love, being 'one's brother's keeper', carrying the Christian message to the rest of humankind, and bringing the latter within a common spiritual fold. These duties were binding because they were divinely enjoined, and should be discharged not merely as a matter of justice as the Stoics had thought but out of the love of God and in the spirit of human brotherhood.

The 17th century represents a third stage in the development of universal morality. Like the Stoic natural law tradition, the Seventeenth century reflections on the subject occurred in the context of European expansion and the increased contacts between different societies. European countries were beginning to discover non-European peoples, with whom they traded and whom they also colonized. This raised the same question that the earlier natural law theorists had faced, namely, what principles should govern the relations between human beings in general? The currently dominant Christian principles were not much help, both because they had no relevance to non-Christians and because some people in Europe were themselves losing their faith in Christianity. The principles of universal morality had to be secular in nature and derived from a universally shared secular source, for which human nature was thought to be the only available candidate.

While the 17th century writers were thus far travelling in the same direction as the Stoics, they differed in the way they defined human nature and what they derived from it. Human nature for them included not only reason but also common needs and vulnerabilities. Human beings feared violent death, desired self-preservation, liberty, means to the satisfaction of their basic needs, and so on. Since all civil authority in their view was socially derived, 17th century writers argued that human beings were naturally free and independent, masters of their lives and owners of their powers and capacities. As independent individuals freely pursuing their interests, all human beings enjoyed certain rights. Since these rights, such as those to life, liberty and property, were derived from the basic dispositions or laws of human nature, they were called natural rights. Unlike its Stoic and Christian predecessors, the modern natural law tradition was individualist, articulated in the language of claims, and made natural rights rather than natural duties the content of universal morality.

All human beings had certain natural rights, and that entailed a duty on others to respect them. Given the way in which the rights were derived, the duty involved was negative in nature and consisted in non-interference with others' exercise of their rights. There was no positive duty of love, benevolence, mutual care or helping the needy. The natural right to life, for example, implied that one had a duty not to harm others, but not a duty to provide food to the starving or to help those in desperate need. In this respect the modern natural law tradition was closer to the Stoic than to the Christian. The latter stressed the positive duty to help others in need, to share with them what one had and could spare, and some Christian theologians including Thomas Aquinas went so far as to argue that a starving person had a right to help himself with the surplus food of others. The modern natural law tradition was too individualist and negative to allow this.

The modern natural law tradition remains the basis of much contemporary thought on universal morality. The U.N. Declaration of Human Rights, as well as most other international covenants and agreements, are good examples of its continuing influence. They lay down universal principles of morality which take individuals as the primary moral agents and endow them with certain rights. The rights generate claims on the state, which is assigned the duty to establish and protect them. Citizens are the exclusive responsibility of their state, and all their claims are addressed to it. Outsiders have a negative duty to respect their rights and not to interfere with them, but no positive duty to help them acquire the resources necessary for the exercise of these rights or even to help establish them in societies where they are absent. If some societies are desperately poor and their members are dying of starvation or malnourishment, their members have no right to demand the help of more affluent societies and to require them to share their surplus resources with them. Others may help them if they feel so inclined, but they have no duty to do so and are not morally delinquent if they offer no help. Like the Stoic and the modern natural law traditions in general, the United Nations and other declarations of human rights presuppose and remain limited by a statist perspective. They lay down universal principles of morality in the shape of the rights that all human beings should enjoy, but place the responsibility for realising them exclusively on individual states.

In spite of these and other limitations, the U.N. Declaration marks a significant fourth stage in the development of a statement of universal morality. For the first time in human history, official representatives of large parts of humankind met, discussed, agreed on and freely signed the Declaration. It embodies a broad universal consensus on the basic principles of civil and political morality, and has become a benchmark against which state practices are judged. People in different countries appeal to these rights in their struggles against their governments, and elicit at least some international support for their struggles. The fact that the Declaration is associated with the U.N. also gives it an organizational basis and a quasi-official status. It is not a political orphan; it has an accredited global agency which takes ownership of it and provides a global public space in which to discuss its implementation and debate its content.

The world today is quite different from what it was when the U.N. Declaration laid down a clear statement of the universal principles of morality for a traumatized humanity. It is far more interdependent than ever before and all societies, including the most remote and isolated, are part of a global pattern of interaction and integration.[1] Thanks to the great technological advances in the means of transport and communication, space has shrunk, news spreads instantaneously, and different parts of the world are within easy reach of each other. The massive migrations of people and the growth of transnational communities mean that almost every contemporary society includes groups who link it to several others, act as visible reminders of the world beyond its borders, and give it some idea of the great diversity of the human species. An economic crisis in one part of the world affects all others in varying degrees, and calls for a global action. Although some economies affect others more, none is devoid of at least some impact, as we saw when the economic troubles of the East Asian countries impacted on the economies of the G7 as well as the rest of the world. Domestic policies of rich countries, such as the subsidies they give to their farmers and industries, the tariffs they impose on imports from developing countries, and the weak regulatory regime to which they subject and the political protection they give to their multinationals profoundly affect the vital interests of millions in the rest of the world. Civil wars in distant countries affect the supply of new materials, and hence the prosperity and well-being of the rest of the world including the rich west. And they also lead to a flow of refugees, who knock on our doors and whom we cannot turn away as we would stray dogs and intruders, at least without some moral unease. Disease and environmental damage know no boundaries, and one country's pollution or deforestation affects the climate and the economic and physical well-being of others.

Thanks to the global reach of the media, human suffering in distant parts of the world comes to us in vivid images, gets under our skin, and calls for a response. Feeble though it is, some concern for the suffering of unknown others is becoming an integral part of our consciousness and paving the way for a vague but unmistakable sense of a global moral community. It is this that explains the historically unique phenomena of humanitarian aid, popular pressure on governments to help societies in distress, the great personal risks taken by aid workers, doctors, nurses, journalists, and others working in unstable countries, the

Live Aid Concert that raised millions from ordinary citizens, and the global campaign to cancel the debts of poor countries. The growing sense of human unity is also reflected in and reinforced by the increasing interest in the great scientific, philosophical and artistic achievements of other civilizations, translations of their literary works, and the preservation of the common human architectural and ecological heritage.

The profound transformation of the world presents new moral challenges and radically alters the context and content of the traditional discourse on universal morality. Our actions, directly or indirectly, affect people in distant lands and, as moral beings responsible for the consequences of our actions, we need to ensure that they take full account of and do not harm others' interests. As the consequences of our actions spread across territorial boundaries, outsiders no longer remain outsiders but form an integral part of our moral universe. We are increasingly bound together not only by common interests but also by a spirit of mutual concern and shared fate. Human beings entertain certain expectations of one another, especially of those in the affluent and powerful West because of their greater capacity to cause harm and offer help. And as the latter respond appropriately, the expectations acquire moral legitimacy, set new moral and political norms, and reinforce the growing awareness of a global community. As the 'we' that constitutes and defines a political community expands to encompass outsiders, humankind begins to acquire some of the features of a *political community*.

Not only is the scope of moral consciousness widening to encompass the entire humankind, the content of our duties to outsiders is also undergoing a profound change. Much of the earlier discourse on universal morality took a thin, negative and individual-centred view of the duties to other outsiders. That view is no longer tenable in the modern context. Since our actions have consequences across our territorial boundaries, the outsider/insider distinction makes only limited sense. Thanks to the growing sentiment of human interdependence and solidarity as well as for reasons of enlightened self-interest, it deeply matters to us how other human beings live. And since many of their problems and frustrations arise because of the sorry state of their economic and political life, the latter becomes a matter of deep moral concern in a way it never did before. Our duties therefore acquire a collective dimension in two interrelated respects. We feel concerned about the quality of collective life in other countries, and our efforts are directed not so much at helping individuals as at helping struggling societies cope with their problems. And since we can help them effectively not by individual actions but by acting collectively through our governments, our moral response too takes on a collective character. While individuals do have duties to relieve the suffering of other individuals as the earlier theories of universal morality had argued, these duties in our historical context are politically mediated and take the form of political communities helping each other directly or through international institutions. This inescapable collectivization and political mediation of our moral duties has no historical parallel.

Another unique moral feature of our age has to do with the fact that for the first time in history, humankind faces common collective problems, has to find collective solutions, and needs to act as a collectivity. Climate changes, pollution, and environmental degradation cannot be tackled by any society on its own. As the world becomes economically integrated, no national economy can be managed on its own, and we need to design an appropriate global economic order. Civil wars, failed or failing states, regional instability, etc. affect us all and call for a new global political order. All this calls for appropriate institutional structures and that, in turn, requires guiding principles to determine their objectives, functions, composition, and modes of operation. Such institutions as the U.N. and its various agencies, the IMF, the World Bank, and the WTO, many of which were set up soon after the Second World War, are informed by a particular set of moral principles and a distinct vision of the world. Both require reassessment.

In the light of our discussion, it is clear why we need universal principles of morality, why the traditional discourse on them is inadequate, and how it needs to be revised. Since our actions have consequences for those outside our society and we cannot uncritically impose our values on them, we need universally agreed principles to guide our actions. Others ask for our help and we need agreed principles to decide what human well-being consists in, whether and when their plea is legitimate, what help we should give, who among us should give it, and on what conditions. We also need universal principles to help us decide what claims human beings may rightly make on and what duties they owe each other in our interdependent world. And we also need them to decide how to address common global problems, how to design international institutions, what goals they should pursue, how they should decide their priorities, how they should be composed, and to whom they should be accountable.

Some of the moral questions we face today are then wholly new to our age. Some of the old ones have taken new forms. And even those that remain constant need to be discussed in a vastly different historical context. It is this radical transformation in the traditional discourse on universal morality that the term 'global ethic' highlights and which, at least partly, explains why it is generally preferred to the older term 'universal morality'. Unlike the term 'universal', the term 'global' stresses the collective and integrated nature of our moral life, and captures the threefold fact that humankind is getting increasingly integrated and forming a single moral community, that it faces common problems requiring collective solutions, and that the effects of many of our actions reach out to the farthest corners of the world and require us to create a global order. Unlike the term 'moral', the term 'ethic' highlights the facts that not just the individuals but also political communities, multinational corporations, etc. are moral agents or at least bearers of duties, that we are concerned with institutions, policies and practices and not just with individual actions, and that our primary focus is not on the intentions, motives, and character of individuals but on the structures of social relations. Global ethic is not a new name for the centuries old discourse on universal morality but a historically novel form that the latter takes in response to the unique moral demands of our times.

Developing a Global Ethic

In the previous section I concluded that we need a global ethic to provide us with principles that can guide us in addressing the problems thrown up by our globalising and interdependent world. This raises the question as to how we should go about developing it. The question has received several answers, many of which contain valuable insights but none is wholly satisfactory.

The Stoics, the modern natural law theorists and their contemporary successors appeal to human nature, teasing out what they take to be its distinguishing features and dispositions and using them to arrive at statements of universal values. Although this approach has its value, for no moral principle can be taken seriously if it demands what is beyond human capacity, it is open to serious criticisms.[2] Human nature is generally taken to refer to what is distinctive to human beings and distinguishes them from the animals, their nearest cousins. Countless features distinguish human beings, such as that they walk on their two feet, engage in sexual activity all year round, laugh, kill for fun, hate, act in a vengeful manner and are able to think and reason. It is not clear which of these is to be the basis of morality. The usual tendency is to stress rationality, but there is no obvious reason why it should be singled out in preference to all the others. We do so because we value rationality and would like it to be the basis of the good life. Different normative assumptions would be involved if we singled out any of the other human features. In other words all definitions of human nature are normatively embedded, and their underlying norms are not themselves derived from human nature. Furthermore, singling out a particular human capacity, be it reason, will, choice, self-transcendence or any other, ignores or underplays the role of other human capacities and dispositions, introduces an implicit hierarchy among them, and gives a highly simplistic and reductionist account of human nature. Human nature at best tells us what human beings can and cannot do, not what they should or should not do, unless we take a teleological view of it, which is not easy to substantiate and raises its own problems.

There are also other difficulties with the appeal to human nature. Over the millennia, human nature has been so heavily overlaid and shaped by social influences that we have no direct access to its 'inherent' or 'original' content. Reason itself develops at a certain stage in human evolution, and cannot be regarded as inherent in human nature except on the basis of an arbitrary cut-off point. Again, in the course of their history, human beings have displayed such unusual and unexpected capacities for good and evil that we cannot say what new surprises lie in store for us. Human nature is not a finished product and all statements about it are necessarily tentative. Furthermore, our culture and the kind of historical identity and self-understanding that we develop shape us profoundly, and become so integral a part of us that we call it our 'second' nature. The distinctly modern notions of selfhood, self-authorship, individuality and choice, for example, are not part of human nature, but they are central to the make-up of the modern western individual. Any moral theory that only appeals to human nature and ignores the 'second' or historically acquired nature is necessarily incomplete and lacks the power to guide people.

Some moral philosophers turn not to a theory of human nature, at least not directly, but to certain procedural tests to arrive at universal principles. These include Kant's universalisability principle, Rawls's veil of ignorance, Habermas's ideal speech situation, and an appeal to what is supposed to be common to all societies. Although each of these has its strengths, none takes us very far. The last is the least tenable, because hardly any principles are common to all societies as comparative sociologists since Montesquieu have pointed out. And such principles as we do find common to many societies, such as racism, inferior status of women and discrimination against outsiders, are obviously unacceptable.

Kant's universalizability principle runs into several difficulties.[3] The requirement that one's maxim of action should be capable of being willed by all assumes that all human beings have equal dignity and worth and deserve equal respect and consideration. The universalizability principle, therefore, cannot stand on its own and makes sense only if one accepts the principle of equality. Kant realizes this and grounds equality in a dualist metaphysic, involving a transcendental and noumenal view of human beings. His arguments are unconvincing. Equality of human beings at the noumenal level has no empirical content, and does not by itself entail equality at the level of human needs, resources and conditions of the good life. The maxim that we should not render assistance to those in need can be universalized, as Kant himself admits, but we rightly resist it just as Kant did. He argues that it is impossible to will such a maxim because instances are bound to arise when every human being would want the love and sympathy of others, the possibility of which would have been ruled out by the maxim. This is not a moral but a prudential argument. It assumes that all human beings are bound to want sympathy and love, which is open to question, and that even if they do, some might not be prepared to forgo them. In other words Kant ignores the basic fact that what can be consistently willed and universalized cannot be decided in ignorance of empirical facts about human beings and their circumstances. And once we introduce these, the application of the universalizability principle becomes far more complex than he realized.

Even if we abstracted the universalizability principle from its Kantian framework, difficulties remain. It is possible to universalize and consistently will the principle that one should always tell the truth irrespective of its consequences. It is equally possible to will consistently that one should tell the truth unless it causes harm to others. Since the Kantian test is met by both, it does not tell us which one to opt for. As this example illustrates, moral principles can also conflict, and Kant's test does not tell us how to resolve it. Another difficulty with Kant's universalizability principle arises out of the fact that it takes the individuals alone as the basic moral agents. Although this is an attractive view of morality, others are equally plausible. Since the universalizability principle is tied to one view of moral life, it is not a morally and culturally neutral procedural test and is ill-equipped to cope with the complexity of a cross-culturally valid global ethic.

John Rawls's view that universal principles are best arrived at by exploring what individuals would agree upon behind the veil of ignorance fares no better.[4] It is not easy to decide what human features are contingent and should be abstracted away. Rawls abstracts away envy, greed, concern for status and the impulse to gamble, but not self-interest, self-respect and individuality, without explaining how he defines contingency and moral irrelevance and determines what does and does not fall under it. What is more, it is difficult to see how the principles arrived at under the veil of ignorance can be applied or even be relevant once individuals know full facts about themselves, their circumstances and the social world. They might then take a different view of the principles, want to revise them, and would not be persuaded by an appeal to the veil of ignorance which they have now penetrated. Rawls's method is particularly inappropriate for a project of global ethic. His original position is territorially bounded, and individuals in it deliberate about what principles should apply within their political community. Rawls does not explain why he does not abstract away the territorial boundaries, why he considers them morally so significant as to circumscribe the scope and content of the principles of justice, and why he bases the relations between human being across the boundaries on very different principles to these obtaining between fellow-citizens. Even when he addresses the question of global justice in his later writings, he remains trapped within the statist framework and gives an untenably minimalist and ultimately arbitrary account of duties to outsiders.

The Habermasian view that universal principles should be based on the best arguments in an ideal speech situation runs into similar difficulties. The idea of an ideal speech situation is logically incoherent. All speech occurs within a language, and all languages are culturally shaped, charged with historical memories, and limit what can be said and how. A culturally neutral speech that is equally hospitable to a variety of world views is inherently impossible. Habermas talks of universalizable interests, and that runs into similar objections to those raised earlier in relation to Kant's universalizability principle. Habermas wants the best argument to win, and defines it as one that is logically most powerful. This is too rationalistic a view of reason to be convincing or to be true to reality. Moral discourse does not occur between pure intelligences or exclusively reason-driven beings, but between historically situated and culturally embedded human beings with their hopes, fears, emotions and memories. Arguments, therefore, are not abstract intellectual exercises but engage the participant's self-understanding, individual and collective identity, and so on. We need to aim not only to convince others, which is only sometimes possible, but also to persuade them, to win them over, to woo their assent as Kant put it. This gives us a very different view of the 'best argument', assuming that we wish to use the expression at all. Moral and political discourse involves reasons, but they are of several different kinds, arguments being only one of these.

Some writers look to religion to provide universal principles. This approach runs into obvious difficulties. Belief in God is not self-evident and cannot be established to the satisfaction of those who do not share it. It also creates the familiar puzzle as to whether a principle is right because God wills and commands it or because we have independent reasons to accept it. If the latter, God is not its source. If the former, then in theory God could have willed an opposite principle. We find this inconceivable because God could never will what is wrong, thus presupposing that His will is subject to limits and that we have at least some independent knowledge of what is right and wrong. God might still be introduced to play a moral role, such as sanction or supplement morality, but He cannot be the sole source of our moral principles. God, again, speaks differently in different religions and we have no means of deciding which of them represents His true or authentic will.

It is often suggested that we should look for principles that are common to all religions.[5] All religions do share certain attitudes and sensibilities, such as the spirit of transcendence, the deep sense of human fallibility and finitude, and the sense of the sacred and the holy. However, it is doubtful if they share moral principles in common and whether those that many of them do, such as a low view of women and hostility to outsiders, are morally acceptable. Many religions do not value human equality. Although they value human life, they do not place equal value on that of outsiders, heathens and idolaters, and hardly any on that of the apostates. They value human dignity, but again limit it in various ways, and some even make it dependent on acceptance of the 'true faith' or belief in God. Some value the service of fellow-humans, but others either do not or consider it inferior to the life devoted to the solitary contemplation of God. Some value the environment and respect for nature, others do not. We can, of course, reinterpret religions and find different degrees of support for some or even all of these values, but that only shows that the values are derived from other sources and read back into a religion. This is not to deny that moral values acquire energy and depth when backed up by religion and that religion is a source of morality for many, but rather that it is not the sole source of morality and that its morality can and should be evaluated in terms of independent moral principles.

A global ethic then cannot be derived from human nature, God, the prevailing consensus, or any of the several Kantian-inspired abstract procedural tests. It can only be arrived at by means of a cross-cultural dialogue. Morality is a human institution created and sustained by human beings, and its content is determined by human deliberation. Religion is one source of morality, but it is subject to human judgement and is filtered through human deliberation. The better the quality of deliberation, that is, the more it involves all those affected by it under conditions of equality and in an atmosphere conducive to a radical exchange of ideas, the greater are our chances of getting the moral principles right. Since the principles are meant to apply universally, all societies should participate in the deliberation. This shows respect for them, gives them ownership of the principles, makes it easier for them to accept these, and ensures their uncoerced compliance. And as we are inescapably conditioned by our background and ethnocentric assumptions and tend to universalize the familiar, an open-minded dialogue with others alerts us to our biases, creates a space for their critical examination, and increases the possibility of a richer and truly universal perspective.

The dialogue involves critically examining various candidates for universal principles, weighing up reasons for and against them, appealing to the historical experience of humankind, human nature, the nature of the world we inhabit, etc., and settling on those that withstand critical scrutiny and enjoy a broad cross-cultural consensus. The dialogue is inevitably multistranded, multilayered, and includes different kinds of argument. It involves correcting factual errors, refuting flimsy and incoherent arguments, exposing untenable assumptions and conceptual confusions, and criticising each other's biases. This takes us much further than many imagine. Racism in the sense of a belief in the natural hierarchy of biologically classified human groups and the inherent and irremediable inferiority of some is largely discredited today because we have successfully challenged its 'factual' basis, imprecision of the concept of race, the confused identification of the limited cultural contributions or educational attainments of some groups with the natural inferiority of their members, false fears about the consequences of miscegenation, and so on. This is also largely how the institution of slavery was undermined earlier, and the belief in the inherent inferiority of women is increasingly being discredited today. This is not to deny that some people still continue to hold these and related beliefs, but rather that they do so with less and less conviction and are widely considered as mistaken as the believers in the flat earth.

Some beliefs are not amenable to such a fairly decisive refutation. Although there are no moral beliefs to which ascertainable facts about human beings and the world are wholly irrelevant, they are less or less directly relevant to some beliefs than to others. Some beliefs, again, are less amenable than others to rigorous reasoning. They might be grounded in metaphysical or religious views of the world which are not easy to refute or even criticize. In such cases we obviously cannot convince others and should aim instead to persuade them, to win them over, by appealing to their interests, ambitions, suitably reinterpreted cultures, lessons of history, experiences of other societies, the nature of the modern world, compulsions and constraints of modernity, and so on. This is how modernizers in many parts of the developing world have won over or undermined the dogmatism of the traditionalists and the revivalists, arguing that traditional institutions and practices simply do not make practical sense in the modern world, that they provoke opposition and disorder, that they stand in the way of strong and prosperous societies which the traditionalists want, and that traditions are often invented and can only survive by adopting to changing circumstances. This is also how we can reason even with the religious fundamentalists, showing them by examples how identification of religion and state corrupts both, that the religious texts do not really say what they think they do, that they cannot realize their dream of creating powerful and cohesive societies by the means they propose, that their actions provoke dissent and disorder, that the desires and aspirations stimulated by modernity cannot be long suppressed, that past religious leaders have often been proved mistaken in their interpretations of the scriptures and that this can just as easily happen to their successors. The nationalists, the communists, the libertarians and others can be similarly challenged, as indeed they have been. In each case we aim to show our dialogical partners why their views are muddled, self-contradictory or poorly thought out, to allay their fears, plant self-doubt, loosen their rigid frameworks of thought, stimulate internal debates, draw in their excluded members and so on, and endeavour to reach a broad consensus.

Some might remain obstinate and resistant to arguments, withdraw from the dialogue, or insist on going their own ways even when shown to be mistaken. While fully appreciating the limits of dialogue and finding other ways of dealing with such people, the dialogue remains our best hope. Even when it fails to convince or persuade, it encourages people to think, leaves a residue of doubts and destabilising thoughts, and challenges them to come up with better defences of their views. Given time, all this is likely to work its way through deep disagreements and generate some common ground. Take the U.N. Declaration of Human Rights. When it was first discussed, several countries strongly disagreed with its contents and even its very relevance. The communists saw it as a bourgeois document and a cunning device to embarrass and destabilize them, and pressed for economic and social rights. Their first criticism was shown to be misplaced. There were also internal debates and pressures within communist countries, and eventually they came round. Although their second criticism was initially rejected, it provoked internal debates within western societies and was eventually incorporated in the subsequent Covenants on social, economic and cultural rights. Muslim countries too initially objected to the U.N. Declaration. They had to give reasons, some of which were shown to be flimsy. Their own people debated the rights, and some of them reached different conclusions to those of their governments. Thanks to the rethinking that this has provoked, the moral pressure of world opinion and the Muslim diaspora, and the desire for international respectability, Muslim societies are increasingly beginning to come round to at least some of the rights and democratic freedoms advocated in the U.N. Declaration. There is evidence that the ideas of individual liberty, human rights, basic democratic freedoms, etc. are increasingly acquiring a global consensus and continuity.

When a cross-cultural global dialogue generates an agreed body of universal principles, we need to be careful how we understand the nature of these principles. The claim we make for these principles is that they deserve the allegiance of all human beings, that we can give good reasons why we reasonably expect them to respect them. It is not necessary that they should all accept and respect them for the same reasons. Equality of human worth, for example, could be shown to be a universally valid principle, but some may be persuaded by religious and others by different varieties of secular reasons. The universality of the principle refers to its scope or range of validity, not to its grounds. Universal principles, again, are not and need not be absolute in the sense of disallowing qualification and compromise. Absoluteness refers to their moral status, universality to their scope, and the two should not be confused. Since we have several universal principles, each limits the others. They can also conflict, and we need to decide how much each needs to be compromised in order to achieve the best possible reconciliation between them. This does not mean that we may not consider some principles absolute and non-negotiable. We might, for example, hold that the principles of equal human worth and ban on torture should never be violated. While a few formal principles may be viewed in this way and allowed to trump others, we cannot give such a status to all. Universal principles are not all of equal moral importance any more than all human rights are. They are also bound to conflict in different situations, and the conflict cannot be resolved if each of them is regarded as absolute and non-negotiable. A principle need not be absolute in order to be universal.

Like all general statements, universal principles are formal and indeterminate in different degrees. They have to be interpreted and adopted to the circumstances and traditions of different communities. If they are to become an integral part of a community's way of life and not remain an alien and indigestible import, they need to be indigenized and brought into a reasonably harmonious relationship with its traditions and values. For these and other reasons universal principles are invariably mediated by the self-understandings and circumstances of different communities, are interpreted and lived differently, and give rise to different practices and institutional structures. Take the principle of the sanctity of human life. In a society which believes in reincarnation and blurs the sharp dividing line between humans and animals, human life is not easy to define and demarcate. Views also differ about when it begins and ends, whether it persists in some form after the dissolution of the body and continues to make certain claims, whether the duty to respect it involves only non-interference or also active assistance, and what is to be done when this duty conflicts with respect for human dignity or the duty to eliminate injustices. While rightly insisting that universal principles are binding on all human beings and societies, we should not make the mistake of thinking that their meanings, internal relations, modes of articulation and forms of realization must also be universally identical.[6]

The dialogically generated global ethic derives its moral authority from two separate but related sources. It is based on good reasons which the participants find persuasive and because of which they give it their assent. It is also based on their freely given consent to the agreements in which the consensus is embodied and given a formal status. Assent implies intellectual approval, consent a commitment to accept and live by it. Assent is an exercise of rational judgement, consent that of moral and political freedom. The two are closely related and equally important. The fact that a global ethic is based on good reasons is not by itself enough to make it binding; those involved should freely undertake to abide by it, both because this is demanded by respect for their autonomy and because it restrains the authoritarian impulse to force people to be rational. Conversely their consent is by itself not conclusive because it could be manipulated, misguided or given under pressure; it needs to be based on their well-considered intellectual assent, their genuine belief that the ethic is based on good reasons and deserves their allegiance. Both rationality and freedom or autonomy are central to morality, and a global ethic is no exception.

Toward a Global Ethic

I have argued that the principles of global ethic can only be arrived at by means of a dialogue within and between societies. The dialogue has been going on since at least the end of the Second World War, has been conducted in a reasonably free and egalitarian spirit since the end of European colonialism just over two decades later and has generated a broad and limited consensus. The project of developing a global ethic should begin with the prevailing consensus, correct its incoherences and limitations, take account of the criticisms currently being made of it, and develop a coherent set of principles. The prevailing consensus as embodied in many an international agreement includes several principles that are unexceptionable in the sense that compelling reasons can be given in support of them. They include respect for human dignity, equal human worth, civil and political liberties, democratic freedoms, the rights to life, personal autonomy and collective self-determination, and so on. There are several others, however, that also have equally strong moral claims to become part of the universal consensus. I shall briefly discuss three of them.

We can take it for granted that human beings have equal worth and make equal claims to the good life.[7] They have therefore negative and positive duties to each other. The former involve non-interference with others' pursuit of their self-chosen goals, not harming their vital interests, not taking advantage of their weaknesses and vulnerabilities, and so on. The latter involve the duty to offer such help as others need to lead fulfilling lives and which one can provide within the limits of one's abilities, resources and knowledge. Although negative and positive duties overlap and cannot be easily separated or even distinguished, they arise differently. The idea of human dignity plays a central role in the case of negative duty, that of human worth and value in the case of positive duty. The negative duty derives from the fact that, as unique and self-determining beings who have the capacity to plan and organize their lives and best know what satisfies their deepest aspirations and is in their interest, they should be left free, or what comes to the same thing, should have a right to live the way they like and learn from their mistakes. Their dignity is the basis of their right or claim to autonomy, and generates the duty of non-interference on the part of others.

The positive duty has a more complex moral basis in human worth, vulnerability and interdependence.[8] As beings capable of creating a rich world of meaning and values and a unique form of life, human beings deserve to be valued and cherished. One cannot consistently claim to recognize and respect their worth and value, and remain indifferent if they lead frustrated, empty, miserable and meaningless lives. Such lives degrade their humanity and diminish their worth, and no moral being aware and proud of his humanity can fail to be addressed by them. Human beings, further, are not masters of their circumstances. They might inherit a disadvantaged background, fall on bad times, run into problems with which they cannot cope, or become victims of bad luck or an economic and political crisis. Since these are not their fault and are beyond their control, they need and can rightly ask for others' help to overcome them.

The positive duty to help others is reinforced by the moral logic of the shared communal life. When some members of our society are poor, frustrated or deeply discontented, they are not only unable to discharge their share of communal obligations but also do damage to themselves and others. This affects the quality of the collective life, adds to its moral and social cost, and denies the rest such contributions as they might otherwise have made. Both morality and enlightened self-interest dictate that we address their problems and enable them to lead worthy lives. Unlike the negative duty which presupposes and arises out of others' rights, the positive duty is independent in origin and neither presupposes nor even entails rights.

While we have negative and positive duties to all human beings, we also have special duties to the members of our own community.[9] The latter arise out of the ties of identity and attachment, mutual expectations, a shared past, present and future, common interests, and the compulsions of living together. The universal and special duties regulate each other, and neither of them automatically trumps the other as the ethical universalists and the nationalists maintain from their different perspectives. We may not therefore so define our national interest that it ignores that of others, nor so pursue it that it harms theirs. We also have a duty to help other societies lead decent lives within the limits of our resources, and the greater our resources and capacity to help them, the greater is our duty. In earlier times this duty was severely limited by technological, administrative, economic, cultural, emotional and other factors. This is no longer the case today. We know how others live, what help they need, and how to get it to them; their problems and actions affect our interests as ours affect theirs; we feel emotionally involved in their lives and have a strong sense of a shared fate; and the difference in the interdependence between societies and that within them is only one of degree and is diminishing. As territorial boundaries become morally less important and as humankind becomes more integrated, the sharp separation between the duties to our fellow-citizens and to outsiders makes less sense.

In the light of our discussion, it is easy to see the limitations of the United Nations and other declarations of human rights. They take rights as the central moral category, and fail to see that some important duties are independent of rights. They also remain trapped within the statist framework, making the state solely responsible for creating the regime of rights and securing the conditions of their exercise, and say nothing about the duties of outsiders. They ignore failed or failing states and those too poor to ensure decent lives for their members, too torn by internal conflicts to ensure even the minimally necessary level of civil order, or too heavily manipulated or exploited in the past to have the self-confidence and the capacity for self-management. The declarations of human rights therefore need to be supplemented by the declarations of the negative and positive duties that individuals and states owe each other. Like the former, the latter should indicate in fairly specific terms how states should help each other, share their skills, resources and technical knowledge, address problems of global poverty and injustice in a spirit of partnership, and meet a firm collective commitment to creating decent lives for all.[10]

Once we appreciate that we have duties across territorial boundaries and cannot remain indifferent to how others live, the traditional doctrine of state sovereignty becomes morally problematic. Citizens of a state are not its responsibility alone, for outsiders too have duties to them, and the state is accountable to the rest of humankind for the way it treats them. Its sovereignty therefore can never be absolute and unconditional. If it engages in genocide or massive violations of basic human rights and freedoms, it fails to show respect for the dignity of its citizens and forfeits its claim to others' non-interference. Outsiders may then legitimately intervene and render such help as its citizens need to restructure the state.

Rather than undertake such interventions on an *ad hoc* basis, we need to establish clear norms of international law.[11] The norms should lay down the conditions under which such an intervention is justified and the limits to which it is subject. It cannot be left to the whims and self-interest of individual states and should be authorized by the United Nations. It should be undertaken for limited and clearly stated purposes, should have a reasonable chance of success, should involve minimum violence, and should be accompanied by a clear plan of reconstruction. Although the state has forfeited its sovereignty, the community concerned retains its right to independence. External intervention must respect this right and should not become an excuse to occupy the country or dictate its future.

Along with the principle of humanitarian intervention, the related doctrine of just war also needs to be reconsidered, especially as its assumptions about the nature of the world and war make only a limited sense today.[12] As traditionally formulated, it limits the discussion of war to those who are directly involved, and has little to say about the role of international institutions and third parties. It says little about the role of international law and the legality of war. It is silent about the warlike activities of non-statal agencies. It evaluates the morality of war solely in terms of justice, and that is too narrow, for a war might be just but ill advised because of the precedent it sets or its likely consequences. The traditional doctrine is also innocent of such other ways of securing the objectives of war as economic sanctions, pressure of world opinion, suspension from international institutions, and recourse to the international court of justice. If we are to discourage states from making up their own specious doctrines of justified war and using pre-emptive violence to counter hypothetical threats, we need to develop a new doctrine of ethical war, indicating not only when it might be justified but also laying down rules concerning its conduct, post-war responsibilities of combatants, and the treatment of prisoners.

The second important but neglected principle of global ethic has to do with the global cultural and moral diversity. Since different societies have different histories, traditions, cultures, ways of organising their affairs and values, respect for human beings requires that, subject to the constraints of universal principles, they should be not only free but encouraged to experiment with diverse visions of the good life. Such a diversity is also a global common good. No culture has the monopoly of truth, and represents the only truly human or even the best way to understand and order human life. All cultures are partial, realising some human capacities and forms of excellence and marginalizing others, cherishing some aspects of human life and ignoring others. A dialogue between them increases their capacity for self-consciousness and self-criticism, widens their horizons, and benefits them all. A world dominated by a single view of it would be not only culturally bland and impoverished, but would also lack a critical interlocutor and the space to look at itself from the standpoints of others, thus losing the vital capacity for a dialogue with itself.

Although diversity cannot be preserved like a museum artefact, we can do much to foster it. We can create conditions in which it is cherished and able to flourish by requiring international institutions to include it among their goals. We can also assign a special status to cultural products, exempt them from the usual terms of trade agreements, and allow societies to subsidize and protect their cultural industries within certain limits. Even if we have other reasons not to do this, we can at least refrain from undermining the global diversity by pressurising all societies to follow a uniform path of development and seeking to reshape them in the image of some hubristic vision of the world.

Thirdly and finally, a well-considered global ethic needs to value democratic participation and design international institutions accordingly.[13] All societies have a stake in the conduct of global affairs. They are deeply affected by it and have their own views on what principles should guide it. The kind of egalitarian intercultural dialogue we talked about earlier needs to take place in all international institutes and shape their deliberations. All states should therefore have an equal voice in the running of these institutions. The fact that they are vastly unequal in their economic and political power does not negate the case for equality any more then such inequalities within a political community detracts from the principle of political equality. As long as states remain political units for the purposes of international representation, they are all equal *qua* states. Indeed one might say that it is precisely because they are vastly unequal that we need equality of representation to counter it. Since governments alone do not speak for their citizens, the principle of democratic participation requires that we should find ways of representing nongovernmental organizations and ordinary citizens in global institutions, if not as their formal members then at least on their advisory councils. This enables us to hear neglected voices and to give these institutions and their policies a much-needed democratic legitimacy.

Conclusion

I sketched above some of the important principles of a global ethic. Some of these are increasingly being recognized, but they have not yet become part of a universal consensus. We need to press their case until they become as central to our moral and political discourse as human rights. The principles I have sketched are only illustrative, for there are many others that a fully worked out global ethic would need to include. Since ethics is not just about principles, norms and rights but also about virtues, a global ethic needs to explore the intellectual and moral virtues that citizens all over the world need to cultivate in order to cope with our interdependent and diverse world. This paper, is therefore, no more than a tentative prolegomenon to such a fully worked out global ethic.

Notes

[1] For good anthologies on globalization, see Benyon and Dunkerley (2000) and Scholte (2000).
[2] I have explored this in detail elsewhere. See Parekh (2000: chapter 4).

[3] For a critique of the limitations of Kant's universalizability principle, see Jones (1999: chapter 4), and Skorupski (1999: chapter 8). For an attempt to save the principle by radically reinterpreting it, see O'Neill (1986: chapter 7, especially pp. 130ff).

[4] See Parekh (2000: 81ff).

[5] See the *Declaration Toward a Global Ethic* by the Parliament of the World's Religions, September 1993. Its Introduction asserts that 'a common set of core values is found in the teachings of religions and that these form the basis of a global ethic'. The list is a mixed bag and includes common aspirations rather than shared values. Hans Küng, who influenced the Declaration, is one of the ablest champions of a religiously grounded and shared global ethic.

[6] See Parekh (2000: 126ff).

[7] For a fuller view, see Parekh (2003). I take it for granted partly because it is already part of the prevailing moral consensus.

[8] See Scheffler (2001: chapters 2 and 3); Honderich, (2002: chapters 2 and 4).

[9] For a good discussion, see the articles by David Miller and Cécile Fabre in Seglow (2002).

[10] I develop this argument more fully and propose a global welfare state in Parekh (2003: 3f).

[11] See the articles by Todorov, Ignatieff and Singer in Owen (2003); Wheeler (2000); Parekh (1997).

[12] For useful discussions, see Gilbert (2003: chapters 1, 5 and 6) and Walzer (1977). Walzer's discussion of just war does not escape some of the basic limitations of the traditional doctrine.

[13] For interesting ideas on how to restructure international institutions, see Commission on Global Governance (1995: chapters 4 and 5) and the articles by Anthony McGrew and James Goodman in Anderson (2002).

References

Anderson, J. (ed.) (2002), *Transnational Democracy: Political Spaces and Border Crossings*, London, Routledge.

Benyon, J. and Dunkerley, D. (eds) (2000), *Globalisation: The Reader*, London, Athlone Press.

Commission on Global Governance (1995), *Our Global Neighbourhood*, Oxford, Oxford University Press.

Gilbert, P. (2003), *New Terror, Just Wars*, Edinburgh, Edinburgh University Press.

Honderich, T. (2002), *After the Terror*, Edinburgh, Edinburgh University Press.

Jones, C. (1999), *Global Justice: Defending Cosmopolitanism*, Oxford, Oxford University Press.

O'Neill, O. (1986), *Faces of Hunger: An Essay on Poverty, Justice and Development*, London, Allen & Unwin.

Owen, N. (ed.) (2003), *Human Rights, Human Wrongs*, Oxford, Oxford University Press.

Parekh, B. (1997), 'Rethinking Humanitarian Intervention', *International Political Science Review* 18 (1).

Parekh, B. (2000), *Rethinking Multiculturalism*, London, Palgrave.

Parekh, B. (2003), 'Cosmopolitanism and Global Citizenship', *Review of International Studies* 29.

Scheffler, S. (2001), *Boundaries and Allegiances: Problems of Justice and Responsibility in Liberal Thought*, Oxford, Oxford University Press.

Scholte, J-A. (2000), *Globalisation: A Critical Introduction*, London, Macmillan.
Seglow, J. (ed.) (2002), *Ethics of Altruism*. A special issue of the *Critical Review of International Social and Political Philosophy* 5 (4).
Skorupski, J. (1999), *Ethical Explorations*, Oxford, Oxford University Press.
Walzer, M. (1977), *Just and Unjust Wars*, New York, Basic Books.
Wheeler, N.J. (2000), *Saving Strangers: Humanitarian Intervention in International Society*, Oxford, Oxford University Press.

Chapter 3

Cosmopolitan Political Community: Why does it Feel so Right?

Kate Nash

Introduction

> Nature should thus be thanked for fostering social incompatibility, enviously competitive vanity, and insatiable desires for possession or even power (Kant, 1991: 45).

We are all Americans (*Le Monde*, 12th September 2001).

Identification with a national community is typically associated with 'hot' emotions, and opposed to 'cool' cosmopolitanism as an ideal (Turner, 2000). 'Hot' communicates intensity of feeling experienced as such: while the causes and the precise coordinates of feeling may be questioned or confused (the premise of psychoanalysis), that there is emotion is not in doubt. 'Hot' emotions also suggest a direct link between emotion and motivation to act that is relatively unreflexive: these are the emotions that overwhelm reason and self-interest. 'Cool' emotions are experienced as more diffuse, where there is questioning of what is felt and where motivation to act is taken to be based on reflection.[1] In this chapter we will consider how the oversimplified characterization of national feeling as 'hot' and cosmopolitanism as 'cool' tends to reify the former and idealize the latter. We will consider cosmopolitanism in the neo-Kantian terms of human rights, in which, although emotion has not been addressed directly, 'hot' national feeling and 'cool' cosmopolitanism are implicitly opposed in this way. I will argue that the dichotomy makes it difficult to see how 'warm' cosmopolitanism is actually developing in political communities organized by western national states, in less rationalist ways than is suggested by neo-Kantians and in association with, rather than in opposition to, national feeling.

Despite the wide variety of groups that have considered themselves and been considered as nations, and despite differences of emphasis in accounts of nation-building and nationalism, most sociologists working in this area agree on three points. Firstly, a nation is distinguished from other, superficially similar groups, like ethnic or racial 'peoples', in that nations are linked to the ideal of self-determination through a state, whether as an aspiration, or, at the very least, as the memory of an administrative unity that approximated a state. This is clear from the very conflation of 'nation' as nation-state (in the United Nations, for example), and 'nation' as 'people living in a state' (see Billig, 1995: 24). In this sense nations are political communities. Secondly, it is widely agreed that nations are socially constructed. There have been a variety of paths to nationhood, depending on whether it has been imposed by elites, taken up as a national-popular movement, or linked to decolonization (Hobsbawm, 1990). But nations are not what nationalists take them to be: timeless communities 'naturally' based on shared 'race', culture, or language; they are modern phenomena that have been 'imagined' out of selectively appropriated and invented traditions. Thirdly, since there are no objective criteria upon which to decide which social groups are 'really' nations and which are not, it follows that the emergence of a particular nation depends ultimately on self-identification as such. As Gellner (1983) has it, 'it is nationalism which engenders nations, and not the other way around'.[2] An important peculiarity of the nation is, then, as Benhabib (1998) has argued, that it is socially constructed and yet experienced by those it for whom it forges a 'special unity and belonging' as essential: as having clearly delineated and coherent boundaries which exist over time.

Sociologists also agree that, in its essentialist mode, the nation is 'an emotionally charged object' (Guibernau and Rex, 1997: 4). For Anderson, the nation creates 'deep attachments' of fraternity that have made possible extraordinary sacrifices (1991: 7). For Gellner, nationalism involves righteous anger at the violation of the principle that nation and state should be congruent, or satisfaction at its fulfilment (1983: 1). Feelings of national belonging are also seen as central to the extension and consolidation of citizenship since they support a political community that requires sacrifice, seen primarily in gendered terms of military service and taxation (Habermas, 200: 64-65).[3] It is important to distinguish between different degrees of emotion that are felt for the nation, but also to note that they are differences of degree rather than of kind. As a feeling – rather than an ideology or a movement – nationalism is the same as patriotism, which is generally taken to involve love, but also pride in one's country, and usually a measure of hatred of the Other too. Once a nation-state is established, in times of peace feelings of national pride and solidarity may rarely be made explicit, though, as Billig has argued, it is in the 'banal nationalism' of everyday life that ideological parameters are set, as the assumptions and symbols of 'our' nation are 'flagged' (1995: 24). 'National feeling' encompasses a range of emotions, from jingoistic patriotism to the tacit acceptance that nationality confers more than just a passport – an acceptance exhibited by the practically universal willingness to consider stereotypes of national character plausible. National feeling invariably involves a degree of loyalty, affection, and pride: feelings of belonging are also feelings of attachment to a nation that is, if not good in absolute terms, certainly better than its immediate neighbours, and that, whatever else the individuals and groups who make it up may have in common, has had and will continue to have a historic destiny.

As an ideal, cosmopolitanism is invariably opposed as 'cool' to the 'hot' emotions of nationalism. It is also opposed to national feeling as such: a cosmopolitan, according to the *Oxford English Dictionary*, is 'free from national limitations and attachments' (Held, 1995: 227). There have been recent attempts to think beyond this opposition (Delanty, 2000; see also the discussions in Cohen, 1996, and Turner, 2000), as well as studies of 'actually existing cosmopolitanism', which are difficult to distinguish absolutely from transnational ethnonationalisms (Robbins, 1998). In this chapter we will focus on neo-Kantian understandings of cosmopolitan citizenship to be realized in legitimate human rights (Habermas, 1999, 2001; Held, 1995). In this usage, cosmopolitanism is close to that of the original Stoic idea of human beings as rational creatures with universal rights as citizens of the 'cosmopolis' (Held, 1995: 227). In terms of identity, it involves, above all, dis-identification from the nation.

The emotional 'coolness' of neo-Kantian cosmopolitanism is related to its basis in liberal-democratic human rights rather than in political community. This form of cosmopolitanism is secured by a commitment to autonomy that guides normative principles rather than by affective identification with one's fellows. Human rights are emotionally charged only by love of justice, altruism, or, as implied in Habermas's proposals for strengthening the legitimacy of human rights, by rationalized emotions of anger and resentment that have been worked on in deliberation to produce agreement on universals (2001: 110-111). It is hard to conceive of cosmopolitanism in terms of feelings of belonging to a political community because of the lack of global state, or even a world federation of states. Globalization does produce increased mutual interconnectedness and, arguably, a growing orientation towards global awareness (Albrow, 1996). There are overlapping political constituencies of belonging that cut across national borders, of which transnational social movements and INGOs are the most significant organizations. These political movements are, however, very far from forming a global movement that might displace national feeling. In the absence of a global political community, then, how might cosmopolitanism compete with nationalist particularisms?

For neo-Kantians, the development of a cosmopolitan political community is necessary if human rights are to be legitimate. As Held (1995) argues regarding his proposals for cosmopolitan democratic law, human rights require the consent and support of voters in national political communities, not only for strategic reasons, but also in order to be genuinely democratic. For Habermas too, existing forms of politics provide only 'weak legitimacy' for human rights, involving as they do the participation of elites rather than full debate in democratic societies (2001: 108-109). Processes of globalization have undoubtedly weakened the nation-state, but it is far from redundant. Since it is states that make, administer, and police human rights agreements, human rights claims may paradoxically reinforce the legitimacy of the national political community while at the same time altering traditionally indivisible state sovereignty (Soysal, 2001). For human rights to be democratic, then, it is necessary that members of national political communities learn to think and feel beyond the limits of national interests, otherwise governments will continue to address voters on this basis and the gross inequalities of the New World (Dis)Order will remain, both within national borders and beyond (Habermas, 2001: 112).

The Social Construction of National Feeling

To investigate the possibilities of creating a cosmopolitan political community, it is useful to study the emotions of 'actually existing' cosmopolitanism. On the basis of such an investigation, I will suggest that, in some significant cases at least, national feeling is constructed within a moral order in which 'real' emotions are figured as 'human'. This means that, under certain conditions, far from conflicting with national feeling, cosmopolitan emotions are actually implied in national feeling as such.

Since, as we have seen, it is generally agreed that the nation is socially constructed, an obvious place to begin enquiry into these issues is by considering the social construction of emotion. Indeed, the 'social constructionist' aspect of both theories has much in common: like nations, emotions are not to be seen as 'natural kinds', concrete, bounded 'things' that exist in and of themselves; they are rather contingent, historically and contextually specific. The chief empirical difference between nations and emotions in this respect is that the nation is not embodied, even if it is sometimes symbolized in this way (in the tomb of the Unknown Soldier, for example). Harré argues that the temptation to abstract and reify emotion is particularly strong because of experiential embodiment: it is tempting to treat emotion as an 'it' because of the way emotion is felt, often as a physiological agitation. However, this is to be resisted: once we begin to ask 'what is an emotion?', our answers will only uncover the commonsense ways in which emotion has been constructed in the usage of particular languages. Emotions are nothing other than the meanings they are given by the use of 'emotional vocabularies' in particular contexts (Harré, 1986).

A theory of the social construction of national feeling risks being circular. Benhabib argues that in nationalism, and indeed in identity/difference movements in general, essentialist versus constructivist perspectives may be seen as corresponding to the standpoint of the participant in social and political life and the observer, respectively (1998: 93). In terms of emotion, however, understanding of the participant position seems to do no more than replicate the rhetoric of nationalism itself: nations exist, endure, and command self-sacrifice because they feel right to those who identify as nationals. For social constructionists, national feeling is nothing more than what is socially identified as such in particular contexts by those who experience and witness it.

There is a further consideration that complicates this simple account, however. In comparison with personal emotions like jealousy, anger, envy, or grief, love of one's country – while it must surely be considered as an emotion – is rather abstract. It may be thought of, following Barbalet's insightful sociological analysis of emotions, as a 'macro-emotion', experienced collectively on a large-scale, beyond the face-to-face micro-social contexts that are the main focus of psychological studies of the social construction of emotion (2001: 71). This gives rise to particular theoretical and methodological difficulties. National feeling fulfils all the criteria social constructionists of emotion have identified for the use of emotion words: it may well involve bodily agitation; it is intentional – it is 'about' the nation; and it certainly involves a local moral order of rights, obligations, duties, and conventions of evaluation (Harré, 1996: 8). However, its abstract status as a 'macro-emotion' complicates national feeling and makes it peculiarly suspect in any particular case. As Barbalet puts it in his discussion of class resentment: 'One problem ... with any account which focuses upon groups rather than individuals, is that the actual emotional experience of any given person at any time will not correspond with the analogous 'micro-emotion' (Barbalet, 2001: 71). Using an analysis of media coverage of the 'war against terrorism' following the attack in New York on September 11, I want to suggest that national feeling is indeed complex, both 'micro' and 'macro', involving personal emotions that are encompassed as aspects of national feeling. Moreover, national feeling is understood in precisely this way by many of those who experience it: as consisting of empathetic identifications with others who feel certain emotions because they are human. It is because personal emotions and 'humanist' sympathy are reflexively intertwined in national feeling in this way that 'actually existing' cosmopolitanism is, under certain conditions, experienced as an extension of legitimate national feeling rather than as opposed to it.

The analysis will be focussed on the website set up to canvass 'Readers' Opinions' on the 'Portraits of Grief' series that ran in *The New York Times* until December 31, 2001. It is important to note that the example is not intended to *prove* that national feeling and 'humanist' sympathy are intertwined emotionally, but nor is it being used simply to *illustrate* the theory. The point of using this example is rather to contribute to thinking through the relationship between national feeling and 'humanist' sympathy in a concrete case. The example allows us to explore how at moments of heightened emotion national feelings of belonging are experienced temporally in a way that makes them impossible to separate absolutely from strong feelings about people who are 'like us', not just as fellow nationals but also as human beings. It is not difficult to find counterexamples in which the non-national Other continues to be interpreted as less-than-human. I am suggesting, however, that the logic of national feeling is such that under certain conditions, even where it is at the 'hot' end of the scale, as it was in the US after 9/11, it may be 'convertible' into what I will call 'popular cosmopolitanism'.

The 'war' on terrorism is, of course, unlike typical wars in many ways. It did, however, intensify national feeling in the US and this intensity is prominent in 'Portraits of Grief'.[4] The 'Portraits of Grief' themselves are short, simply written obituaries of those who died in the Twin Towers. They emphasize the 'ordinariness' of those who died and are far from explicitly patriotic. The fact of American nationality is not even noted – it is assumed – and other countries appear to be mentioned only as incidental facts of some people's lives: one man retained his Indian citizenship, for example; another married a woman from his hometown in Italy. In this respect, the 'Portraits of Grief' are celebrations of individuality rather than of nationality. Nevertheless, *The New York Times* is a national newspaper and, as we would expect, many of the readers who wrote to the web forum express themselves as belonging to the 'imagined community' of America through these reports.

Many of the emails, unsurprisingly, explicitly enact a sense of national belonging 'To the families of the victims: the whole country shares your grief' (from 'thechunk' Dec 5); 'to pay homage to all the beautiful lives *we* lost' (italics added; from 'tkeene' Dec 5); 'with love to my fellow Americans and to those in the world that are standing with us' ('melmunch' Dec 7); and so on. Furthermore, many of those that do not thematize American belonging explicitly nevertheless end their messages with 'God Bless America' (though, as a marker of belonging, this is complicated by the fact that one of these identifies herself as Chinese and living in China ('jo-jo lam' Dec 31)). There are also a number that enact a more cosmopolitan sense of solidarity, explicitly criticizing American patriotism and calling for wider identifications: 'let us be aware that we alone do not suffer this trauma, but it happens all over the world' (from 'Andrew' Dec 11); 'I suggest that we spend a lot more time asking each other what it is we value about being Americans. If it's living without regard for the rest of the world, we are fools' (from 'derrelldurrett' Dec 20); 'We need to see 'Portraits of Grief' for the victims of the bombings in Afghanistan and Iraq' (from 'dclearwaters' Dec 23).

The expressions of national solidarity here are self-evidently 'hotter' than those of cosmopolitanism, which appear to be more critical and reflective than emotive. Importantly, however, these 'hot' expressions of national feeling gain much of their emotional charge from the context in which they are embedded: they are almost invariably intertwined with personal feelings of shock, grief, or sympathy. In a way this is simply produced by the question 'How has your own life changed since the attacks?' that solicited responses to the 'Portraits of Grief'. The writers almost always make reference to the suffering of individuals and families who died, or who were close to or knew someone who died, as a result of the attack on the World Trade Centre. The implication, sometimes made explicit, is that we know, understand, and share what they are feeling because we too have suffered injury or bereavement in our personal lives. In this way, national feeling is constructed out of empathetic identification with the personal feelings of fellow nationals.

However, many of the emails also implicitly point beyond the limits of nationality in their appeals to empathize with personal suffering: they rely on an understanding of what others must feel because they are human. Often the writer invokes the commonality of 'human' suffering by describing how they themselves feel: 'Just imagining how many grieving families and friends are out there seemed overwhelming' (from 'stefr' Dec 5); 'I find every day to be a struggle, to see faces on the train that also see life as a struggle' (from 'dtsalvati' Dec 6). Sometimes the writers link 'human' suffering to more personal feelings of loss and pain, making reference to loss in their own life, whether directly related to the events of September 11 or not. More usually, however, they simply assume that 'we', the readers, understand and share these feelings, or they demand what 'should be' a shared response: 'if we imagine the pain of the victims' families, this should make us realize how precious life is and not to worry about little things' (from 'shahla7' Dec 5); 'I am Californian and felt my heart was broken the day of Sept 11, 2001. Everybody at work was feeling the pain every person that has a heart felt'

('123456162' Dec 31). Alternatively the grief is felt to be unimaginable, and therefore knowable as such: 'I cannot imagine the sorry and grief they friends and families feel, but nevertheless, my thoughts and heart will be forever with them' ('sansan16' Dec 20).

In this way, then, feelings of national belonging are constructed through personal emotions that are understood to be common to all humans. National feeling is constructed in 'Portraits of Grief' as a 'macro-emotion' in that it is assumed that fellow nationals all feel the same way about the same events: 'we' feel together as a nation who is reading and writing to a forum organized in the name of a national newspaper. However, the feelings themselves are not oriented to the nation, nor, in the great majority of cases, are they expressed for others specifically as Americans. They are shared and understood as feelings 'anyone would/should have' if they were to put themselves in the position of individuals and families who feel the 'human' emotions of love, grief and loss. In this respect, the 'micro-feelings' that bring us together as a nation are not limited to fellow nationals: they are universal, personal emotions. 'Humanist' sympathy is occasionally made explicit in these emails: 'It is a blessing to be reminded of the sanctity of every human life, even as we are happy to learn and celebrate all the ways the lost beloved fold lived life to its fullness' ('hill634' Dec 13); 'People were mourning and sad, but at the same time the tragedy brought the best out of everyone – people going out of their way to help others, people consoling perfect strangers – in a city that is renowned to be all rush, rush, rush...' ('sansan16' Dec 20). 'Humanist' sympathy is nevertheless implicit, where it is not explicit, in all the appeals to a common sense of emotional experience.

Implicit 'humanist' sympathy is clear if we consider how inappropriate an expression of emotion that articulated *nothing but* a love of country and sympathy for others only because they are fellow nationals would be in such a context. The moral order within which national feeling makes sense is evident in these emails insofar as, although it is not an interactive forum, 'excesses' of emotion do receive correction. There are actually only two types of emails that produce a response from readers of 'Portraits of Grief' who write in to *The New York Times* website. The first is in response to expressions of grief that seem excessive in proportion to the writer's direct personal experience of bereavement. The second is in response to those, relatively rare, interventions that vow revenge on 'our' enemies in the name of those fellow nationals who are suffering. The two are often linked in that excess in the first case is rebuked as giving fuel to excess of the second kind, as in the following message:

> OK, I'm going to offer what may be a 'politically incorrect' statement, but bear with me... Unless you had someone that you know directly die in the attack(s), I don't believe that you should still be in grief. Personally, my life hasn't really changed that much... I worry more about the future now, I guess, since the anti-terrorism hyperbole that has erupted after 9/11 has helped push two countries to the brink of nuclear war, and I'm afraid that, in the future, it will be easy to simply point a finger at someone and yell 'terrorist', as easy as it was to point a finger and yell 'witch' in the past ('tamcmahan66' Jan 2 2002).

This was followed next day by a supporting message: 'it is time to stop revelling in our schizophrenic patriotism and grief, which has done nothing more than stoke the fire of national hate' ('nadimk' Jan 3). It would seem that, in this context at least, it is more legitimate to suffer personal emotion as an individual or a member of a family who has been bereaved, or to offer sympathy to those fellow nationals who have suffered, than it to express abstract 'national grief' or 'militaristic nationalism'. There is a moral order at work here within which national feeling is being constructed: 'proper' national feeling is limited to sympathies for others based on 'what they must feel as we would feel if it were our personal grief'. It is not that nationalism necessarily gives way to cosmopolitanism in such a moral order. It is rather that 'humanist' sympathy enables the contestation of what is reasonable and right as a response to the nation's enemies. In these responses to the events of September 11, nationalism is contested primarily in terms of emotions: both strategic and normative reasoning is secondary. What is right as a response to the nation's enemies must be grounded in proper emotions, which are personal and human rather than simply patriotic.

This analysis shows how 'humanist' sympathies, personal emotions, and nationalist sentiments are interrelated in twenty-first century America, even – or perhaps especially – at times when national feeling is heightened. The specificities of the analysis may be limited to the setting of liberal America. *The New York Times* is a liberal newspaper in which we would expect to find nationalism tempered by 'humanism', in comparison with other US media. The question 'How has your own life changed since the attacks?' may be seen as peculiarly productive of emotional response from those schooled in 'intimate citizenship' (see Berlant, 1997). Finally, insofar as 'humanist' sympathy is historically and culturally specific, it may be that nationalism outside the West is not experienced in the same way. Nevertheless, there are reasons to suppose that the analysis made of this particular case may have more general significance. Firstly, the geopolitical importance of the US makes it particularly significant for the extension and securing of cosmopolitan human rights. We will examine this issue more closely in the final section of the paper. And secondly, there seems no reason to suppose that national feeling is less complex in other settings if we consider that emotion is necessarily experienced as embodied and temporal.

Barbalet's temporal theory of emotions gives us a way to think the complexity of the social construction of national feeling. If, he argues, social life is understood as process, in which actors, structures, and institutions are always becoming rather than in a state of fixed, essential being, then emotion too should be understood as social process (rather than as a product of social management). Moreover, emotion should not be understood in exclusively cognitivist terms, a tendency Barbalet criticizes in social constructionism. He argues that 'emotion can be neither hindered nor removed except by another emotion' (2001: 181; following Spinoza, 1996).[5] In the case of national feeling, then, it is necessarily provoked in relation to, and temporally limited by, other, equally strong emotions. As we have seen, personal feelings, feelings for others, and feelings for the nation succeed and strengthen each other in the process in which attachments to the nation are constituted. National feeling is also limited in relation to personal emotions and 'human' sympathies in the moral order through which nationalism is constructed. This moral order – at least in twenty-first century America, influenced historically by 'sentimental citizenship' requires that national feeling *should* exist in relation to other, deeply-felt but limited personal emotions and 'human' sympathies. To return to Benhabib's puzzle over how it is that the nation is constructed and yet experienced as essential, nationalism does involve the feeling that 'I belong to a nation that is unified, coherent, and enduring', but those feelings of belonging are not themselves unified, coherent, and enduring.

Cosmopolitan Citizenship

In the absence of a world state, the extension of human rights gives some substance to the idea of cosmopolitan citizenship. Human rights are being extended by 'non-coercive' means through the institutions of the UN and the EU. They are also, more dramatically, being extended through new forms of war, both in 'humanitarian interventions' and in peace settlements (Kaldor, 1999).[6]

Western governments, ultimately answerable to the electorate, must justify getting involved in wars of humanitarian intervention that may lead to loss of citizens' lives and that cannot be described very convincingly as serving national interests. Humanitarian wars require compassion and support for altruistic action on the part of governments and voters who are also taxpayers. The ongoing 'war against terrorism' is undoubtedly ambiguous in this respect: declared on the grounds of US national security, the bombing of Afghanistan was, however, carried out by the military coalition in the name of humanitarian intervention, to overthrow the Taliban and restore Afghanistan to its people. Martin Shaw (1996) has argued that the impetus for humanitarian interventions has generally come less from national states than from the media, which solicit compassion using the themes of 'humanist' sympathy that, as we have seen, are also productive of nationalist feeling. We are by now all familiar with the portrayal of war leaders who bring ruin to the country and distress and suffering to 'innocent people'. The separation of 'the people' from warmongers enables an identification across national differences that is solicited on the basis of human feelings: though they differ from us in various ways, nevertheless 'ordinary people' suffer the same 'micro-emotions' we would feel in their situation, losing friends, family, homes, jobs, and education as a result of religious persecution and war. In the case of the war in Afghanistan, the emphasis of human interest stories was on refugees and on women's lives under the Taliban.

It is in the soliciting of human identification across national differences that we see 'popular cosmopolitanism' as an extension of the complexity of emotions that make up national feeling rather than in dichotomous opposition to it. In some cases, 'popular cosmopolitanism' certainly is in tension with national feeling. As one contributor to the 'Portraits of Grief' (who had lost his sister and who was not 'corrected' for excessive emotion) wrote: 'I am filled with hatred for people I do not know nor understand. I have no pity for the starving children or their parents. I only feel they deserve it for all the death their people have caused here' ('jsaladino1' Jan 11). On other occasions, however, it is possible to go so far as to figure 'popular cosmopolitanism' as a hybrid form of 'cosmopolitan patriotism'. In response to President Bush's suggestion that every American child give $1 to help Afghan children survive the winter, one child wrote: 'there is a lot that we can do to help people, not only Americans but the children that are starving and hurting inside ... Doing this wonderful act of kindness just shows what a wonderful country we are' ('Gina' http://www.nytimes.com/learning/students/letters/).

'Popular cosmopolitanism' is, of course, highly volatile and erratic: it seems only rarely to extend to asylum-seekers, for example, especially where conflicts over local resources are in question, and it rarely implicates individuals in acts of generosity or independent action against injustice (Cohen, 2001). The uneven and contradictory development of 'popular cosmopolitanism' is no doubt linked in part to its emergence as 'consent to global rule' by Western powers extending human rights by military force. Is it possible that in this respect 'popular cosmopolitanism' is following an historical trajectory much more like that of nationalism than would be expected, given an understanding of 'hot' nationalism as opposed to 'cool' cosmopolitanism? It may be that, in extending human rights by force, western states acting in coalition are a 'state conglomerate', a multinational bloc that forms an effective centre of power through which successful wars can be prosecuted (Shaw, 1999). In this sense, 'popular cosmopolitanism' may be closely tied to the development of the 'Western state', just as nationalism is tied to the development of the nation-state.

I have argued that the distinction between 'hot' nationalism and 'cool' cosmopolitanism reifies the former and idealizes the latter. In relation to the western state, cosmopolitanism is less likely to be based on 'cool' altruism than on sympathy with human suffering, understanding of personal emotions, and even, paradoxically, heightened feelings of national feeling in 'new wars'. Although fear and hatred of enemies both outside and inside the nation should not, of course, be underestimated, what makes humanitarian intervention 'right' for the citizens of the West is less likely to be the reasoned principles with which cosmopolitanism is associated in neo-Kantianism, than sentimental 'popular cosmopolitanism' that makes it *feel right*. As Arendt argued, compassion justifies violence against those who cause suffering, obviating the need for 'wearisome processes of persuasion, negotiation, and compromise' (1990: 187). The media is much better at representing people in conflicts as victims than as protagonists; newspapers and TV reports rarely take seriously the self-representations of those in conflict situations, and they tend to take their cue from Western governments and international organizations (Shaw, 1996: 182). The extension of human rights by military means that is justified by 'popular cosmopolitanism' does not require a highly engaged, democratic process of negotiation.

Clearly, 'popular cosmopolitanism' is very far from the neo-Kantian ideal. It may therefore be argued that it is not cosmopolitanism at all. However, neo-Kantians tend to be ambivalent about the extension of human rights by force (including Habermas, 1999; Held, undated). The most difficult question for those committed to cosmopolitan democracy is surely whether the democratic institution of human rights is made more or less unlikely by their extension into undemocratic countries, however that is achieved. A further pragmatic question concerns the emotional resources on which substantive human rights might draw. If citizenship rights within state borders have relied on national feeling to underpin political community, might not substantive human rights that require redistribution of wealth, ecological awareness, and self-sacrifice have to rely on the rather dubious emotional identifications of 'popular cosmopolitanism', rather than on the rational deliberations of an informed and impartial democratic public?

Notes

[1] The distinction between 'hot' and 'cool' is similar to Hume's analysis of 'calm' and 'violent' emotions. According to Hume, 'calm' emotions are often confused with reason, though '[r]eason is, and ought only to be the slave of the passions' and 'violent' emotions that are relatively constant are most likely to motivate us to action (Hume, 1978: 415).
[2] The chief opponent of the view that nations are modern social constructions is Anthony Smith (1995: 39-40). We will not deal with this debate here, except to note that one of his objections to the argument is that social constructionists under-estimate 'hot' loyalty to the nation.
[3] The direct 'emotion work' that women as citizens are required to do generally goes unacknowledged in mainstream writing on citizenship. On this, see Pateman (1989).
[4] http://www.nytimes.com/pages/national/portraits/ (downloaded 15.1.02).
[5] Barbalet is also close to Hume (1978) on this point.
[6] The principle is not itself new. Kant considered intervention into states torn apart by civil strife legitimate, though he otherwise upheld the principle of state sovereignty. In fact, it may be seen as a principle that is integral to state-building and the construction of the interstate system itself. On this, see Badie (2000).

References

Albrow, M. (1996), *The Global Age: State and Society beyond Modernity*, Cambridge, Polity Press.
Anderson, B. (1991), *Imagined Communities: Reflections on the Origins and Spread of Nationalism*, London, Verso.
Arendt, H. (1990), *On Revolution*, Harmondsworth, Penguin.
Badie, B. (2000), *The Imported State: The Westernization of the Political Order*, Stanford, Stanford University Press.
Barbalet, J. (2001), *Emotion, Social Theory and Social Structure: A Macrosociological Approach*, Cambridge, Cambridge University Press.
Benhabib, S. (1998), 'Democracy and Identity: In Search of the Civic Polity', *Philosophy and Social Criticism* **24** (3), pp. 85-100.
Berlant, L. (1997), *The Queen of America Goes to Washington City*, Durham, Duke University Press.
Billig, M. (1995), *Banal Nationalism*, London, Sage.
Cohen, J. (ed.) (1996), *For Love of Country: Debating the Limits of Patriotism*, Boston, Beacon Press.

Cohen, S. (2001), *States of Denial: Knowing About Atrocities and Suffering*, Cambridge, Polity Press.

Delanty, G. (2000), *Citizenship in a Global Age: Society, Culture, Politics*, Buckingham, Open University Press.

Gellner, E. (1983), *Nations and Nationalism*, Oxford, Blackwell.

Guibernau, M. and Rex, J. (1997), 'Introduction', in M. Guibernau and J. Rex (eds), *The Ethnicity Reader: Nationalism, Multiculturalism and Migration*, Cambridge, Polity Press.

Habermas, J. (1999), 'Bestiality and Humanity: A War on the Border between Legality and Morality', *Constellations* 6 (3), pp. 263-72.

Habermas, J. (2001), *The Postcolonial Constellation: Political Essays*, Cambridge, Polity Press.

Harré, R. (1986), *The Social Construction of Emotions*, Oxford, Blackwell.

Held, D. (1985), *Democracy and the Global Order: From the Modern State to Cosmopolitan Governance*, Cambridge, Polity Press.

Held, D. (undated), 'Violence, Law and Justice in a Global Age' at http://www.ssrc.org/sept11/essays/held.htm (downloaded 21.1.2002).

Hobsbawm, E.J. (1990), *Nations and Nationalism since 1780: Programme, Myth, Reality*, Cambridge, Cambridge University Press.

Hume, D. (1978), *A Treatise on Human Nature*, Oxford, Clarendon Press.

Kaldor, M. (1999), *Old and New Wars: Organized War in a Global Age*, Cambridge, Polity Press.

Kant, I. (1991), *Political Writings*, Cambridge, Cambridge University Press.

Pateman, C. (1989), *The Disorder of Women*, Cambridge, Polity Press.

Robbins, B. (1998), 'Actually Existing Cosmopolitanism', in P. Cheah and B. Robbins (eds), *Cosmopolitics: Thinking and Feeling Beyond the Nation*, Minneapolis, University of Minnesota Press.

Shaw, M. (1996), *Civil Society and Media in Global Crises: Representing Distant Violence*, London, Pinter.

Shaw, M. (1999), 'The Kosovan War, 1998-99: Transformations of State, War and Genocide in the Global Revolution', *Sociological Research Online* 4/2 http://www.socresonline.org.uk/4/2/shaw.html.

Smith, A. (1995), *Nations and Nationalism in a Global Era*, Cambridge, Polity Press.

Soysal, Y. (2001), 'Postnational Citizenship: Reconfiguring the Familiar Terrain', in K. Nash and A. Scott (eds), *The Blackwell Companion to Political Sociology*, Oxford, Blackwell.

Spinoza, B. de (1996), *Ethics*, Harmondsworth, Penguin.

Turner, B.S. (2000), 'Liberal Citizenship and Cosmopolitan Virtue', in A. Vandenberg (ed.), *Citizenship and Democracy in a Global Era*, Basingstoke, Macmillan.

Turner, B.S. (2002), 'Cosmopolitan Virtue: Globalization and Patriotism', *Theory, Culture and Society* 19 (1-2), pp. 45-63.

Chapter 4

Towards an Embodied Global Ethic

Luigi Esposito and John W. Murphy

Introduction

The current world order is said to be one where all social institutions are organized around rationality, and where humans have achieved an increased 'mastery' of the world through new technologies and advances in science. Considering all this, one cannot help but ask why, despite unprecedented advances in technology, science, and trade, the present world order also continues to promote extreme inequality and the disenfranchisement of the majority of the world's population?

Recent writers answer this question by pointing to the lack of an appropriate global ethic. Stated simply, an ethic of global responsibility – one that is representative of all cultures and people – is missing from the current world order (e.g. Küng, 1991). Accordingly, the global capitalist economy and the political relations among nation-states are organized and managed in a way that excludes the identities and interests of various segments of humanity. Thus, for example, exclusion and oppression – practices that are antithetical to ethics – are exercised in the name of 'the good', while all ideals and practices that diverge from dominant interests (dressed up as moral universals) are vilified as irrational and uncivilized. Claims to 'moral purity' (e.g. the good), in other words, are called on to legitimize domination and oppression.

A thorough understanding of this problematic paradox requires a critical analysis of how morality/ethics has been traditionally understood. Throughout much of Western history, human conduct has been evaluated on the basis of moral standards that are divorced from the purposeful efforts of people. Standards of correct action are, therefore, assumed to be derived from non-contingent grounds (Murphy, 1989: 73). Accordingly, as people conform to these standards, dismal social conditions engendered by the resulting institutional practices are typically assumed to be neutral, although unfortunate, outcomes that carry no ethical burdens, for they reside outside all human intention and reflect the laws associated with a reality *sui generis*.

Ethics and the Quest for Moral Absolutes in the Western Tradition

Throughout much of the history of Western ethics, attempts have been made to find moral absolutes that can be used to evaluate and determine the true worth of all human actions. Among the classical Greeks, this effort begins with Socrates (as revealed in Plato's works). In the name of true knowledge, Socrates developed his rendition of ethics as a critique of the arbitrary morality advanced by the Sophists. According to Socrates, ethics are predicated on virtue – an innate rational knowledge of what is truly good. This knowledge contains invariable laws that could be called on to evaluate (and determine) the quality of all human conduct. These laws, moreover, are independent of the fluctuating choices of individuals (Rogers, 1945: 33-35). Therefore, Socrates's assertion that virtue represents pure wisdom unencumbered by passion opened the possibility for establishing an unquestionable foundation for moral absolutes.

In the writings of Plato, such standards are found in a metaphysical order and are embodied in 'ideal forms'. These forms are basically flawless archetypes that contain the essence of all things, and thus provide the necessary basis on which to build a moral and just society. Plato's central point is that morality is not found in the purposeful intentions of people; morality, in other words, is not something people contrive. Instead, morality is found in the basic and eternal metaphysical order that governs the entire universe. Ahistorical archetypes, in effect, dictate true moral standards.

Subsequently, Aristotle followed both Socrates and Plato's directives and sought non-contingent moral standards. But while Plato had found a basis for ethics and justice in archetypes that were thought to exist outside quotidian concerns, Aristotle sought to develop an ethics grounded on moral principles that were not separate from, but rather reflected human considerations. Simply put, ethics are inextricably tied to specific assumptions, interests, and intentions that are thoroughly mediated by thinking agents who attach a specific finality to their actions as they exercise reason. Nonetheless, Aristotle also suggests that human reason, and all the institutions and conventions that are produced through the exercise of reason, are also reflections of an ahistorical, and seemingly perfect, natural order. Although Aristotle breaks from Plato's supernatural basis for morality, reason is nonetheless simply a reflection of nature. Here again, reason is not something people create but rather constitutes an *a priori* source of wisdom.

Much later, in the medieval period, divine law became the basis for ethics. In other words, the sources of morality that Plato found in ideal forms and Aristotle in reason, were replaced by the notion of God. In point of fact, during this time, the notion of reason seemed unholy to many theologians and philosophers. Reason, in effect, was too closely associated with the glorification of secular knowledge that, to many thinkers of the time, was synonymous with heresy.

This tendency to associate reason with blasphemy was eventually called into question by Saint Thomas Aquinas. Stated simply, Aquinas (re)discovered classical Greek thought, and sought to reconcile Aristotle's notion of reason with faith in God. He maintained that reason and faith were not antagonistic forces. Instead, combining the two would actually lead to a greater understanding of God. According to Aquinas, there exist natural laws that govern the universe, and these laws are communicated by God to people through reason. Reason, in effect, is a gift from God, and not a form of heresy.

Beginning in the late 16th and early 17th centuries, in the wake of the Reformation, reason became separate from faith and tradition, thus spawning the so-called Enlightenment era. During this time, rationality replaced piety as the ultimate source of moral wisdom. Nonetheless, Western writers of the modern era continued the quest to find moral precepts in non-contingent sources of knowledge. Morality originates neither in a supernatural realm, nor in the purposeful efforts of people, but rather in the laws of nature. This assumption inspired further efforts to develop a 'science of right living' that, in turn, would produce a moral and perfect society.

Morality in Modern Western Philosophy: Naturalism, Utilitarianism, and Evolutionism

Thomas Hobbes is widely recognized as a central figure in natural law theory. In the 17th century, Hobbes made the claim that morality does not reside in some extra-sensory realm, such as God or a metaphysical order. His central point is that morality depends on establishing a centralized state. Specifically, morality is predicated on forging a social contract – enforced by an omnipotent state – whereby those in power secure their self-interests by safeguarding the needs of the ruled majority. In effect, Hobbes assumed that a stable order, even if repressive, is morally superior to one where people are unconstrained, for they – because of their very nature – cannot be entrusted to secure a moral order.

Following the naturalist tradition of Hobbes, David Hume also suggested that morality does not come automatically, but rather must be achieved through a social covenant that ensures the common good (MacIntyre, 1966). Although Hume accepts that reason enables persons to distinguish between truth and falsehood, reason itself does not produce a sense of morality. Instead, sentiment and reason interplay to produce moral judgement. However, while morality is essentially an experiential phenomenon, people possess a "moral sense" that is intrinsic to human nature. People, in effect, are epiphenomena of instinctual impulses that are governed by nature, and behave on the basis of pre-social moralistic axioms that they 'feel' or 'sense' in a passive, mechanical way. In the end, Hume appears to embrace a Platonic form of morality organized around specific human traits.

Hume's work went on to inspire the utilitarian ethics of Jeremy Bentham and John S. Mill in the nineteenth century. Consistent with the British naturalist tradition, Jeremy Bentham suggested that "nature has placed man under the governance of two sovereign masters, pain and pleasure. It is for them alone to point out what we ought to do, as well as to determine what we shall do" (Bentham, 1789: 4). But how can this so-called principle of utility be considered moral, if individuals are exclusively (and naturally) concerned with seeking their own pleasure? Bentham answers this question by making the claim that there is harmony between private and public pleasures. In effect, ethical relations are possible because individual actors are, as if by accident, beneficial to one another. Specifically, in using each other as the means to fulfill their respective ends, all individuals automatically aid others.

J.S. Mill also developed an understanding of morality based on the principle of utility, but sought to break from 'psychological hedonism' espoused by Bentham. Specifically, Mill argued that if people are assumed to act *solely* on the basis of self-interest, there was no possibility for establishing a moral society. To avoid this dismal outcome, Mill returned to Hume's idea that, although an element of egotism in human nature is undeniable, rational people are also naturally endowed with conscientious feelings that vouchsafe the common good. Here again, human action becomes ancillary to morality in Mill's utilitarian ethics, for people's moral conscience is not necessarily something that is contrived, but rather constitutes an external force that operates through the psychological make-up of people.

This lack of meaningfulness is later exacerbated in the ethics of Herbert Spencer, who combined Bentham's utilitarianism with Darwin's evolutionism. People, in Spencer's view, compete with one another for both survival and pleasure, and this condition is inscribed in the laws of nature. Accordingly, evolution provides a filtering process whereby life's pleasures – and, indeed, survival itself – are allotted to the most deserving individuals. Moral conduct and ethical relations are those that comply with the laws of evolution and, thus, guarantee that only the most adept and virtuous of all people survive.

In sum, throughout the mainstream Western tradition, morality has been understood dualistically. From classical Greek to post-enlightenment philosophy, a moral order is achieved either through widespread conformity to reified, pre-social archetypes associated with Platonic forms, God's wisdom, natural laws, and ahistorical reason; or, in an automatic fashion, as people passively follow abstract 'moral instincts'. Conceived dualistically, a moral order becomes a lifeless order, one divorced from human purpose. As a result, morality becomes disassociated easily from social conditions and human concerns and transformed into a fetish that may promote oppression, extreme inequality, and exclusion. At this time, the moral philosophy underpinning liberal capitalism has led to this dismal outcome.

Neo-liberalism, Moral Absolutism, and Ethical Bankruptcy

Advocates of neo-liberalism continue the quest for moral absolutes and find them in the laws of free trade. This claim, of course, is predicated on the reification of the market. In fact, recent Latin American writers (e.g. Serrano-Caldera, 1995; Hinkelammert, 1995) have criticized neo-liberalism for supporting what they call a 'Total Market'. Stated simply, the market is granted a *sui generis* status and assumed to require no basis for legitimacy outside its own logic. Human relations are thus organized around specific market norms that are presumed to be impartial and ethical, but yet are divorced from quotidian concerns and social conditions. Alejandro Serrano-Caldera (1993) describes this condition as a type of "social schizophrenia", whereby ethical principles are disassociated from institutional practices. For example, although countries of the so-called free world embrace modern values such as liberty, justice, and democracy, the majority of people in these societies have very little control over economic affairs, how technology is applied, what objectives should guide scientific research, or how political decisions are to be made and enacted. This paradox is also at the heart of what is commonly referred to as the 'crisis of modernity', a condition whereby powerful actors secure their power and privileges by rallying around ideals that are supposed to be impartial, and, most importantly, are identified to secure democracy and improve overall social conditions. This crisis, moreover, is predicated on a type of rationality that is purely instrumental rather than creative, and thus represses the human dimension of social life, where uniqueness is expressed, social needs and desires are made known, and all innovations and social alternatives are spawned.

Most important for this discussion, however, is that because the market order is assumed to be predicated on the rational intellect of individuals, and, moreover, rationality is assumed to be instrumental and guided by the universal and ahistorical laws of trade, ethics/morality is little more than rules that legitimize market demands, thereby sustaining current relations of power and inequality. In this sense, morality becomes little more than blind faith in the market, and this means that ethical relations afford individuals the right to compete freely. Almost invariably, there are losers and winners in these relations (many more of the former than the latter). And yet, there is very little moral concern with securing the needs and rights of those who 'lose' (i.e. the majority). At most, measures are taken to ensure that all players stay in the game (e.g. structural adjustment programmes), while the game itself (i.e. free trade) survives through a form of moralistic fatalism that dismisses social injustice and human oppression as natural outcomes.

In sum, by sundering ethics from purposeful and meaningful human interaction, ethical concerns become secondary to formal rules and procedures that channel actions into acceptable modes of (rational) behavior. Thus, ethics becomes little more than conformity to reified institutions. Ethics, in other words, is disembodied from human considerations and tied to an institutional order associated with a reality *sui generis*, or a Total Market. In the end, the Total Market is simply another Platonic form that promotes ethical emptiness. Because the market is treated as an ahistorical/apolitical entity, ethical principles are presumed to be disinterested and impartial.

Hans Küng and the Search for a New Global Ethic

How can people hope to break from this oppressive state of affairs? Recent writers have argued that the solution lies in developing a new global ethic. In recent years, Hans Küng has gained international recognition as one of the most prominent advocates for such an ethic. In 1993, Küng met with some of the world's religious leaders at the Parliament of the World's Religions and produced a document titled 'The Declaration of a Global Ethic'. He contends that only through an ethic that is truly representative of all cultures and people can humanity hope to correct the present global crisis. As stated by Küng:

> Never has there been such a need for a mechanism to counter global distress.
> Fortunately, a common ethic already exists within all the religious teachings of the

world. This can supply the moral foundation for a vision to lead men and women away from despair, and society away from chaos (quoted in Holland, 2000: 1).

Although Küng makes the claim that a global ethic must be based on an inter-religious dialogue, this exchange is nonetheless constrained within various cultural interpretations of a *universal* source of moral wisdom. This central source of moral wisdom can, in turn, provide a common set of ethical standards that all humans should agree on.

Nonetheless, achieving consensus can be problematic. Specifically, consensus runs the risk of constraining dialogue by presupposing moral imperatives that define with certainty what is right or wrong, moral or immoral, good or evil. Indeed, Küng seems to be espousing a deterministic position by proposing the existence of unconditional and transcendental moral absolutes, similar to Platonic forms, that lie outside human *praxis*. Küng (1991: 53) writes:

> The quality of ethical [conduct] ... cannot be grounded by human beings, who are conditioned in many ways, but only by that which is unconditional: by an Absolute which can provide an overarching meaning and which embraces and permeates individual human nature, and indeed the whole of human society. That can be the ultimate, supreme reality, which while it cannot be proved rationally, can be accepted in a rational trust – regardless of how it is named, understood, or interpreted in the different religions.

In the end, Küng's project of a global ethic fails to correct the present 'moral crisis' that plagues the current world order. In seeking ahistorical ethical standards, Küng dismisses the social context where these standards are validated. Because a 'moral high ground' is retained to anchor ethical standards, dialogue is reduced to technicalities, and, as a result, substantive social change is unlikely.[1] In this sense, Küng does not break away from the Western tendency to conceive morality dualistically.

The Demise of Dualism and the Need for an Embodied Global Ethic

Recent trends in social philosophy have called into question the legitimacy of dualism. A basis for morality outside human contingencies is understood to be impossible, for knowledge is inextricably tied to people and thus is inevitably contextual and limited. The absence of neutrality revealed by this theoretical maneuver has been given a specific form in the works of Latin American philosophers associated with liberation philosophy (notably Enrique Dussel), as well as in the writing of Alejandro Serrano-Caldera. According to these writers, when conceived dualistically (i.e. as existing independently of humans) morality is transformed easily into a tool for legitimizing domination and repression. To counteract this adverse condition, dualism is attacked. Subsequent to the demise of dualism, ethical norms/ideals do not simply organize behavior, as if they represented *a priori* referents; instead, these ideals are found precisely in the actions themselves.

Accordingly, because ethical norms emerge out of the purposeful actions of people, immoral social outcomes promoted by institutional beliefs and practices can no longer find legitimacy in reified abstractions such as a Total Market. Indeed, once ethics becomes embodied and purposeful, institutional barriers no longer have the status necessary to silence anyone. Instead, the voices of *everyone* require serious attention; after all, the voices themselves, and nothing else, become the only available source of morality.

(i) Continental Philosophy

The works of Karl Marx and Emmanuel Levinas are especially significant at this juncture. Although Marx does not deal directly with the issue of ethics, there should be little doubt that his critique of human relations in capitalist societies demands the creation of a new ethic. Specifically, Marx, especially in his early work, wrote about the injustices of capitalism and emphasized the material conditions that made capitalism antithetical to a moral order. To Marx, an optimal (and one could say moral) order was one where: (1) people interact with one another as equals; (2) all people are guaranteed basic needs such as food, shelter, education, work, and medical care; (3) everyone is afforded the opportunity to express their creativity in concert with other people; and, (4) all economic and social relations are organized around norms of cooperation and community.

Marx claimed that capitalist systems made this form of moral order impossible. Because workers are objectified and turned into commodities, the capitalist-worker nexus becomes a master-slave relationship. Moreover, the hierarchy and oppression entrenched in all social and economic relations are sustained by legal norms enforced by the state as well as by cultural norms and institutional practices that serve to support the status quo.

In Marx's view, the only way out of this sort of alienation was for the oppressed proletariat to understand their conditions and interests, break completely from the dominant ideology, envision an alternative order, and *achieve* this vision through revolution. Morality, in other words, involves a concerted effort among people and hence does not reside outside human contingencies. In this sense, morality must be achieved through a critique that inspires an alternative vision of society, which becomes real through revolutionary *praxis*. A moral world is thus achieved and not simply 'reached'.

Marx's central contribution is to bridge the *praxis*-theory link, so that an ahistorical moral wisdom becomes increasingly difficult to imagine. Thus, Marx seeks moral validation not in abstract principles, but in the site where all people seek to ensure their survival and well-being. The basic idea is that that human affairs should govern morality and not *vice versa*. In point of fact, Marx, at least in his early work, saw this sort of embodied morality as a requisite for justice and equality.

Much like Marx, Levinas is also concerned with promoting social justice and equality, and, as part of this effort, he develops an understanding of ethics that is anti-dualistic and bound to human relations. Central to Levinas's understanding of ethics is the idea that people think and act in the presence of other people. In his view, morality is not inscribed in the laws of the cosmos, reason, or any universal desire for pleasure. Instead, ethics is first and foremost *human encounter*.

Starting from the premise that ethics involves an encounter between people, Levinas argues that humans understand and define the world. Subjectivity, therefore, opens the world for all people. However, subjectivity is not an appropriate source of moral knowledge, for morality/ethics is necessarily relational (i.e. to be 'good', one must do good to others.) On the other hand, objectivity is problematic and runs the risk of reducing ethics to formalities. For example, if the other is reduced to 'essential' (i.e. objective) categories (e.g. race, gender, etc), then the alterity of the other is eliminated along with the other's humanity. In other words, if one has a certain idea about a person and equates this idea/category with the real person, then contact has been closed off with that real person. And in truncating the autonomy of the other in this way, relationships are 'totalized' and become easily repressive.

Most important in this discussion is that because human encounters involve nothing other than the people themselves, human relations are joined through *praxis* as opposed to some underlying natural order. Specifically, in the case of Levinas, persons actually become their conversations. And because language is always contingent and inextricably connected to a specific context and perspective, there is always an element of mystery when one comes face to face with another person. In the view of Levinas, to act ethically is to act not as if one has a 'grand vision' of the world, but rather to act in the face of the other, taking the other's difference into account, and viewing the other as a self-determined human being that can never be easily summarized.

As a result, an ethical order requires that persons encounter one another without recourse to some primordial or *a priori* intermediary. Nonetheless, the old absolutes require that the other be ignored; all attention is directed away from the world in order for moral standing to be established. Persons simply pursue their own aims, similar to atoms, and a moral order is achieved. But what if during this process, as in the case of capitalism, persons advance at the expense of others? Ethics, in short, requires an ongoing effort to be ethical in the presence of other people, and hence ethical norms must never be detached from what occurs in social or institutional relationships.

(ii) Liberation Philosophy

Recent writers such as Enrique Dussel (1985) and Jung Mo Sung (1993) have drawn from continental philosophers such as Marx and Levinas to critique current social conditions. These writers are part of a Latin American tradition of philosophy and theology that began under the general rubric of *filosofía de la liberación* ('liberation philosophy'). At the heart of liberation philosophy is a rejection of the sort of ontological realism that continues to legitimize relations of oppression between the core and the periphery.

Writing from social contexts where the flaws of world capitalism are especially pressing, and their remedies are particularly urgent, these Latin American writers seek to (de)reify social reality in order to envision an alternative vision of a moral society. Morality, therefore, begins with the assumption that social change is needed. In this sense, morality now requires the creation of a new order – social, economic, and political – where all people become subjects rather than objects. Morality, in other words, must necessarily begin by paying close attention to those who are oppressed and disenfranchised by an 'ontology of dependence'.

The suggestion is made that in the present world system, all social options are predetermined and streamlined into structures of domination. Writers such as Leopoldo Zea (1963) and Enrique Dussel (1985) suggest that domination is not only sustained by politics or the economy, but also, and perhaps most importantly, by cultural habits, customs, and modes of thinking. Most important is that the self-annihilation witnessed in Latin American is the product of the instrumental rationality that governs the so-called modern world. Humans encounter one another as mere means to instrumental and reified ends that reaffirm the autonomy and hegemony of the dominant system.

Thus, according to Dussel (1985: 41) and other proponents of liberation philosophy, the other is revealed as truly other only when a person is viewed as someone (a being of *praxis*), rather than something (a means to an end). Morality, therefore, involves an 'ethical conscience' that Dussel (1985: 59) defines as "the capacity one has to listen to the other's voice, the transontological world that breaks in from beyond the present system". In sum, to be ethical means to listen to the voices of others, to recognize their alterity, sensitize oneself to their plight, and engage in an active effort delegitimize the system – cultural, political, and economic – that oppresses them.

(iii) Alejandro Serrano-Caldera: The Need to Ground Ethics in Intersubjectivity

Although Nicaraguan philosopher Serrano-Caldera embraces the basic premises of liberation philosophy, he also extends this project in significant ways. In his view, the need for self affirmation of one's unique identity, interests, and needs, is a *necessary but insufficient* objective in the effort to promote a truly ethical order. Specifically, Serrano-Caldera emphasizes an intersubjective ethical order that requires constant effort on the part of all participants, and not just the oppressed. As a result, self-affirmation is not necessarily synonymous with liberation or emancipation. Instead, liberation must necessarily entail a rethinking of *human relationships*, the building blocks of any social system. Hence, Serrano-Caldera (1993: 5-6) maintains that ethics must be derived from an 'intercultural dialogue', whereby all human differences criss-cross in the creation of a new, concrete, and moral universality – what he calls "unity within diversity" – and this implies a new image of social reality.

However, the justification for these efforts is not some abstract notion of morality. Instead, these efforts are derived, again, from unconstrained dialogue. Once this sort of open dialogue is established, people – as opposed to metaphysical standards – can begin to mediate the course of history and shape all aspects of the social world. Indeed, once ethical norms are disengaged from inviolable moral standards, and instead become attuned to the voices and interests of all people, a new world order could be developed from below that does not violate the participants.

Conclusion: Toward a New Global Ethic

The works of continental philosophers such as Marx and Levinas, along with philosophers of liberation such as Dussel, and other progressive Latin American thinkers such as Serrano-Caldera, offer viable possibilities for promoting a new global ethic, and, taken together, some basic directives can be discerned for the purpose of its development.

First, ethics are not mere principles but rather modes of purposeful action that must take others into account in all their alterity – including their different cultures, identities, needs and interests. Second, morality can no longer seek validity outside its human content. The point here is that the grounds for morality can no longer be found in instinct, natural law, or ahistiorical standards, but instead are predicated on an interpersonal realm, or what is often referred to as 'intersubjectivity'. Third, rather than simply exploiting some 'moral right' for self-affirmation in the form of opposition, the dominant system that requires opposition must be called into question. In other words, instead of pitting groups of people against each other in order to promote their respective interests, the entire moral system that has put their legitimacy in doubt must be called into question. And fourth, a redistribution of resources is a key objective in any effort to promote a moral order. In this regard, the other has the right and the necessary means to exist.

In the end, morality/ethics must be understood as a never-ending process; in fact, a totalized morality ceases to be moral. Ethics, in other words, must be the outgrowth of an ongoing human effort, and not simply the product of specific norms of conduct. Once human differences are allowed to flourish, ethics will require constant innovation to foster this condition.

Notes

[1.] For example, the ethical standard of 'respecting human life' that Küng sees as a moral imperative (and one that is championed by the world's religions) could, in practical political/economic action, amount to little more than endorsing policies of free trade. And this objective may be legitimized easily by making the claim that such policies will produce viable economies that will eliminate world hunger, thereby saving human lives. Ethics, therefore, could be reduced to technical procedures that sustain the efficiency of the socio-economic order in place without necessarily responding to human needs and interests.

References

Dussel, E. (1985), *Philosophy of Liberation*, Maryknoll, NY, Orbis Books.
Hinkelammert, F.J. (1995), *Cultura de la Esperanza y Sociedad Sin Exclusión*, San José, Costa Rica, DEI.
Holland, D. (2000), 'Hans Küng: In Search of a Global Ethic' at http://www.shareintl.iorg/archives/religion/rl_dhHansKung.htm, retrieved June 2000.
Küng, H. (1991), *Global Responsibility: In Search of a New World Ethic*, New York, Crossroad Publishing Co.
MacIntyre, A. (1966), *A Short History of Ethics: A History of Moral Philosophy from the Homeric Age to the Twentieth Century*, New York, Macmillan.
Murphy, J.W. (1989), *Postmodern Social Analysis and Criticism*, Westport, CT, Greenwood Press.
Rogers Reginald, A.P. (1945), *A Short History of Ethics: Greek and Modern*, London, Macmillan.
Serrano-Caldera, A. (1993), *La Unidad en la Diversidad*, Managua, Editorial San Rafael.
Serrano-Caldera, A. (1995), *Los Dilemas de la Democracia*, Managua, Editorial Hispamer.
Sung, Jung-Mo (1993), *Neoliberalismo y Pobreza: Une Economia sin Corazan*, San Jose, Costa Rica, DEI.
Zea, L. (1963), *The Latin American Mind*, Norman, University of Oklahoma Press.

Chapter 5

Consequentialist Cosmopolitanism and Global Political Agency

Raffaele Marchetti

Introduction

Modern theories of political philosophy, concerned with striking a legitimate balance between the two traditional levels of political action – individual and state – have proposed a variety of different interpretations, but have often failed to expand their arguments to the wider vision necessary for a comprehensive theory of political justice. Concentrating on the domestic political sphere, conventional political theory seems ill-equipped to deal with the repeated challenges generated by recent global transformations, which affect both the traditional socio-political structure of the nation-state and the conventional political concepts underpinning it. Within this context, the relevance of cosmopolitan theories resides in the capacity to enlarge and rebalance the political perspective by including a number of further significant, international aspects, which pertain to the other major level of political action – the global.

Among cosmopolitans, consequentialist scholars in particular have offered since Singer's famous article (1972) several specific contributions to the understanding of global issues of justice but have failed to produce a comprehensive cosmopolitan theory. Whilst respecting the terms within which this debate is framed, this chapter aims to provide the core argument underpinning a multi-layered framework for a comprehensive version of consequentialist cosmopolitanism by focusing on the issue of political agency. While sharing the general cosmopolitan principles according to which the scope of justice should ultimately be global, what characterizes the present account is the use of a single teleological criterion of justice, which is indirectly deployed across different political levels. The recognition of the particular characteristics (i.e. principles and structure) of international ethics extends the theory of consequentialist cosmopolitanism over three major levels (individual, state, and world), which are unified through an appeal to the ultimate principle of improving the world welfare condition.

This chapter proposes, in particular, a new reading of the cardinal concept at stake here – political citizenship – and a reconstruction of its supranational and institutional framework. In opposition to the communitarian *leitmotiv*, according to which the very expression of cosmopolitan citizenship would be an oxymoron, cosmo-political citizenship is here understood to have significant meaning. While communitarian state-centric logic holds that citizenship refers to a limited political organisation and that the attempt to expand it is self-contradicting, it will be argued here that the idea of citizenship is not inseparably tied to the notion of a sovereign state, insofar as its scope comprizes differing political spheres. Hence, no normative obstacles impede the expansion of the traditional notion of polis to the entire cosmos and of that of political agency to a universal constituency composed by diverse political actors.

An interpretation of cosmopolitan citizenship in terms of freedom of choice forms the core of this proposal. Accordingly, the capacity of individuals to navigate the possibility of personal choice within a legitimate political system becomes the primary object of concern for a project trying to maximize the world welfare condition through individual enfranchisement. Endorsing the principle of controlling one's own life leads, then, to recognizing the procedural centrality of democratic reflexivity between choice-makers and choice-bearers, and the need for its institutionalization at every level of political life, including the global, through the mechanisms of representation and public accountability.

In contrast to existing international law and national policies, citizens are recognized as cosmopolitan stake-holders entitled to rights, which extend to a number of differing spheres of political action. Consequently, the argument for global citizenship rests on the capacity of political agents to influence those public decisions made in a foreign or, indeed, a global political sphere of action whose consequences extend across borders. Hence, this chapter advances the fundamental claim that only a multilayered cosmopolitan theory can properly deal with the complexity of global phenomena from a consequentialist point of view, insofar as the right to democratic participation to self-legislation is considered to be the political tool for enhancing individual choice and, thereby, the world welfare condition.

The chapter begins by setting out a number of definitional characteristics and presenting the fundamental rationale of consequentialist cosmopolitanism. It goes on to explore the conceptual relationship between citizenship and institutions, together with the contradictions which are inherent in the current global democratic deficit. It then explores in detail the issue of political agency at the global level and the concept of cosmopolitan citizenship before ending with some concluding remarks.

Consequentialist Global Justice

Consequentialist cosmopolitanism, as a goal-based ethical theory, aims at the promotion of the good, which is assumed to reside in the well-being of human beings.[1] However, due to epistemological constraints concerning the unavailability of reliable interpersonal comparisons of utility, an agency-based notion of well-being has to be adopted. In this vein, well-being is only indirectly identified in the individual capacity of choice, rather than in such experiential states as pleasure or happiness. Accordingly, this theory maintains that only when agents are in a position to freely choose their preferred course of action through a process of informed and effective personal deliberation can genuine well-being be attained. Following from this, consequentialist cosmopolitanism prescribes the promotion of the individual capacity for choice as the ultimate ethical goal.[2]

Consequentialist cosmopolitanism, as a political theory, does not concentrate, therefore, directly on individual utility (thereby undermining the importance of traditional aggregative devices), since it endorses the view that it is possible to identify and provide welfare to the individual uniquely in an indirect manner (Hardin, 1988: 3). Contrary to classical political utilitarianism, the prescribed political rules of the proposed system try to assist each individual in search of an enhanced quality of life through the provision of the necessary means (inevitably minimal, insofar as they should be publicly deliberated and thus universal) to allow for the realization of free choice. Crucially, such a project also pays particular attention to guaranteeing the political right to participate in the process of self-legislation, since only through democratic agreement between choice-makers and choice-bearers can the individual capacity to self-decision be empowered in a comprehensive way (Mill, 1861).

In particular, the method of comparison of alternative institutional schemes adopted by consequentialist cosmopolitanism is one that relies on procedural and participatory guarantees based on the primacy of freedom of choice. In contrast to other methods of comparisons which make extensive use of some sort of interpersonal utility comparisons, the present account is committed to valuing bundles of goods, i.e. legal-institutional entitlements, only indirectly with reference to their contribution to the individual achievement of free choice-maker status. According to consequentialist cosmopolitanism, alternative institutional schemes should be assessed in terms of the access they accord their participants to the status of free choice-makers. Since the capability to achieve freedom of choice depends on the guarantees of a number of prerequisites constituted by vital interests and political participation, these are the two principal variables on which the assessment of alternative institutional frameworks needs to be developed. This is the dual 'currency', through which individual shares are defined in consequentialist cosmopolitanism, so as to support comparative judgements about the justice of institutional schemes.

Moreover, in holding an impartial conception of moral relevance, according to which all morally significant consequences affecting all morally significant persons should be taken into account, consequentialist cosmopolitanism maintains a universalistic form of consequentialism. This amounts to extending the scope of the ethical project to the entire world and, consequently, to acknowledging that the best moral code is one where observance of the political system would produce the best consequences in terms of the increase of world welfare conditions. Hence, the morally ideal world is identified as that which maximizes, through a scheme of public political participation, the citizen's capacity to choose.

In this respect, a number of general distinctions mark out this version of consequentialist cosmopolitanism from other theories of justice. Set against communitarian theories, consequentialist cosmopolitanism argues that the scope of justice should be universal insofar as no discrimination is justified when considering the ultimate entitlement of every citizen to control his or her destiny. No national difference can legitimate a partial hearing of such an individual right. Among the many versions of cosmopolitanism (Caney, 2001; Jones, 1999; Scheffler, 1999), consequentialist cosmopolitanism distinguishes itself by advocating a moderate, institutional, co-operativist and federal cosmopolitanism. This implies, correspondingly, the rejection of the following four contrasting claims: a) only global principles of justice are acceptable; b) global principles of justice are merely ethical precepts; c) the primary agent of justice is the individual; and d) multilateral global governance constitutes a legitimate form of cosmopolitan democracy.

Looking more closely at the normative structure of consequentialist cosmopolitanism as a system of international applied ethics, the following two kinds of rules can be identified as of principal relevance in consequentialist terms. The *ultimate* consequentialist rule, i.e. the maximisation of world welfare conditions and *intermediate* rules. These intermediate rules refer to specific levels, which contribute to the design of the political structure of a consequentialist global political system – the 'human rights regime' and the principle of state self-determination, for example. Within such a scheme, the ultimate principle represents the decisive criterion of validity of intermediate principles, and is therefore deployed in the assessment of the long-term impartial socio-political performance of the intermediate rules, among which those concerning global political agency form the main object of the present examination.[3]

The socio-political rules and practices that primarily influence the world utility outcome are identified through the scrutiny of some action types. These types can be grouped into three sets,[4] which correspond to the levels of the individual, state and world.[5] Unfortunately, these three levels of political analysis are very seldom presented together. From the consequentialist point of view however, it is crucial to handle all the three at the same time, since only by doing this can a comprehensive normative treatment of the world social system be provided. In line with such a triple approach, the political proposal of consequentialist cosmopolitanism, in the context of *intermediate* rules, consists of a threefold political focus on guarantees and rights as the means whereby the maximisation of freedom of choice and, thus, of the world welfare condition can be achieved. This is constituted a) at the individual level, through the protection of a set of minimal universal interests insofar as it works as individual socio-political capabilities to freely choose one's own personal life; b) at the state level, through the protection of a set of collective interests as the foundation of a state capacity to free self-determination; and c) at the global level, through the protection of a set of international means which are needed to rule global phenomena. Accordingly, only through a simultaneous and consistent implementation of these legal-institutional guarantees can a political system offer an adequate political response to a multi-layered social reality.

Contrary to such a normative stance, the opening assumption of this chapter entails recognising the fact that the current world system does not maximize the world's welfare condition because of the serious democratic deficit affecting current international affairs. Here the term *world system* is used in its broad meaning, which includes political, economic, social, legal, and cultural aspects. In particular, within the normative structure of this system, institutions, defined as general patterns or categorizations of activity made up of persistent and connected clusters of (formal and informal) norms, are a central ingredient because of their capacity and potential to promote reform and co-operation (Keohane, 1988: 383 and 393; Hurrell, 2001: 38; Parekh, 2003: 11). As a response to this immoral state, a consequentialist cosmopolitan code is recommended in order to a) update, critically, the interpretation of our current world system and b) propose new normative principles, as constitutive of a comprehensive and consistent moral world, which is able to improve world welfare conditions.

    In the remainder of this chapter, a more detailed outline of the consequentialist cosmopolitan proposal concerning the critical issue of political agency will be offered, while the other two components of the theory (i.e. values and rules) are only summarized in Table 5.1 at the end of this chapter. Equally, despite the fact that the analysis of consequentialist cosmopolitanism is developed over three main political spheres (individual, state and world), the following sections will be devoted solely to the global level because of space constraints. Before analysing the issue of global political agency it is still necessary, though, to introduce a number of features concerning the link between the concepts of citizenship and institutions.

The Relationship between Institutions and Citizenship

Citizenship, understood as the set of entitlements allowing the acquisition of a full community membership, represents the core element of democratic political theory. Conventionally, three different sets of citizenship rights can be distinguished according to their scope: civil, political, and socio-economic rights (Marshall, 1950). These entitlements, which are based on a fundamental principle of equality and reciprocity, are impartially guaranteed to every member of the community, insofar as membership within the collective exercise of self-governance is usually recognized as the minimal precondition of democratic life. The acquisition of such set of rights is, thus, considered crucial in order to participate effectively in social and political life (Delanty, 2000: 1-2).

    The concept of collective autonomy follows from the idea of equal citizenship. Just as agents, at the individual level, enjoy a fundamental right to freely choose their destiny, so groups at the collective level are entitled to make autonomous decisions about their future. Consequently, the legitimate exercise of political self-determination and self-legislation needs to be based on equal citizenship, since only by simultaneously retaining the status of legislators and subjects can citizens remain free and thus pursue their well-being. Since democracy aims at "making the social outcomes systematically responsive to the settled preferences of all affected parties" (Goodin, 2003b: 1), the key mechanism for democratic legitimacy depends upon the congruence between rulers and ruled (Held, 1995, 1996).

This reflexivity between choice-bearers and choice-makers is guaranteed at the domestic political level through a wide variety of institutions. Primary among them is an elected parliament where citizens can express their voice through pluralistic representation. The establishment of such a public, impartial, and predictable institutional system, through which individuals can form and propose their political view on society, forms the premise of democratic life. This is widely recognized as a fundamental formal requirement for the legitimacy of government, and shapes most political systems around the world.

In principle, the correspondence between choice -makers and choice-bearers should be universal in order to guarantee a complete freedom to the individual, so that any exception to this norm has to prove its case. Such congruence should cover all the relational dimensions in which individual life is embedded, i.e. one should be in the position to legislate over the entire range of activities in which one is involved. Until recently, domestic political life has been a dominant influence on an individual's life and, consequently, the political focus has been mainly on institutions, including first and foremost citizenship, within this domestic context. However, given the current world transformations occurring in almost all aspects of social life, domestic-only democracies and their related international institutions are increasingly under pressure, resulting often in self-contradiction.

Current international affairs, characterized by intense processes of global transformations, pose a continuous challenge to the effectiveness and legitimacy of traditional political life, and consequently require the reformulation of the ways in which democratic ideals are politically applied. While the conventional democratic assumption that individuals should have the right to determine their own lives through political legislation is increasingly recognized, both in international covenants and national constitutions, as the cardinal principle of politics, international affairs create a situation where such entitlements are limited and decreasingly guaranteed. Financial markets, environmental crises and migrations vividly remind us of both the intense interdependence of the contemporary international system and its political limitations.

A partial implementation of the principle of universal congruence is for the most part self-defeating in an interdependent environment, because the absence of effective and legitimate political structures at each level of action impedes the efforts of individuals to express their free consent and, therefore, to implement their capacity to be autonomous. Consequently, institutional arrangements need to extend to the global level in order to preserve consistently such congruence and the individual capacity of free choice. A fundamental normative demand thus arises for the strengthening of transnational democratic institutions, intended as viable and comprehensive mechanisms of democratic self-legislation. A strict normative interdependence links democracy, human rights, and peace as three faces of the same principle (Bobbio, 1995), which in turn highlights the urgency of the issue of democratic citizenship at the global level (Annan, 2002; Boutros-Ghali, 1995).

A number of competitive theories, from national realism to cosmopolitanism, have suggested differing responses to this demand for transnational democracy, without offering a viable solution to such challenge. In fact, while realist inter-governmentalism tends to neglect the innovative global aspects of international phenomena, the theory of cosmopolitan governance does not capture completely the necessity of new forms of democratic and direct representation and so fails to satisfy a legitimacy test. This inability to combine properly the features of efficiency and legitimacy (and correspondingly, the serious difficulties suffered by the current international political system in governing global affairs, at the same time, efficiently and legitimately) emphasizes the aforementioned discrepancy, thus emphasising the need for a more satisfying politico-theoretical argument. This urgency moulds the following sections of this chapter which are dedicated to the central feature of the transnationalization of democracy: global political agency.

The Problem of Political Agency at the Global Level

The major distinguishing characteristic of consequentialist cosmopolitanism, as noted above, regards the issue of moral agency in line with a double universalistic conception of responsibility and vulnerability. This feature marks the strength of consequentialist cosmopolitanism as a flexible paradigm, which can adhere more strongly than others to social and political realities in a time of radical transformations. Our world system is increasingly putting the relation between choice-makers and choice-bearers under pressure, with the result that moral and political ties are weakened. Until recently the effects of actions were mostly circumscribed to a defined territory, insofar as everybody could influence (and be influenced by) the lives of a limited number of other people. However, now every action we implement can affect thousands of other peoples, and even if these effects might be imperceptible when taken singularly, they often become decisive when combined with the effects of thousands of similar actions. Consequently, as far as practical possibilities acquire a global dimension, even our moral responsibility needs to enlarge its field of inclusiveness and recognize its new ethical and political capability.

Interdependence is thus an important factor in the moral assessment of international duties in the current situation, though, it should be stressed, it is not a decisive one for what concerns, in particular, positive duties. The fact that we currently influence each other only makes clearer that we are in a position to influence the outcome, but we would still have a duty to improve the fate of the deprived foreigners even if we were not so interdependent. We would, in fact, have the duty to build up relations to create and facilitate the channels of co-operation and help. This marks an important point of contrast with all those theories of justice which are interaction-dependent, such as communitarianism and most versions of contractarianism, insofar as they limit duties to people with whom one interacts. As suggested by Hurrell, 'there is a real danger in tying notions of moral community too closely to networks of economic interaction, particularly when so many of the world's most vulnerable people are precisely those who are excluded or marginalized from such integration processes' (2001, p. 34).

A prominent characteristic of the current socio-economic situation at the global level is the multiple availability of channels of actions, except for those of political representation. Collective agents, such as multinational corporations (MNCs) or international organisations, have the ability to intrude, in multiple ways, into domestic and individual lives. Individuals also have a plethora of private avenues along which to pursue their interests, for good or bad, insofar as 'they have a multitude of new point of access to the course of events' (Rosenau, 1992, p. 285). But unlike previous collective agents, individuals are on the whole denied political access to institutions where they can properly express their public consent. Individual citizens are, therefore, deprived of their collective autonomy of self-determination at the global level. The lack of such corresponding channels of access for political representation at each level of political action is utterly striking when compared with the asymmetrical power of other international agents. Hence the concept of agency constitutes a crucial element of any scheme of international ethics, since it represents the key institutional tool in order to contrast this situation and re-balance the denial of the right to multi-layered self-legislation through the direct empowerment of the choice-bearers.

At the core of the present reading of political agency is the principle of vulnerability, which is centred on a forward-looking responsibility anchored to the concept of capacity to influence outcomes. This principle generates the political identification of both classes of agency and the corresponding political sanction. Choice-makers, i.e. those who decide and carry out an action which produces consequences, are made *responsible* through a precise method of accountability based on the capacity to influence the outcome. Choice-bearers, in contrast, i.e. those who suffer the consequences of that action, are identified as potentially *vulnerable* and consequently protected (Goodin, 1985; Pettit, 1997; Held, 2002). Since there can be multiple agents (including individual and collective/institutional agents) on both sides, a moral theory cannot be complete if it fails to identify clearly' the moral position of every agent involved in the situation under scrutiny (O'Neill, 2001). Such identification can be better deployed in political terms through the construction of institutional mechanisms where choice-makers and choice-bearers can publicly recognize their actions and establish forms of accountable citizenship.

For the class of choice-makers in particular, the present proposal demands a multilevel and synchronic commitment of responsibility, whose enforcement needs to be implemented through a scheme of global co-ordination based on the principle of subsidiarity.[6] Individuals are required to acknowledge their own potential to harm, in line with the various political levels of action, and subsequently their actual responsibility. Along with individuals, all other collective agents (such as NGOs, MNCs, and supranational organisations), which are in a position to prevent situations of vulnerability and guarantee the implementation of the different participatory policies at each social level, are called to action. In sum, consequentialist cosmopolitanism entails a radical revision of the centrality of both states and individuals, insofar as they represent only *some* of the international ethical agents.

While the extension of individual moral agency from the domestic to the international domain is, from a normative point of view, relatively straightforward, the case of institutional moral agency appears, at least *prima facie*, more controversial. Clarifying this latter case is, however, of extreme importance in the global domain, since a number of international actions can be delivered uniquely by collective bodies, such as intergovernmental and supranational institutions. Environmental crises, international migratory flows, and humanitarian interventions are all examples of situations requiring institutional co-operative management rather than individual commitment. Hence the attribution of moral responsibility (and correspondingly of vulnerability) at the institutional level constitutes a major priority on the global political agenda.

In opposition to realist assumptions about the 'immoral society', consequentialist cosmopolitanism claims that it is indeed viable to assign moral agency, and corresponding responsibility, to institutions, be they states or international organisations. Once institutional moral agents are identified through two principal characteristics – the capacity for moral deliberation and action, and the condition of effective freedom to exercise this capacity[7] – the following steps involve assigning precise responsibility within collective agency. Collective responsibility, beyond direct actors, has at least two different meanings in the literature, it can be intended as *separatim* or *collegialiter*. It can assume that members can be held, vicariously or indirectly, liable even though not all of them are personally at fault, since this is a burden associated with group membership. It can also apportion culpability to the entire collectivity or institution, intended as distinct from and superior to individual members. Consequentialist cosmopolitanism presents a third position, where moral responsibility is multiple, by degrees and crucially embedded in democratic reflexivity.[8] This entails that both individual 'non-actors', such as citizens, and collectivities, such as governments, can be identified as responsible, depending on their capacity to influence the final outcome of any course of action at each political level in which they are involved. At the global level in particular, given the specific political nature of the issues at stake, responsible agents are principally considered international institutions and, within them, cosmopolitan citizens.

Cosmopolitan Citizenship

The political discourse on cosmopolitan agency rests on a specific conception of global value and rules generated within the general paradigm of consequentialist cosmopolitanism as outlined in this chapter. In order to conceive who the global agents are, it is necessary to understand which goods are to be pursued at the global level and what kind of political rules are most conducive to such an end.

At the third level of political action, consequentialist cosmopolitanism identifies the global concern as the value which is most appropriate to the objective of the maximisation of world welfare conditions. This entails an enlargement of the traditional sphere of moral consideration towards the recognition of global issues as political problems. The appreciation of humanity as a political subject is essential to the development of a multiple identity, which allows for the comprehensive maturating of the capacity for individual choice. Accordingly, the concept of humanity is understood to be intrinsically linked to that of a single agent, and to require the critical evaluation of where one should stop the process of ethical and political opening beyond oneself. In fact, 'at whatever point universalizability stops, one can raise the question: why stop there?' (Singer, 1988, p. 157). This does not mean, however, that such a form of cosmopolitanism implies the moral deficiency and motivational weakness which worries many communitarian scholars. While not requiring the renunciation of local or state identity, consequentialist cosmopolitanism demands only the addition of a third factor to our identity – humanity at large – through a multi-layered hermeneutical process characterized by impartiality and simultaneity.

The recognition of world society as a 'community of fate', as Held (2000: 224-25) describes it, within which individuals are inevitably intertwined, provides further evidence for the acknowledgement of humanity as a full political subject. The intense global transformations, which shape the fundamentals of the world system, clearly reveal a number of widely shared socio-political elements. The escalating level of world trade, the huge migratory flows, environmental degradation and the spread of disease are all features of a common future. This world-wide overlap of interests is more and more evident and ordinary citizens are becoming increasingly conscious of how much their lives are influenced by global factors. Those, who argue against the innovation of globalization, do not sufficiently recognize the novelty of the changes affecting, first and foremost, citizens' awareness of how interdependent and intrusive global affairs are and how much new global rules to tackle them are required.

As a normative answer to this political demand, consequentialist cosmopolitanism proposes a scheme of cosmopolitan democracy complemented by a number of universal humanitarian rules to be applied in cases of emergency. In requiring the expansion of our ethical concern world-wide, these factors demand the other two sets of political rules, i.e. those regarding individual and state political spheres, to be aligned coherently to the universal requirements of humankind through a new ethical-political equilibrium within a comprehensive and consistent political system. Accountable mechanisms of cosmopolitical government of global issues form the issue here at stake.[9] This political control is needed not only for global phenomena, such as international migration or environmental crises, which cannot be governed by the traditional political forms of state and interstate organisations, but also for local and state phenomena, like the abuse of human rights and local minorities, which are insufficiently guaranteed by local and state authorities. Both global and state domains need the integration of cosmopolitan management, in order to safeguard the heterogeneity of world actors beyond the pure balance of power politics. Similarly to the domestic democratic case, at the global level a cosmopolitan government is needed to foster civil coexistence among political agents endowed with differing power (Ferrajoli, 1999).

A new form of cosmopolitan politics is, therefore, necessary to fill the gap between choice-makers and choice-bearers and to preserve the autonomy of the various agents at the global political level. Due to epistemological constraints, however, this cosmopolitics should be procedural and negative, shaped by the principle of prevention of global harm (Linklater, 2001), and the scope of cosmopolitan institutions should consequently be limited to two main areas of competence: a) insurance, acting as second guarantor, of the possibility of genuine flourishing at both individual and state level; and b) regulation through a world-wide scheme of co-operation to foster public and accountable management of global problems. The latter, in particular, is needed to supervise the increasing global externalities of international affairs, but it cannot be achieved without a new, transnational interpretation of public agency.

World agency entails the enlargement of the current view of political agency, since traditional state-centric politics operates within a conception of responsibility and vulnerability, which is too narrow to deal properly with the ethical problems exacerbated by the global dimension of political life. Only in the post-Second World War period has a new universalistic approach (principally based on human rights) emerged, which disputed the classical interpretation of political agency by accentuating the tension between state legitimacy and cosmopolitan claims of justice (O'Byrne, 2003).

Within this historical trend, world citizenship represents a crucial step toward overcoming the established system of agency and establishing cosmopolitan institutions (Dower and Williams, 2002; Hutchings and Dannreuther, 1999; Linklater, 1998). Rather than acting directly on the agent's welfare, consequentialist cosmopolitanism deploys an indirect strategy which gives the potentially vulnerable the political capability to influence the outcome affecting them. Far from deleting all the other forms of citizenship, this strategy introduces a concept of stakeholder citizenship, according to which individuals and collective agents are entitled to multilevel citizenship and are able to influence decisions at all the political levels which affect them (Goodin, 1996: 363; Sassen, 2002; Sen, 1996). Simultaneously, however, political agents are also made accountable for their actions in the global sphere and to humanity, in general (both directly and indirectly as spill-over effects of their behaviour), and appropriate sanctions are ordered against non-compliance.

Accordingly, at the world level the class of choice-makers – that which is responsible through a co-operative scheme for the international enforcement of cosmopolitan policies – comprises: a) supranational political bodies, such as a federally reformed UN and macro-region institutions; b) supranational collective bodies, such as MNCs, NGOs (international trade unions, international churches, international associations and groups and, more generally, the so-called global civil society); c) states; and d) individuals who act within these collective bodies. These political agents all share a social responsibility toward the class of vulnerable agents. They are under a duty (weighted in correspondence with their actual capacity to influence the outcome) to preserve and maximize the independence of the class of choice-bearers.

Conversely, global choice-bearers, i.e. those agents who are vulnerable in their supranational status, include: a) first and foremost humanity as a broad concept, comprising the entire present human species and future generations; b) supranational collective bodies such as civil organisations, which are characterized by a transnational attitude in dealing with political issues; and c) individuals, insofar as they are the ultimate reference in terms of welfare.

In recognizing such a twofold scheme of global agency, together with the relevance of international institutions where these two classes of agents can be made at once accountable and guaranteed, consequentialist cosmopolitanism aims at re-establishing the congruence between choice-makers and choice-bearers, which is central to any democratic form of politics. Only where such correspondence is universally respected and individuals are in a position to self-legislate over the entire range of activities in which they are involved, can their freedom of choice be preserved.

Conclusions

In response to the absence of a comprehensive consequentialist theory of international political theory, this chapter has offered a cosmopolitan response. The conventional vision, centred on the binomial individual-state, has been criticized through the adoption of a comprehensive perspective which includes other significant aspects of political action in contemporary world. Consequently, a new ethical-political approach has been outlined which both recognizes the most neglected international variables and describes the three main levels of political action to be tied together into a new democratic equilibrium.

An innovative interpretation of global citizenship, entailing differing degrees of responsibility and relative power at all levels of political decision-making, including the global sphere, has been shown to be a normative solution to the narrow-focused perspective, which is one of the causes of the current democratic deficit at international level. Only through such a pluralistic and multi-level interpretation of the concept of political agency can the political potential of the individual be empowered in all its dimensions, as well as personal choices receive an impartial hearing and a path cleared for the maximisation of world welfare conditions. Arguably, such political arrangements represent, for the time being, the appropriate compliance with the requirements of a consequentialist cosmopolitan theory of global justice.

Table 5.1 Summary of the three-levels of consequentialist cosmopolitanism[10]

		Values	*Rules*	*Agency*	
				Responsibility	Vulnerability
Individual		• Choice-based individualism	• System of individual rights • Maximin of vital rights	• All (aggregately)	• Individuals
State	Internal	• Group flourishing	• Minorities and groups rights • Special duties	• States • Local collective bodies • Individuals	• Local collective bodies • Individuals
	External	• State autonomy	• Self-determination • Non-intervention	• International institutions • International collective bodies • Individuals	• States • Individuals
World		• Global concern	• Cosmo-federalism • Humanitarian universal rules	• Supranational institutions • Supranational collective bodies • States • Individuals	• Humanity • Supranational collective bodies • Individuals

Notes

[1] A more extended presentation of the normative fundaments of consequentialist cosmopolitanism can be found in Marchetti (2003), where a more detailed examination of the ultimate principles of this project together with a number of crucial comparisons with the theories of justice developed by Rawls, Sen and Held.

[2] This approach shares a number of relevant theoretical elements with the capabilities approach proposed by Sen and Nussbaum (Nussbaum and Sen, 1993; Nussbaum, 2002; Sen, 1980, 1982, 1985, 1988, 1992). Consequentialist cosmopolitanism and the capability approach are, in fact, distinctive from other consequentialist theories such as utilitarianism in that they aim 'to square the circle' by combining consequentialist evaluation with a number of apparently (or traditionally associated with) deontological intuitions related to the respect of agent-relativity, such as rights and personal values. Despite these similarities, consequentialist cosmopolitanism and the capability approach are nonetheless distinctive in that they are based on two different foundationalist strategy and epistemological assumptions that produce differently defensible, and yet compatible, normative justification of the primacy of freedom of choice as embedded in a consequentialist framework. While the former warrants the centrality of freedom of choice through the combination of the consequentialist principle with some constraining epistemological requirements, the latter combines the consequential evaluation with the account of the positional objectivity, i.e. the parametric dependence of observation and inference on the position of the observer.

³ Intermediate rules are, then, warranted as long as they produce a maximising outcome in the long term, regardless of other arbitrary and a priori principles of justice. The coexistence of a second order consequentialist principle (the final arbiter) and different *prima facie* non-consequentialist principles as first order rules (i.e. the intermediate applicative levels) is, then, admitted.

⁴ Each of these categories represents a realm into which action types of standardized states of the world may be placed. It contains the following elements: a) an empirical description of social and political circumstances, which influence the agents' utilities, i.e. utility structures; b) the subjective utility feedback which the agent gains from the situation; c) a critical point of view concerning the rule structure of the utility outcome. Although utility feedback represents the real core of the issue, it is something that cannot be influenced directly. What can be influenced, instead, is the availability of goods, i.e. the agent's power to choose and to get access to them, which is due mainly to political structures and social institutions (Sen, 1981: 45-47).

⁵ The other levels of political analysis, such as the regional, interstate and local, are currently considered less significant in relation to world welfare conditions, and are, therefore, excluded from the discussion. For a different, more comprehensive view see Archibugi, 2003).

⁶ This kind of responsibility has to be intended by degrees depending on the relevance of one's position within the link between choice-maker and choice-bearers, and has to be assessed aggregately, not iteratively (Hooker, 2000: 166). Finally, it has to be also intended in its omissive version. An agent is, therefore, responsible even when harm is produced by inaction, i.e. he is accountable for both his direct (foreseeable and desired) and oblique (foreseeable and not desired) intended consequences (Hare, 1999: 153-4; Hooker, 2000: 5).

⁷ In particular, the following characteristics have to be met by collectivities or institutions in order to be qualified as moral agents. A collective agent has an identity that is more than the sum of the identities of its constitutive parts, i.e. it is not exhausted by the conjunction of the identities of the members, and therefore extends over time and conceives itself as a unit. Such agent also has internal organisation and/or a decision-making structure, i.e. differing defined roles such as an executive function that allow for the allocation of power within the organisation. And finally, a collective agent enforces different, often more stringent, standards of conduct than those applying outside it (Erskine, 2004: 26; French, 1984: 13-16).

⁸ Accordingly, the *separatim* conception has to be rejected because it does not take into account the possibility of purely group responsibility, whereas the *collegialiter* one remains inadequate for it excludes the recognition of individual objection such as the 'not in my name' attitude during a war conflict. In sum, they are both insufficiently sensitive to the simultaneous forms and different degrees that responsibility assumes in a complex and intermingled world.

⁹ This proposal suggests a version of cosmopolitan democracy different from the recent formulations from Archibugi, Held, and Linklater (Archibugi, Held, and Kohler, 1998; Held and McGrew, 2002). While they tend to recommend a more decentralized and opaquely-cut governance structure characterized by multiple decision-making centres, in which governments still retain a certain degree of sovereignty, consequentialist cosmopolitanism prescribes a more centralized and individual-based system, where states lose part of their authority in favour of federal powers when dealing with global issues. Moreover, in arguing for a central inclusive authority, consequentialist cosmopolitanism avoids the risk of exclusion, which seems inherent in Held's proposal. In suggesting a net of institutions spatially delimited (Held, 1995: 237), Held's proposal fails to guarantee representation to citizens outside that structure and does not offer the chance to compare the effects of uncoordinated decisions taken by different agencies, which are considered equal in political

authority (Thompson, 2000: 143-44). The insufficiently democratic character of cosmopolitan governance is discussed more at length in (Marchetti, 2004).
[10] In this table, each of the three levels is analysed using three conceptual categories: value, rules, and agency, which correspondingly recall the three topical themes of international ethics, i.e. pluralism, multilevel dimensionality, and moral agency. Consequently, each section on value detects the relative good which is to be pursued in that realm; each section of rules indicates those prescribed contextual rules which are most conducive to the maximisation of world welfare conditions in that specific domain; and each section of agency identifies the relative moral persons as agent makers (the responsible people) and agent takers (vulnerable people). It should noted, ultimately, that since each level has to be normatively consistent with the other two, a double co-ordination must be implemented. Hence, while, theoretically speaking, the axiological co-ordination needs to be strictly mono-directional, insofar as the normative primacy is attached to the individual well being, it must, from a political point of view, be also bi-directional, i.e. from above to below and *vice versa*, and synchronic (Goodin, 2003a).

References

Annan, K.A. (2002), 'Democracy as an International Issue', in *Global Governance*, **8**, pp. 135-42.

Archibugi, D. (2003), 'Cosmopolitan Democracy and its Critics', in B. Morrison (ed.), *Transnational Democracy: A Critical Consideration of Sites and Sources*, Aldershot, Ashgate.

Archibugi, D., Held, D. and Kohler, M. (eds) (1998), *Re-Imagining Political Community: Studies in Cosmopolitan Democracy*, Cambridge, Polity Press.

Bobbio, N. (1995), 'Democracy and the International System', in D. Archibugi and D. Held (eds), *Cosmopolitan Democracy: An Agenda for a New World Order*, Cambridge, Polity Press.

Boutros-Ghali, B. (1995), 'Democracy: A Newly Recognized Imperative', in *Global Governance*, **1**, pp. 3-11.

Caney, S. (2001), 'Review Article: International Distributive Justice', in *Political Studies*, **49**(5), pp. 974-97.

Delanty, G. (2000), *Citizenship in a Global Age: Society, Culture, Politics*, Philadelphia, PA, Open University Press.

Dower, N. and Williams, J. (eds) (2002), *Global Citizenship: A Critical Reader*, Edinburgh, Edinburgh University Press.

Erskine, T. (2004), '"Blood on the UN's Hands"? Assigning Duties and Apportioning Blame to an Intergovernmental Organisation', *Global Society*, **18**(1), pp. 21-42.

Ferrajoli, L. (1999), 'I diritti fondamentali nella teoria del diritto', in *Teoria politica*, **1**, pp. 49-91.

French, P. (1984), *Collective and Corporate Responsibility*, New York, Columbia University Press.

Goodin, R. (1985), *Protecting the Vulnerable: A Reanalysis of Our Social Responsibilities*, Chicago, University of Chicago Press.

Goodin, R. (1996), 'Inclusion and Exclusion', in *Archives Européennes de Sociologie*, XXXVII, **2**, pp. 343-71.

Goodin, R. (2003a), 'Globalising Justice', in D. Held and M. Koenig-Archibugi (eds), *Taming Globalisation: Frontiers of Governance*, Cambridge, Polity Press.

Goodin, R. (2003b), *Reflective Democracy*, Oxford, Oxford University Press.

Hardin, R. (1988), *Morality within the Limits of Reason*, Chicago and London, University of Chicago Press.

Hare, R.M. (1999), *Objective Prescriptions, and Other Essays*, Oxford, Clarendon.

Held, D. (1995), *Democracy and the Global Order: From the Modern State to Cosmopolitan Governance*, Cambridge, Polity Press.

Held, D. (1996), *Models of Democracy*, Cambridge, Polity Press.

Held, D. (2000), 'Regulating Globalization', in D. Held and A. McGrew (eds), *The Global Transformations Reader: An Introduction to the Globalization Debate*, Cambridge, Polity Press.

Held, D. (2002), 'Law of People, Law of States', in *Legal Theory*, **8**, pp. 1-44.

Held, D. and McGrew, A. (2002), *Governing Globalization: Power, Authority and Global Governance*, Cambridge, Polity Press.

Hooker, B. (2000), *Ideal Code, Real World: A Rule-Consequentialist Theory of Morality*, Oxford and New York, Oxford University Press.

Hurrell, A. (2001), 'Global Inequality and International Institutions', in T. Pogge (ed.), *Global Justice*, Oxford, Blackwell.

Hutchings, K. and Dannreuther, R. (eds) (1999), *Cosmopolitan Citizenship*, Basingstoke, Macmillan.

Jones, C. (1999), *Global Justice: Defending Cosmopolitanism*, Oxford, Oxford University Press.

Keohane, R. (1988), 'International Institutions: Two Approaches', in *International Organization*, **32**(4), pp. 379-96.

Linklater, A. (1998), 'Citizenship and Sovereignty in the Post-Westphalian European State', in D. Archibugi, D. Held and M. Kohler (eds), *Re-Imagining Political Community: Studies in Cosmopolitan Democracy*, Cambridge, Polity Press.

Linklater, A. (2001), 'Citizenship, Humanity, and Cosmopolitan Harm Conventions', in *International Political Science Review*, **22**(3), pp. 261-78.

Marchetti, R. (2003), 'Consequentialist Cosmopolitanism'. Paper presented at the ISUS Annual Conference, *Utilitarianism, Human Rights, and Globalization*, Lisbon.

Marchetti, R. (2004), 'Global Governance or World Federalism? A Dispute within Cosmopolitanism'. Paper presented at the ISA Annual Convention, *Hegemony and its Discontents*, Montreal.

Marshall, T.H. (1950), *Citizenship and Social Class*, Cambridge, Cambridge University Press.

Mill, J.S. (1861). *Considerations on Representative Government*, reproduced in Mill (1991), *Complete Works of J.S. Mill*, Toronto, University of Toronto Press.

Nussbaum, M. and Sen, A. (1993), *The Quality of Life*, Oxford, Clarendon Press.

Nussbaum, M. (2002), 'Capabilities and Human Rights', in P. De Greiff and C. Cronin (eds), *Global Justice and Transnational Justice*, Cambridge, Mass., MIT Press.

O'Byrne, D.J. (2003), *The Dimensions of Global Citizenship: Political Identity beyond the Nation-State*, London, Frank Cass.

O'Neill, O. (2001), 'Agents of Justice', in T. Pogge (ed.), *Global Justice*, Oxford, Blackwell.

Parekh, B. (2003), 'Cosmopolitanism and Global Citizenship', in *Review of International Studies*, **29**(1), pp. 3-17.

Pettit, P. (1997), *Republicanism: A Theory of Freedom and Government*, Oxford, Clarendon.

Rosenau, J.N. (1992), 'Citizenship in a Changing Global Order', in J.N. Rosenau and E.O. Czempiel (eds), *Governance without Government: Order and Change in World Politics*, Cambridge, Cambridge University Press.

Sassen, S. (2002), 'Immigration and Citizenship in the Global City'. Paper presented at the London School of Economics.

Scheffler, S. (1999), 'Conceptions of Cosmopolitanism', in *Utilitas*, **11**(3), pp. 255-76.

Sen, A. (1980), 'Equality of What?', in S.M. McMurrin (ed.), *The Tanner Lectures on Human Values*, Cambridge, Cambridge University Press.

Sen, A. (1981), *Poverty and Famines: An Essay on Entitlement and Deprivation*, Oxford, Clarendon.

Sen, A. (1982), 'Rights and Agency', in *Philosophy and Public Affairs*, **11**(1), pp. 3-39.

Sen, A. (1985), 'Well-Being, Agency and Freedom: The Dewey Lectures 1984', in *The Journal of Philosophy*, **82**(4), pp. 169-221.

Sen, A. (1988), 'Freedom of Choice: Concept and Content', in *European Economic Review*, **32**, pp. 269-94.

Sen, A. (1992), *Inequality Reexamined*, Oxford, Clarendon Press.

Sen, A. (1996), 'Humanity and Citizenship', in J. Cohen and M. Nussbaum (eds), *For Love of Country: Debating the Limits of Patriotism*, Boston, Beacon Press.

Singer, P. (1972), 'Famine, Affluence, and Morality', in *Philosophy and Public Affairs*, **1**(3), pp. 229-43.

Singer, P. (1988), 'Reasoning toward Utilitarianism', in N. Fotion and D. Seanor (eds), *Hare and Critics: Essays on 'Moral Thinking'*, Oxford, Clarendon Press.

Singer, P. (2002), *One World: The Ethics of Globalization*, New Haven, Conn., Yale University Press.

Thompson, D.F. (2000), 'La democrazia liberale nella società globale', in *Filosofia e Questioni Pubbliche*, **V**(1), pp. 139-54.

Acknowledgements

The author would like to thank Daniele Archibugi, Garrett W. Brown, Keith Dowding, Bob Goodin, David Held, Paul Kelly, and Rolf J. Olsson for helpful comments on previous versions of this chapter. The author is also grateful to the GSA for the bursary received for attending the GSA annual conference in 2002.

Chapter 6

Global Ethics:
Foundations and Methodologies

Heather Widdows

Why Global Ethics?

'Global Ethics' is a new term which has come into use in the last few decades. In this short time it has appeared in very different disciplines, for example in theology (Küng, 1990, 1993, 1998), philosophy (Dower, 1998) and international relations and political theory (Booth, Dunne and Cox, 2001). The proliferation of 'global ethics', especially considering the short time this terminology has been in use, suggests that global ethics signifies something increasingly important in how we construct and address questions concerning how we ought to live in the global context. To state that the terminology of ethics is increasingly used in the political and legal discourse – nationally and internationally – is uncontroversial. It is simply a fact. The controversy lies in two questions; first, why has ethics become prominent; and second, what constitutes – and what should constitute – (global) ethics?

This chapter will address these questions in turn. First, it will describe the return to ethics and consider reasons for the revival, such as the decline of traditional sources of moral authority and the ascendancy of liberal democratic ideology and its policies of multiculturalism. Second, this chapter will outline a particular conception of global ethics one which answers the contemporary need in liberal democracies for communication across value frameworks and belief systems and which goes some way to exploring what a substantive global ethics would look like.

The Revival of Ethics

'Global ethic' or 'global ethics' and the increased prominence of ethical terminology in the public sphere is a new phenomenon. However, 'ethics' is anything but new, and could arguably be considered the oldest Western academic discipline, as its roots are found in the earliest Western philosophy. Taken in its broadest sense, for example using Plato's description from the *Republic*, ethics "is no small matter, but how we ought to live" (1974: 352d). Conceived of in this way ethics cannot be a single, or even a group, of academic disciplines, nor can (or should) it be contained within academia. Rather it crosses the political economic spectrum and the private/public divide. In short, every aspect of life – personal and public, individual and communal – can be viewed from an ethical perspective, found in every attempt to structure our lives as we attempt to answer Plato's question of how we ought to live. This ancient description of ethics fits well with the contemporary revival of ethics, as we find ethical terminology used across the public sphere, from regulating the work place and professions to questions of international relations. Indeed, imagining public debates which ignore ethical factors is almost inconceivable at the present time. Think of the recent (ethical) debate over the war in Iraq and Tony Blair's use of the term 'moral imperative', and the oft-cited 'ethical foreign policy' (whatever one feels about the implementation, or lack of it). Such language and the supporting ideology indicates the central (and presumably vote-winning) nature of ethics (or at least the appearance of ethics) in contemporary political debate.

Undoubtedly, determining how we ought to live is a fundamental part of all human action, and unavoidable both individually and collectively. Moral decision-making is a given, a necessary part of human living. However, what is not given is the manner and the framework of this decision-making. The question to be answered, therefore, is why these fundamental issues are now being framed in ethical terminology. Employing ethics as a methodology to address these issues has not always been popular and has even been eschewed. As Booth, Dunne and Cox note, "a point of view emphasising the unity of politics and ethics would have struck many students and practitioners of international relations over the years as misconceived" (Booth, Dunne and Cox, 2001: 2). The first question we must address, then, is what has changed to make ethics the preferred (or at least one of the central) perspectives for addressing such fundamental questions. In other words, 'why (global) ethics, and why now?'.

Until this recent revival of ethics as a discipline in its own right and a key component of other disciplines, ethics could primarily be found in the disciplines of practical or pastoral theology and moral philosophy; both disciplines being concerned with the descriptive questions of how people act and the prescriptive questions of how they should act. Yet, although these disciplines continued to engage in ethical discourse and examination at a time when other disciplines ceased to regard ethics as central, in different ways they too partook of the trend away from ethical inquiry and limited the scope of ethics.

From the time of Greek Philosophy until the Enlightenment (albeit in slightly different forms) ethics, theology and philosophy were all part of the same scholarly pursuit: "theology was simply the name for that same rational investigation of all reality" (Mackey, 2000: 3). Only post-Enlightenment did the fracturing of disciplines take place leading to particular aspects becoming specialisms and eventually the separate disciplines that we find in today's academia. As a result ethics in theology and philosophy became only a small part of each discipline, rather than a holistic perspective and analytical framework. Thus, in theology ethics became Christian Ethics, concerned with correctly determining moral rules derived from divine commands; generally an exclusivist ethic concerned with only those within the Church (and usually only the particular denomination of the theologian in question). Moral philosophy continued to wrestle with fundamental ethical questions, yet, changes in philosophy meant that philosophy increasingly attempted to emulate science and, as a result, scepticism about values (found in various philosophies – non-cognitivism, emotivism, intuitionism and relativism) became increasingly prominent. Due to this uncertainty (particularly when concerned with the prescriptive questions about 'how we ought to live'), "value becomes difficult to discuss ... Scientific views and methods spread from their proper place in science into peripheral areas. All sorts of theorists (including some philosophers) begin to feel that they must eschew value preferences and discussions of value, and offer themselves as neutral scientific workers" (Murdoch, 1992: 50-51). The division of the theory from the practice of ethics meant that ethics, as presented by philosophers, tended to be descriptive and analytical rather than prescriptive and practical (the practical reduced to a small section of philosophical ethics, somewhat dismissively referred to as 'applied ethics'). In this manner the sphere of ethics was vastly reduced, rendering philosophers inarticulate on the fundamental questions of ethics, those key practical questions of how we ought to live.[1]

The revival of ethics can be seen in the gradual return to the field of moral philosophy by philosophers, as well as moral philosophers becoming again involved in multidisciplinary work, practical issues and ethics in its broader public aspects.[2] Along with philosophers many others are entering the fields of ethics and it is in the so-called fields of applied ethics that the revival of ethics is most marked; for example, medical ethics, business ethics and environmental ethics. Medical ethics, the longest established of these applied ethical disciplines, is a clear example of the gradual increased importance of ethics over the last century. As a recognisable discipline medical ethics first appeared in the 19th century as a professional ethic which developed as the medical profession was refined and distinct roles and duties of doctors and nurses to their patients were formalised. Since this time it has grown in prominence and since 1993 has become a compulsory part of the medical curricula in the UK (GMC, 1993). In addition to the increased importance of medical ethics in the training of medical professionals, medical ethics and the somewhat wider field of bioethics has become increasingly important in the public sphere. The ethics of medical procedures, capabilities and interventions have dominated the media and are issues of public concern and controversy. This can be seen in the area of genetics; for example, in public fears about genetic manipulation, such as the possibility of cloning and parents creating so-called 'designer babies', as well as in worries about the uses of genetic material in all areas of life from the medical to the behavioural and criminal.

In light of the scientific and technological advances and increased capabilities it could be argued that ethics is a new discipline create to address the new dilemmas being raised by these advances. For example, the 'genetic revolution' raises questions about how identifying information is to be processed and to whom it belongs,[3] as well as deeper questions about meaning and identity.[4] Parallel arguments can be used for other young ethical disciplines; for example, environmental ethics as a response to the environmental crisis, and business ethics (or issues of corporate responsibility) to the globalisation of business, organisations and IT beyond the nation state and traditional spheres of governance. Taken together medical ethics, business ethics and environmental ethics could be seen as a step towards global ethics – as none of the dilemmas raised in each of these applied disciplines can be adequately addressed by one community or one nation state.

This said, even if it is the case that new dilemmas are driving the revival of ethics, it is not clear why it should be ethics – as a language as well as a discipline – which should be adopted to address these new dilemmas, rather than alternative political, cultural or religious frameworks and methodologies. Therefore, the question we must consider is 'why ethics?' – that is to say, why has this revised concept of ethics become the chosen methodology for resolving dilemmas, taking the place of more traditional forms of moral authority and moral reasoning?

Liberal Democracy and the Failure of Traditional Sources of Moral Authority

One answer is to claim that, in the West at least, traditional moral sources are no longer functioning effectively, and are failing to address not only the new dilemmas, but also traditional moral dilemmas. Such a view is expressed by those who talk of a 'moral crisis' and a 'process of demoralisation' occurring in the West.[5] This is perhaps best, and famously, described by MacIntyre, who states that, "we have – very largely, if not entirely – lost our comprehension, both theoretically and practically, of morality" (MacIntyre, 1991: 2). This supposed erosion of a shared moral framework is now broadly accepted as a fair description of the situation in the West, and "it is now a commonplace about the modern world that it has made these [value frameworks] problematic" (Taylor, 1989: 16).

The traditional source of moral authority in the West is Christianity. Christianity as the 'official religion' (Luckmann, 1967) upheld and legitimated the moral framework and the social order. Thus, the argument from the moral crisis perspective is that Christianity can no longer function as a shared moral source within the pluralistic context of liberal democracies, which tolerate and even embrace competing value frameworks and belief systems.

The historical process by which the liberal democratic ideology replaced the Christian ideology (in which it has its roots) as the prominent ideology responsible for shaping the socio-political environment was long and drawn out. The decline of Christianity, the official religion, occurred gradually, through the process of 'secularisation'. Secularisation is most often regarded as a linear process which can be traced and its crucial moments mapped: for example, the Renaissance, the Reformation, the Enlightenment, the Scientific Revolution, the Industrial Revolution, globalisation, to name but a few landmarks along the way. This picture of secularisation assumes a time when the Christian value framework was absolute and universally accepted, a picture which is an over-simplified account and one which was never completely true. The nearest approximation to this picture is medieval Christendom, a time when a relatively homogeneous belief system was endorsed by the majority of the population of Europe.[6] However, even in Christendom, competing belief systems were not unknown: in the conflicts with the Moors, in the Jewish communities – persecuted to a greater or lesser extent – and in the ongoing enculturation of so-called 'pagan' religions, particularly in the Celtic parts of Europe. However, the impact of these opposing systems could be contained or countered. Therefore, for the most part, the value framework was shared and the Church was accepted as the mediator of moral authority. Yet, crucially, at this time of supposed uniformity, competing belief systems were very much a reality of everyday life and yet did not serve to undermine a shared sense of value.

In light of this it cannot be simply the experience of competing belief systems which undermines religion as a moral source. Instead, it is the rise of an incompatible liberal democratic ideology and the way that pluralism is embraced that makes religious, and other sources of traditional moral authority, untenable as carriers of shared moral value in contemporary liberal democracies.[7] Thus, it is with the ideology, structure and values of liberal democracy that traditional sources of moral authority cannot compete, not with the mere existence of competing world views. As Bhikhu Parekh argues, "in order to consolidate itself both politically and ideologically and to create an individualist moral and political culture, the state set about dismantling traditional institutions, communities and ways of life, with liberals providing the necessary ideological justification" (Parekh, 2000: 34). If we consider other contemporary responses to competing belief systems – a reality for all communities in the current global context – it is clear that religious and other traditional moral sources can continue to function as shared moral sources in non-liberal democracies. Non-liberal democracies continue to endorse such all-encompassing value frameworks, and examples are found in the return to 'traditionalism', such as the lauding of 'Asian values'[8] and the rise of theocracies, which endorse divine command theories and are gaining ascendance particularly in the Muslim world.[9]

It is the incompatibility of liberal democracies and other forms of value framework which has undermined traditional sources of moral authority. For, liberal democracies have overtly adopted 'thin' procedural values and have refrained from endorsing 'thick' value frameworks (Dworkin, 1978). In other words, they claim not to endorse any one conception of the good life, but to provide a framework within which any conception of the good life can be chosen. The overarching value of liberal democracies is tolerance – a commitment to equal respect for the views of all, irrespective of belief system – and tolerance is implemented in political and moral spheres. Not only do liberal democracies not endorse a conception of the good life (although they do so implicitly by asserting tolerance and the other values of liberal democracy and explicitly by endorsing and permitting certain practices[10]), but they regard any attempt to do so as heterogenous. Thus, in the liberal approach, 'political decisions must be, so far as possible, independent of any particular conception of the good life, or of what gives value to life' (Dworkin, 1978: 127). Rather than expect citizens to share a conception of the 'good life', all that is required is agreement to comply with the laws of the society – which mediate between different views and essentially protect the rights of individuals and groups to engage in their chosen way of life. Thus liberal democracies have embraced pluralism and explicitly implemented policies of multiculturalism (i.e. the incorporation of a pluralism of belief systems and value frameworks). However, such a requirement is demanding and undermines alternative value systems since:

> All citizens are expected to privilege their territorial over their other identities; to share in common as citizens far more important than what they share with other members of their religious, cultural and other communities; to define themselves and relate to each other as individuals; to abstract away their religious, cultural and other views when conducting themselves as citizens; to relate to the state in an identical manner and to enjoy an identical basket of rights and obligations. In short, the state expects all its citizens to subscribe to an identical way of defining themselves and relating to each other and the state. This shared political self-understanding is its constitutive principle and necessary presupposition. It can tolerate differences on all other matters but not this one, and uses educational, cultural, coercive and other means to ensure that all its citizens share it (Parekh, 2000: 184).

The power of the liberal democratic ideology and its primary value of tolerance is often underestimated, or more dangerously regarded as a neutral backdrop against which groups and individuals can continue to endorse their chosen belief systems and value frameworks. However, the enforcement of tolerance (and ironically intolerance with regard to those who do not adhere to this fundamental value) has profound consequences for alternative and particularly traditional moral frameworks, as it effectively prohibits the endorsement of any moral framework which claims to be absolute, unless the values of the liberal democracy – particularly tolerance – are part of the framework. As a result traditional sources of moral authority, such as religion, are unsustainable as shared sources of moral value in a liberal democracy. As a consequence of this incompatibility in liberal democracies religion (and all questions of ultimate significance) have been fully relegated to the private sphere and the ability of other forms of moral authority to function as a shared source of value are undermined.

Yet relegation of value to the private sphere cannot ultimately be successful, as public forms of moral decision-making are essential and value judgements cannot be purely a matter of individual choice. States must make laws and regulate behaviour – at the very least they must define the limits of private decision-making – and all these decisions are value-judgements and, as such, based on a certain (explicit or implicit) value framework and conception of the good life. As a consequence of their privatisation of value liberal democracies have difficulty in giving reasons for their positions and value judgements. Moreover, the claim to assert only procedural values makes any attempt to promote one position as superior to another tenuous. However, as we have seen, liberal democracies do in fact endorse powerful value frameworks and promote certain values (and consequently certain ways of life) over others. Yet, because of the structure of the ideology – based on the premise of not endorsing one value perspective over another – articulating and arguing for these values is problematic. Thus, liberal democracies need to find a means to discuss value in the public sphere in order to articulate the logic of their own position and to enable them to effectively engage in moral debate. It is here we return to ethics and suggest that ethics could provide a language and a methodology which is capable of framing moral decision-making in liberal democracies. Before discussing the role of ethics in this context we must further examine the underlying values of liberal democracies and the need for them to be articulated.

The Values of Liberal Democracy

As discussed above the liberal democratic ideology makes the articulation of substantial values problematic in its very premises. However, clearly liberal democracies do endorse substantial values – despite the claim that they only endorse 'thin' procedural values. This of course is not to say that all liberal democracies are the same. For example, France is more explicit about the liberal secular values around which the society is built and to which citizens are expected to conform and therefore is not a multicultural society (Parekh, 2000: 7). Yet, although there are differences between liberal democracies, the core values of the liberal democratic ideology are similar and rarely, if ever, explicitly stated. As a result their consequences and impact are not fully realised or understood. This is a problem both within the boarders of liberal democracies, in establishing order and governance, and in matters of global communication, affecting international relations and policy-making in the global context.

Within liberal democracies the problem is particularly acute when minority groups challenge the values of the liberal democratic ideology, particularly the key public value of tolerance. Unless the value framework which supports liberal democracy and the key values which it upholds are articulated liberal democracies are unable to provide reasons and explanations for the prominence of tolerance and other values. They simply assert their importance, declare them foundational values and the corresponding ways of life as those to be preferred, rather than offering reasons and arguments for such suppositions. Minority groups and those with distinct belief systems are explicitly accommodated within liberal democracies, which advocate respect for different belief systems in the private sphere – formalised in policies of multiculturalism. As long as groups respect the public value of tolerance and the procedures for interaction between individuals and groups in the public sphere different belief-systems and value-frameworks can be accommodated. Such accommodation reinforces the division of public and private and it upholds the individual's right to adopt a value system of their choice in private as long as the public value of tolerance is accepted. This public/private division undermines (as we saw in the case of Christianity) the authority and efficacy of other sources of moral authority and so successfully endorses and upholds the liberal democratic ideology. However, if a minority group resists the pressure of liberal democracy to conform to this value structure, and rejects the public/private divide and the primacy of tolerance then the liberal democracy finds it difficult to respond. There are two options for liberal democracies faced with such a challenge: either the legitimacy of the group or individual must be rejected – for example, by denying the 'reasonableness' of the opposing group – or the ideology must be modified to accommodate such differences (Rawls, 1993). Modifying the ideology is no easy task primarily because the core values of liberal democracy are rarely explicitly articulated. For the most part, minority groups and individuals within liberal democracies do not, as yet, provide a great threat, as those who actually, rather than rhetorically, reject the ideology are numerically small. However, the lack of dissent is due to circumstance and is open to change, therefore, clearly it would be wise for liberal democracies to devise a means at least to understand and so dialogue with those of different persuasions. At the moment liberal democracies tend to regard those who do not endorse tolerance as either unreasonable or mad – judgements which preclude dialogue and communication.

One example of how liberal democracies can address such dissent within their boarders is to follow the French example of insisting that those who wish to be citizens do endorse the values of the secular liberal democracy in the public sphere:

> To be a French citizen is to be integrated by an act of will into the French nation and to enjoy the same rights and obligations as the rest. The tradition recognises only citizens and has no space for a concept of minority ... the French nation is supposed to embody and protect the French culture, which its citizens are expected to accept as a condition of their citizenship (Parekh, 2000: 6).

In this manner France has a more articulated value system – evidenced, for example, by the national ethics commissions – than many other liberal democracies.[11] Yet it has not embraced multiculturalism and while arguably ensuring some measure of homogeneity within its borders it fails to address the problem of communication with those who disagree, both with minority groups within the country (who exist despite the lack of structural recognition) and with other nations who adopt different value frameworks and belief-systems.

Adopting such a non-multicultural policy is one model which other liberal democracies could adopt. In other words they could embrace a somewhat exclusivist view and reject those who hold worldviews which run counter to their own. However, modifying the liberal democratic ideology in this way severely limits the value of tolerance which is at the centre of the ideology. Moreover, it is questionable whether the ideology – especially in the forms and nations which have embraced multiculturalism – could withstand such a redefinition and remain liberal democracies. In addition, such reversal of policy would be impractical if not impossible and highly destructive of the groups and individuals within multicultural societies.

More importantly, particularly for global ethics, the consequences of adopting exclusive values in an overt manner – rejecting radical tolerance, the key value of liberal democracy – puts liberal democracies not only into conflict with minority groups within the society, but also with those who hold different value frameworks in the global context. If all liberal democracies can offer is a judgement that those who hold alternative positions are mad or unreasonable then communication across value frameworks and belief systems is impossible. Such a conclusion is utterly undesirable, not least as the consequences of being unable to communicate across dissimilar world-views are potentially devastating. Yet, although dismissing those who do not hold the same values is an unsatisfactory position (especially in the global context), at least in such judgements the values are articulated and clear which, it could be argued, is preferable to no articulation and the consequent dumbness which besets many contemporary liberal democracies.

Until the values of liberal democracies are articulated liberal democracies will be unable to advance effectively their ethical causes and defend their principles. Instead of real communication and debate they can only assert the rightness and superiority of their position – using various languages of morals, rights and values. They cannot fully engage in dialogue, present reasons and argue for their position, nor can they recognise that other reasonable perspectives are possible. This inability to communicate has often led to a lack of comprehension of other cultures, contributing to misunderstanding and mistrust of those who hold different value systems. In addition to lacking comprehension of other value frameworks, the lack of articulation and understanding of the underlying values and assumptions of liberal democracies has led to a failure of those endorsing liberal democratic positions to understand their own presumptions and perspectives. As a result, advocates of liberal democratic values can fail to recognise that they are asserting the particular values of the liberal democratic ideology which arise from a particular moral framework in a particular historical socio-political context. Unfortunately, as a result the tendency is to assume that they are endorsing not the values of an ideology, of one belief system and value framework, but universal values, which depict the correct and only reasonable moral position.

The lack of defence, debate and argument about moral assumptions is evident in the heated debate about human rights. Such rights, claim critics, are not universal but particular, the attempt of one group (the West) to impose its belief system on everyone else. For example, human rights have been criticised by non-Western groups (such as advocates of Asian values[12]) as being fundamentally Western and individual and thus a form of imperialism (Howard, 1993; O'Neill, 1996; Rorty, 1993). In order for liberal democracies to engage with minority groups within their own borders, as well as with those countries that endorse different belief systems and value frameworks, an articulation of the values of liberal democracy (and different liberal democracies) is fundamental and needed with great urgency.[13]

Ethics and Liberal Democracies

It is here that we return to ethics and the part that ethics could play in both articulating the values of liberal democracies and providing a language of moral communication across belief systems and value frameworks, both within the borders of liberal democracies and in their communications with non-liberal democracies. Ethics, as noted at the beginning of the chapter, is already established in the intellectual and public life of liberal democracies, which places it in a good position to provide the theoretical analysis of the liberal democratic ideology and its underlying values. Ethical analysis, with its philosophical heritage and current application in the social sciences, is multidisciplinary and well placed to unmask the hidden (to a greater or lesser extent in different forms of liberal democracy) core values, both in theory and as they function in practice as ideals, standards and guidelines for regulation in the public sphere. Once the values of liberal democracy are articulated then liberal democracies should be in a position to engage with those of other value frameworks and belief systems both within their own borders and in the international arena. In addition, ethics can operate as an inclusive language which enables those of different perspectives to enter the debate, as all positions can use the familiar language of ethics to frame their positions and so engage in the public moral debate.

Envisioned in this way ethics first serves to articulate the core values of liberal democracy, revealing the underlying assumptions of the ideology and providing an analytical tool for articulating and defending the value positions of liberal democracies. This in itself will serve to enhance communication by clarifying the liberal democratic position and removing the misconception that liberal democracy provides a neutral backdrop whose values must be adopted wholesale before dialogue can occur. Once liberal democracy is understood as a powerful value framework in itself, not unlike other value frameworks and belief systems, then proponents of liberal democratic values are in a position to engage with those of other perspectives, argue for their stance and even (possibly) modify the ideology in recognition of the validity of other positions, or in a willingness to compromise and reach workable accommodations with others. In the second sense ethics provides a framework and forum for debate about moral issues which is open to those who hold different perspectives. Ethics here provides the terminology and common language (universal rather than communitarian) for moral debate in the public sphere and global context.

A More Substantive Global Ethics?

To suggest that ethics could serve as a means to articulate the values of liberal democracy and moreover to provide a common moral language is already to make huge claims about the potential of ethics, and we could (or arguably should) leave the debate here. But to do so would be to leave untouched the eternal question of what constitutes global ethics. If global ethics is to be prescriptive and engage in the ethical debates of our time then ethics is more than a language of debate (not to negate this important function of ethics). The aim of communication across value frameworks and belief systems is not simply to understand alternative world-views (although this is important and an essential first step), but also, especially in the context of globalisation, it is to find compromises and to discover a more substantive global ethics. To aim merely at understanding would be to endorse relativism in one form or another, and indeed it has been suggested that all that could be expected from any form of global ethics is a form of ethical relativism

(Taylor *et al.*, 1994). Yet relativism cannot be enough for global ethics, which must engage with ethical debates and issues across national boarders and value frameworks. Therefore to say that differences should be accepted as unchangeable is untenable, particularly when one considers the practical issues of making international laws and agreements, from bioethics to human rights. In any event, relativism is far from established and by some is regarded as philosophically incoherent (Dickenson, 2002, 2003). Individual relativism denies the possibility of a shared value framework at any level, and cultural relativism holds that although individuals within cultures may share the same value system, value frameworks are dissimilar and therefore there is not enough common ground between cultures to achieve adequate minimal agreement on moral matters. Relativism, then, is not an option for global ethics because a view which regards the value frameworks of different cultures to be distinct and separate denies the possibility of real communication which can result in agreement and compromise about moral matters across cultures.

Therefore, the process of substantiating a more universal global ethics is a creative process and one which must remain provisional and flexible. Strivings towards this project are underway in the work of various academics, organisations and evident in the international language of human rights (despite its many difficulties). The task of defining global ethics is one of continuous construction and redefinition – indeed will always be such, as 'how we ought to live' is a context-dependent question. Even if we can attain a shared ethical framework with some universal conceptions of value the values will always need to be interpreted in specific contexts. Global ethics, then, must consciously take account of values and beliefs that affect and substantiate local ethics (including economic, social and political factors) and yet insist that the local must be understood in the global context. Not to recognise the importance of differences in race, gender, religion, community, and to attempt to impose a single ethic for all people at all times, is at best naive, resulting in a vague and therefore inapplicable and meaningless moral framework, and at worst arrogant, resulting in reductionism and oppression of other substantive and potentially enriching moral frameworks. Without a doubt it would be wrong not to recognise the danger inherent in the universalism of Western moral neo-colonialism and the tendency of Western ethics to pretend to take difference into account when often any such accommodation occurs only at a very superficial level.

A good example of this tendency in Western ethics is found in the bioethics of Third World research. Researchers and ethicists recognise that informed consent (the main mechanism for ensuring research is ethical) is Western and individualist. However, they respond to this by attempting to find ways to make informed consent acceptable and comprehensible to those of different cultures (for example by seeking additional communal consent) (Nuffield Council, 2002; National Commission on Bioethics, 2001). Thus, researchers and ethics committees fail to question whether individual informed consent is relevant in the particular context and continue to focus on informed consent as the key ethical issue for research in the Third World. Instead issues that should be addressed include, access to healthcare, inducement to participate in research trials and trial aftercare, all of which could arguably be claimed to be more important issues for the Third World.

This said, recognising the imperialist tendency (at least historically) of universalism should not mean we abandon any attempt to recognise substantive global ethics. Rather we should accept that universal does not have to mean, and from the perspective of global ethics should not mean, homogenised. To avoid relativism – cultural or individual – global ethics must go further than this. We must move towards a modified form of universalism (although not in the sense of imposition of one particular viewpoint), a universalism informed by concrete situations which, by definition, must be context and locality specific, and therefore flexible and open to interpretation and able to accommodate cultural differences (without subscribing to cultural relativism). For instance, some have attempted to state that universals may at least be 'followable' in many cultures and while not attempting to claim any of these as a global ethic (or worse *the* global ethic), it is desirable to claim that such ethics can and should exist (O'Neill, 1996; Barry 2001; Dickenson, 2003).[14] This is not to claim, as a global ethic (singular) would imply, that certain values, principles or codes as defined now will be valid at all times and all places. However, using this global ethics schema, one could claim that certain values, principles and codes are correct (or at least better than the available alternatives) and should be applied at the moment, either locally, regionally or globally as part of what constitutes global ethics.

Such a position is open to criticism and could with justice be said to be attempting to 'have the best of both worlds'. As such it could be deemed a failed venture and over before it is begun. Perhaps such a criticism has some validity and clearly further work to substantiate the content of global ethics is necessary. Yet moves in such directions do suggest that global ethics is possible and that not only better understandings of moral matters but also agreement and common practice may also be achievable.

So Why Global Ethics?

In order to answer the question, 'why global ethics?', we have traced the rise of (global) ethics as the means of defining and addressing moral matters in the public sphere. It was suggested that the rise of ethics was not brought about by the creation of new dilemmas which beset the modern world – although these dilemmas may have increased the sense of moral crisis and panic. Rather, ethics has gained ascendancy as a result of traditional sources of moral authority being unable to compete with the dominant liberal democratic ideology. We then explored the inarticulation of the values of liberal democracy and the desperate need for such articulation if liberal democracies wish to communicate with those who hold alternative value frameworks and belief systems. It was suggested that ethics could meet this need and not only provide a means to articulate the values of liberal democracy but also to provide a shared framework and language for moral discussion in the public sphere and global context. Finally we tentatively considered what a substantive global ethics would look like and how it could be arrived at.

In short then, the answer to the question 'why global ethics?' is simple: Ethics provides (or could provide) a means of moral communication in the public sphere across value frameworks and belief systems; something which is urgently needed in the current pluralistic global context.

Notes

[1] This is of course not universally true, and there are some notable exceptions, such as Bertrand Russell and his involvement in the campaign against nuclear disarmament. Nonetheless, although a caricature, it does accurately capture the trend in, particularly British, moral philosophy.

[2] Academics from many disciplines are playing a wider role in the public sphere, for example, Baroness Warnock's role as chair of the inquiry that lead to the HFE Act and the setting up of the HFEA and Professor Brazier's role as chair of the Retained Organs Commission.

[3] Genetic information is different in kind from other medical data, as it provides information not just about the individual, but about consanguineous relations and the wider ethnic group, it also continues to be potentially identifying for current and future generations. Leading to fears of its misuse, for example, by insurance companies, employers and those with discriminating political and racial agendas, now or at any time in the future.

[4] Exactly how genetics will effect our conceptions of human being is unclear, however there are two identifiable, and somewhat contradictory, strands of thinking about genetics evident in the public arena. On the one hand, there is the fear that the mapping of the human genome will allow for individual genetic blueprints and comprehensive testing, providing information about each individual's future health and lifespan. Such assumptions (although arguably derived from misunderstanding genetic susceptibility and risk) lead to theories of genetic determinism and reductionism, which threaten notions of human dignity and individual identity (Nelkin and Lindee, 1995). In addition, such information would lead to discrimination and a genetic underclass could be created, so limiting individuals' opportunities according to the capabilities indicated by their genetic blueprint (Rothstein, 1997; Shickle, 1997). On the other hand, genetics is portrayed as the answer to all human ills, allowing humans to manipulate and design life and explain the previously inexplicable (e.g. behaviour, emotion, sexuality). This train of thought is manifest in the language surrounding genetics, for example referring to the genome as 'the book of life', and genetically treated/chosen babies as 'designer babies' (Harris, 1998). Such responses to genetics are deeply embedded in popular culture, and key issues such as fears of cloning and genetic manipulation are evident in popular films and books (Nelkin and Lindee, 1995). These cultural reactions to genetics and new medical technology are influencing core concepts of meaning and identity, and reshaping our beliefs about life, health and death. As such, the genetic revolution is impacting on the moral frameworks within which human beings live and according to which their lived reality is constructed.

[5] Concern about the 'process of demoralisation' is evidenced, for example, by the Institute for Public Policy Research conference on 'Demoralisation: Morality Authority and Power' in 2002.

[6] Ignoring for the present the previous schisms of the Church, such as the break with the Eastern Orthodox, as largely irrelevant to people's perception of the overriding Christian ideology.

[7] This is not to say that religion and other sources of moral authority are not carries of individual and community value. Traditional sources of moral authority remain potent

carries of value which continue to have influence in the public sphere through the voices of their adherents. However, such traditional sources of moral authority can no longer serve as carries of moral value for the whole of a society in the pluralistic context.

[8] These values are communitarian: they support the political and religious order, emphasise hard work and thriftiness, link business to government and promote loyalty to the family and the wider community. Associated particularly with the leading regimes of Malaysia and Singapore, particularly Noordin Sopiee in Malaysia and Tommy Koh, George Yeo and Kishore Mahbubani in Singapore.

[9] In Islamic theocracies, political authority is in the hands of religious leaders and society is organised according to the religious law, the *Shari'a*. Examples of theocracies are Iran and Afghanistan (when controlled by the Taliban). There are political movements in favour of establishing theocracies in Algeria, Pakistan, Egypt, Sudan and Turkey.

[10] As Parekh notes "even if a state scrupulously avoided substantive goals, it would need to decide whether or not to allow slavery, polygamy, polyandry, incest, public hangings, euthanasia, suicide, capital punishment...If it does not legislate on these matters, it indicates, that it does not consider them sufficiently important to the moral well-being of the community to require a uniform and compulsory mode of behaviour. If it legislates, it takes a moral stand and coerces those taking a different view. Whatever it does, its action have an inescapable moral dimension" (Parekh, 2000: 201).

[11] In France, where articulation of the secular values of the liberal democracy is perhaps more advanced than elsewhere ethics is often the language of values and meaning, substantiating the secular values of the French state – the Enlightenment values of liberty, equality and fraternity. France has avoided some of the difficulties of minority groups by placing overt limits on the public value of tolerance (or equality and liberty construed in this way) – all are equal and have the freedom to live the life they choose, but only within prescribed limits. Once these limits are broken and these values are undermined the rights are forfeited. Thus tolerance is conditional – conditional on a minimum acceptance of the values of the society, in particular the division of private and public values and adherence to tolerance (equality and liberty). The primacy of the values are articulated and thus the liberal democracy ideology is somewhat unmasked.

[12] See endnote vii.

[13] It is important to remember that liberal democracies vary from each other dramatically as we have seen in our discussion of the UK and France. This is particularly important in the case of the US when despite overt claims to privatisation of religion and separation of church and state the practice is very different and far less multicultural than the UK, despite the established Church in the UK.

[14] In a not dissimilar manner, in the sub-discipline of global bioethics Ruth Macklin has defended a modified principlism as a form of universalism (Macklin, 1999).

References

Ayer, A.J. (1988), 'Critique of Ethics and Theology', in G. Sayre-McCord (ed.), *Essays on Moral Realism*, New York, Cornell University Press.
Barry, B. (2001), *Culture and Equality*, Cambridge, Polity Press.
Booth, K., Dunne, T. and Cox, M. (2001), *How Might We Live? Global Ethics in the New Century*, Cambridge, Cambridge University Press.
Dickenson, D. (2002), 'Global Ethics: Black and White and Right All Over?', Inaugural lecture presented at Birmingham University, 23 May (available at http://www.globalethics.bham.ac.uk/DD_inaugurallecture.htm).

Dickenson, D. (2003), *Risk and Luck in Medical Ethics*, Cambridge, Polity Press.

Dworkin, R. (1978), 'Liberalism', in S. Hampshire (ed.), *Public and Private Morality*, Cambridge, Cambridge University Press.

GMC (1993), 'Tomorrow's Doctors: Recommendations on Undergraduate Medical Education', http://www.gmc-uk.org/med_ed/tomdoc.htm (visited 16.01.03).

Harris, J. (1998), *Clones, Genes and Immortality*, Oxford, Oxford University Press.

Howard, R.E. (1993), 'Cultural Relativism as Cultural Absolutism', *Human Rights Quarterly*, **15**(2), pp. 315-38.

Küng, H. (1990), *Global Responsibility: In Search of a New World Ethic*, London, SCM Press Ltd.

Küng, H. (1993), *A Global Ethic: The Declaration of the Parliament of the World's Religions*, London, SCM Press Ltd.

Küng, H. (1998), *A Global Ethic for Global Politics and Economics*, Oxford, Oxford University Press.

Luckmann, T. (1967), *The Invisible Religion: The Problem of Religion in Modern Society*, London: Macmillan.

MacIntyre, A. (1991), *After Virtue: A Study in Moral Theory*, London, Gerald Duckworth & Co. Ltd.

Mackey, J.P. (2000), *The Critique of Theological Reason*, Cambridge, Cambridge University Press.

Macklin, R. (1999), *Against Relativism*, Oxford, Oxford University Press.

Murdoch, I. (1992), *Metaphysics as a Guide to Morals*, London, Vintage.

National Bioethics Advisory Commission (2001), 'Ethical and Policy Issues in International Research: Clinical Trials in Developing Countries' http://www.georgetown.edu/research/nrcbl/nbac/pubs.html (visited 16.01.03).

Nelkin, D. and Lindee, S. (1995), *The DNA Mystique: The Gene as a Cultural Icon*, New York, W.H. Freeman & Co.

Nuffield Council on Bioethics (2002), *The Ethics of Research Related to Healthcare in Developing Countries*, http://www.nuffieldbioethics.org (visited 16.01.03).

O'Neill, O. (1996), *Towards Justice and Virtue: A Constructive Account of Practical Reasoning*, Cambridge, Cambridge University Press.

Parekh, B. (2000), *Rethinking Multiculturalism: Cultural Diversity and Political Theory*, Basingstoke, Palgrave.

Plato (1974), *Plato's Republic*, Book One, 352d. Translated into English by Desmond Lee London, Penguin Books.

Rawls, J. (1993), *Political Liberalism*, New York, Columbia University Press.

Rorty, R. (1993), 'Human Rights, Rationality and Sentimentality', in S. Shute and S. Hurley (eds), *On Human Rights: The Oxford Amnesty Lectures 1993*, New York, Basic Books.

Rothstein, M.A. (ed.) (1997), *Genetic Secrets: Protecting Privacy and Confidentiality in the Genetic Era*, London, Yale University Press.

Shickle, D. (1997), 'Do "All Men Desire to Know"?: A Right of Society to Choose Not to Know about the Genetics of Personality Traits', in: R. Chadwick, R. *et al.* (eds), *The Right to Know and the Right Not to Know*, Aldershot, Ashgate.

Stevenson, C.L. (1963), *Facts and Values: Studies in Ethical Analysis*, London, Yale University Press.

Taylor, C. (1989), *Sources of the Self: The Making of Modern Identity*, Cambridge, Cambridge University Press.

Taylor, C. *et al.* (1994), *Multiculturalism*, Princeton, NJ, Princeton University Press.

Chapter 7

Informal Sociality, Cosmopolitanism and Gender among Transnational Professionals: Unravelling Some of the Linkages between the Global Economy and Civil Society

Paul Kennedy

Introduction

This chapter is based on an exploratory study of transnational architects and related professionals working in the building-design industry. The latter constitutes merely one sector where a growing number of companies flourish in what Sassen (2000) calls the 'producer service industries'. These have become "a central feature of current growth in developed societies" (*ibid*: 61) as the degree of 'service intensity' (Sassen, 2002: 16) required in all industries and sectors has grown. At the same time, firms in these producer service industries are responding to economic globalization, the de-regulatory, market-opening consequences of neo-liberal policies and the rise of post-Fordist flexible capitalism worldwide. Thus, they seek to extend their provision of essential support services made available not only for the benefit of transnational corporations (TNCs), as the latter spread their operations globally, but also for other producer service firms in adjacent sectors – such as certain law firms which have followed not just their corporate manufacturing but also their accountancy and banking clients across the world (Beaverstock, Smith and Taylor, 1999, 2000). Like other businesses providing producer services, the assets and investments of firms in the building-design industry are grounded primarily in human skills rather than in material assets; in intellectual or symbolic capital (Bourdieu, 1984). As such, they are quintessentially at the heart of the symbolic-wealth economy.

   This shift towards 'globalized regimes of flexible accumulation' has given rise to the "new transnational functionaries of global capitalism" (Nonini and Ong, 1997: 9). These functionaries provide certain 'integrative competencies' (*ibid*: 11) required if businesses are to be effectively managed across vast distances while taking appropriate account of local/national cultural, design, legal or other embedded practices (Beaverstock *et al.*, 2000). In recent years this new professional/business class has attracted the attention of a growing number of commentators. Featherstone (1990: 8), for example, refers to this "coterie of new specialists and professionals" who work outside the "cultures of the nation-state". Castells (1996: 415) points to the dominant "technocratic-financial-managerial elite" who, aided by information and communication technology and the key locations which act as the nodes and hubs of globally networked capitalism, direct the space of flows that now constitutes the world economy. Sklair (2001) has written extensively about the transnational capitalist class whose various fractions are mostly grounded within, or linked indirectly to, the TNCs. Similarly, Micklethwaite and Wooldridge (2001) describe the twenty million or so global 'cosmocrats' – managers, professionals, financial experts and creative entrepreneurs – who now make the global economy run effectively.

Problematizing Transnational Professional/Business Elites

Three central issues are clearly discernible in the literature on this expanding class of transnational professionals and business elites. Firstly, there is an emphasis on the need for them to demonstrate certain 'cosmopolitan' leanings but also a claim that such orientations are already evident. Although the precise nature of these leanings is rarely defined there is a basic presumption of the necessity to cope with transnational and multi-cultural situations. Thus, Featherstone (1990: 8) points to the importance of 'inter-cultural communication' among today's global professionals and their empowerment by "a new type of habitus". Sassen (2000: 24) suggests that global businesses not only require 'denationalized elites' comfortable with reduced "national attachments and identities" but that boosted by the critical mass of commercial resources and networks concentrated in global cities such businesses are also contributing to the 'denationalization' of certain 'deeply rooted' institutional areas that have hitherto obstructed global capitalism (*ibid*: 25) Sklair (2001: 55-56) claims that "globalizing companies needs managers with cosmopolitan outlooks" and TNCs increasingly "train their top cadre of managers to expect to work in any part of the world" (*ibid*: 55). Overseas experience, especially a period of training abroad, can also play a crucial role in creating highly professional managers. Thus Beaverstock *et al.* (2000: 101) describe how some American law firms rotate partners between different overseas branches and seek to expose 'outstanding younger foreign lawyers' to the "global finishing schools" provided by a spell in the home company. Contreras and Kenney (2002) point to the necessity to connect local Mexican managers of TNC subsidiaries operating in the maquiladora border region with the USA into the "wider 'social world' of the industry" and to ensure that local managers engage "in a network whose skills and values are defined by a transnational community of experts" (*ibid*: 137). In similar vein, Micklethwaite and Wooldridge (2001) are emphatic that their "cosmocrats are defined by their attitudes and lifestyles rather than just their bank accounts" (*ibid*: 230) and this includes a respect for meritocratic values, intelligence, gender equality and effective networking (*ibid*: 232-33).

Another issue encountered in this literature is the ambivalence with which the roles and lifestyles of transnational elites are often perceived by analysts. On one hand, as we have seen, the cosmopolitan leanings – though often outlined in rather vague terms – evinced by these transnationals are strongly designated as essential to the effective working of the global economy. Yet, at the same time, commentators may be suspicious and even downright critical towards what they perceive to be the privileged lifestyles and attitudes demonstrated by these elites. Here, whatever 'cosmopolitanism' may be, it is a two-edged sword; a quality we hope is strongly evident yet one we despise or fear in equal part. Thus, much of the recent literature on globalization depicts the transnational elites and classes who supposedly determine global economic policies as wielding power in often irresponsible and uncontrollable ways while a vast gap exists between them and everyone else. For Bauman (1998: 3) there is an increasing breakdown of communication between the "global and extraterritorial elites and the ever more 'localized' rest" and while economic globalization has further disempowered the poor it has left elites unaccountable: "emancipated from local constraints". Similarly, Burbach *et al.* (1997: 117-21) describe the rise of a 'barbaric' global bourgeoisie since the fall of communism whose members adhere to few values which might incline them to retain some accountability to the remainder of humanity. Carroll's and Carson's analysis (2003) of the overlapping world economic policy-making groups and top interlocking company directors who together form a 'global corporate elite' (*ibid*: 39) of around 620 individuals – drawn from the leading 350 corporations and five key intergovernmental organizations (IGOs) – again reinforces this sense of elite inaccessibility. Castells (1996) insists that the dominant managerial elites who direct the space of flows in which the global economy is embedded preserve their social cohesion and cultural codes by running their businesses and conducting their increasingly similar lifestyles in "carefully segregated spaces" that are "clearly distinct from the populace" (*ibid*: 416). While "elites are cosmopolitan, people are local" (*ibid*: 415).

Moreover, the lifestyles revealed by these elites demonstrate a fake 'consumerist cosmopolitanism' (Calhoun, 2002: 105) which may involve searching the world for cultural knick-knacks with which to adorn their expensive lives and abodes. As if their rootlessness, detachment from national responsibilities and privileges were not sufficiently adverse traits, Calhoun (2002: 106) further argues that the close dependence of these selfish elites upon global capital means that 'cosmopolitanism' is now identified with a particularly exclusivist and divisive form of neo-liberal capitalism. Despite their undoubted ability to appreciate cultural diversity these elites are unable to take on the 'traditional' mantle of responsibility we equate with cosmopolitanism and for which they are well equipped; namely, to play a leading role in reforming global capitalism so helping to extend a global civil society and democracy (*ibid*: 108). This concern that contemporary transnationalism and cosmopolitanism probably inhibit the strengthening of a global civil society, with clear political and ethical agendas for wider human liberation, is one to which we will return later.

Thirdly, while most observers are in little doubt that the main driving forces of global capitalism are blatantly economic, there is also wide consensus that the imperatives of market competition and profit alone are not sufficient to make global capitalism work. Social scientists have always been aware of what Mitchell (1995: 365) calls the socially and historically "embedded quality of economic activity" such that "specific local traditions actively co-produce and rework global systems". Arguably, though, this reality has been marginalized and perhaps rendered less 'respectable' by the dominant discourse of neo-liberalism during recent years. Of course, this embeddedness has been particularly well documented for immigrants, past and present, who have always utilized the socio-cultural resources generated by particularistic ties, especially the immediate family but also kinship/clan, locality and ethnicity, in their struggles to cope with daily economic and social life in the host country (Boyd, 1989; Basch *et al.*, 1994; Faist, 2000). Included here, too, would be the rather special case of long-distance, dispersed businesses sometimes involving very large investments conducted by such ethnic diasporas as the 'overseas Chinese' from their various bases in South East Asia (Chan, 1997; Mitchell, 1995; Nonini, 1997; Zhou and Tseng, 2001) and where business success depends critically upon family and ethnic support systems. Recently, however, there appears to have been a revival of interest in the need for all capitalist enterprises to be firmly embedded in socio-cultural relations including those based in the West. Indeed, and paradoxically, it seems that economic globalization coupled to neo-liberal policies of widespread market de-regulation, increased competition and the demands for flexibility have together created tensions and pressures that massively *increase* the relevance of various kinds of strong social relationships and interactions within the workplace (Mitchell, 1995; O'Riain, 2000; Beaverstock *et al.*, 2000; Sassen, 2002).

In large part, this is linked to what Boden and Molotch call the "compulsion to proximity" (1994: 257) and the "thickness of co-present interactions" (*ibid*: 259). Thus, only face-to-face interactions can generate the forms of human exchange – including "not just words but facial gestures, body language, voice intonation" and so on – and the effective contextualization of meanings that are sufficiently nuanced and focused to allow business people and professionals to achieve "complex understandings, arrange informal trade-offs, and deal with unanticipated tensions" (*ibid*: 272) among other advantages. Accordingly, they suggest, it is hardly surprising that business leaders seek co-presence and 'flock together' (*ibid*: 272) at conferences, meetings, clubs, key business districts and other venues. Nor has the massive recent uptake of information technology by businesses worldwide fundamentally altered the significance of co-present intimacy and 'personal micro-networks' (Castells, 1996: 416) in business life though clearly the former has brought enormous advantages in its own right. Moreover, the speeding up of business transactions and their extension across vast distances may actually intensify the need to re-capture particular places in the space of global flows and then to construct particularized interpersonal relations within such terrains (O'Riain, 2000: 178). Thus, successful global businesses require the kind of economic reflexivity that produces innovation, continuous learning and the ability to deal with complexity (Storper, 1997) by providing sites where it is possible to gain access to "ensembles of localized relations" (Beaverstock *et al.*, 2000: 98). Similarly, much business activity depends not only on the capacity to tap into local/national as well as wider knowledge, in order to deal with the needs of clients and cope with national regulations and cultures, but also the ability to bring together in particular locations a "mix of talents and resources" (Sassen, 2002: 23) so as to draw upon specialized information and to make appropriate "interpretations and inferences" as well as evaluations (*ibid*: 22).

Recognition of the central role that intensified communication, hugely strengthened by close face-to-face relations, plays in today's global economy is clearly to be welcomed. However, with some interesting exceptions, (for example, Beaverstock *et al.*, 1999; O'Riain, 2000) what is less often stressed is the equal importance of the trust, mutual liking and genuine friendships that not only make possible "solidarity-building within the team" (O'Riain, 2000: 178) but also the construction of highly affective social networks that may endure over time and space. What we are talking about here is a kind of global lifeworld consisting of numerous informal patterns of sociality that emerge in the interstices between and the crevices within large formal organizations and which seep through and into every aspect of the global system world, co-existing alongside more formalized rule-bound relations. They provide a loose framework within which the necessary interactions between key players can take place effectively and creatively while providing the orientations based on trust and mutual liking that engender collaboration. *With increased economic globalization and as the need to forge viable interactions between people of many nationalities becomes ever more compelling, so the significance of these interactions will correspondingly increase.*

In the light of this discussion and using the case study material generated by the study of transnational professionals working in the building/design industry this chapter will explore three issues. One concerns the precise ways in which such friendship relations take root within non-ethnic business organizations and what circumstances and resources enable them to flourish – something that has rather been taken for granted in the literature but which arguably needs to be examined more thoroughly. A second and overlapping question considers the multi-national character of these emergent socialities including the special role that women may play in their evolution. Lastly, I take up the theme of cosmopolitanism and its potential contribution to an emergent global civil society. Here, and despite their manifest privileges, I suggest that some transnational professionals do contribute to the formation of a global civil society, albeit in indirect ways, and that this is because there are many degrees and kinds of cosmopolitan as well as very different roles to be played in constructing a more just and viable world.

The Study

The study explored the work and non-work experiences of professionals working in the building-design industry in the UK. It explored how those who work overseas encounter and cope with transnational social space. Eight enterprises were investigated (seven in London, and one in Manchester) based on previous contacts which were then followed up through a 'snowball' effect. These firms were engaged in the design of various kinds of buildings but they often supervised the implementation of such projects, on site, through sub-contracting to numerous building specialists. Thirty-two professionals were interviewed. Twenty-three had originally trained as architects, though some had since acquired further qualifications, six respondents had trained as building engineers and three were in business management or interior design. It was not possible to select these respondents on a statistically random basis because many employees were on leave, working abroad or otherwise engaged during the research period. However, because the study focused on individuals who had personal experience of working continuously outside their native country at some time during their careers, many employees were excluded from the survey in any case.

Twenty-nine respondents fulfilled these criteria while the remaining three had travelled abroad for shorter periods on numerous occasions. Many had worked overseas in two or more different locations. Twenty-one respondents had worked abroad for more than two years and fifteen people had done so for more than four years. In addition, made many repeated short visits abroad – perhaps two or three days every week or fortnight – as part of their current UK post. The group included an assortment of nationalities: only twelve were born in the UK and/or had single British nationality status. The remaining twenty individuals hailed from seventeen different countries. Working in Britain exposed the latter to the same transnational experiences as their UK counterparts who had previously worked abroad. Eleven of the non-British nationals had worked overseas prior to repeating this experience in Britain.

The 'Resources' Available to Professionals Working Overseas: Forging Transnational Social Space

The building design companies included in the study had attained global reach. They had done so either by forging strong relationships with partner companies overseas – and with whose help they could cope with the local technical, cultural and other demands generated by working on foreign contracts – or they had established their own offices across these countries, or both. Such moves may require companies to send some of their existing employees abroad to work on overseas projects for longer or shorter periods of time while generally encouraging flows of personnel between partner firms and/or overseas and home office. Such flows enable companies to pool design knowledge and experiences, build-up reservoirs of detailed linguistic, cultural and technical skills and to expose local employees to overseas influences. It was exactly these circumstances that had propelled many of the respondents into overseas work though some had also made their first or previous moves into foreign employment by obtaining earlier posts abroad as independent professionals and then later joined one of the more 'global' companies.

The overseas experiences of the professionals included in this study were similar to those of transnational migrants in that their work life revolved around particular locations and social milieus. However, whereas the involvement of transnational migrants in the host society is largely based on their encapsulation within established, multiplex relations constructed around transplanted kinship, village/regional and ethnic ties the overseas social contacts available to most of the professionals in this study were meager or non-existent. They were mostly compelled to construct interpersonal relations, friendships and a supportive social milieu in situ and from scratch. Similarly, their overseas experiences are likely to be somewhat different from professionals or managers who are sent abroad accompanied by their families and by other colleagues, with whom they have previously worked, in order to run a subsidiary owned by the home company.

Though unable to take with them an established network of social relations, there were three other kinds of resources available to these professionals and these enabled them to construct virtually new transnational social spaces. First, there was the bundle of professional skills they had already acquired – their cultural capital or baggage (Bourdieu, 1984) – and which could be adapted relatively easily to meet the requirements of the new work situation and which they shared with colleagues. Both Merton (1957) and Gouldner (1989) distinguished between professionals dependent upon locally-relevant and company-bound attachments and those who relied more on decontextualized knowledge applicable to many locations and who sought the validation of wider peer groups. Intrinsic, therefore, to certain types of professionalism is their inherent transferability between sites and projects and the possession of a roughly shared frame of reference despite national differences in culture and practice. It was evident from the accounts provided by the respondents that they had been able to draw upon just such a shared body of orientations and decontextualized skills (see Kennedy, 2004). Moreover these commonalities outweighed national differences.

It is the remaining two resources that I now wish to discuss in more detail and which are most relevant to the questions outlined earlier. One concerns the dynamics generated by the demands of the work project and the interpersonal interactions and needs of the work team assembled around it. With some significant exceptions (O'Riain, 2000; Hannerz, 2003) these transnational spaces have not received the research attention they deserve. The second involves a discussion of the significance for these multinational professionals of a middle class educational background and its implications for a career spent partly overseas.

Interpersonal Relations and the Dynamics of the Work Project and Team

The work project and the characteristics of the team assembled around it generated an emergent dynamics. This was probably much more important than shared professionalism in enabling the incoming individuals to operate effectively in transnational social space. The work team normally consisted of a core of fellow professionals but clients, suppliers, local sub contractors and artisans were also present. Moreover, this team usually involved a mixture of locals and other foreigners. The interpersonal dynamics of the work project and team normally revolved around four main sets of interacting experiences:

(I) The demands of the project. The project created its own logic and demands. Many respondents claimed that they had worked very long hours; eighty hours a week was not uncommon. This left little energy or time for building a social life outside the firm except for late-night drinking bouts or clubbing with fellow workmates and other team members – though inter-company business linkages might lead to meetings with professionals from other companies. Meanwhile, work hours involved struggling to overcome the problems involved in adapting the original design to local exigencies and in grounding the plan in terms of an actual site and building. Numerous problems arose, from the difficulties of interpreting local technical regulations and procedures, to dealing with the changing demands of clients, sorting out legal and financial issues, coping with in-house and external cultural and language difficulties but also sorting out the complaints associated with an assortment of site contractors, suppliers and artisans. Without the cooperation and support of fellow members of the work team along with good humor, tolerance and above all the trust based on real mutual liking and respect – built ultimately out of friendships that were reinforced by leisure-time socializing – both the work experience of the overseas visitors and the successful fulfillment of the project might be seriously jeopardized. Though, similar problems are encountered at home they are harder to deal with in a foreign cultural situation.

(II) The experience of social exclusion from the host society. Several respondents explained that working overseas had often been accompanied by the feeling of being 'cut-off' from the host society. This was intensified by long hours of work, constant absorption in the demands of the project and the perception of being tied to a particular city given that time constraints minimized travel opportunities. A limited grasp of the national language tended to confine intensive relationships to a circle of other educated locals and non-locals who possessed some language skills. In addition, some countries, for example, in the Middle East, possess very few native professionals and so need to import large numbers of foreigners. Yet, local traditions often impede participation in the host society. Finally, a sense of relative social exclusion may also be linked to age and the stage someone has reached in their life course. Thus, those professionals who are most able to seek overseas work are young individuals probably living outside a permanent relationship and who are still childless. But these circumstances limit the possibilities for extensive socialization with colleagues from the host society unless they, too, are young, single and childless. Older host-society colleagues are likely to be married with families and tied into long-standing neighbourhood, school, kinship and other commitments which leave little time for socializing with visiting foreigners. In short, for many transnational professionals, friendships and leisure time depend on forging experiences with those who share similar personal profiles irrespective of nationality; namely, other non-locals with whom you spend most of your time at work.

(III) Compensating for emotional vulnerability. Being thrust into a new culture, country *and* a work situation involving initially unfamiliar people and practices may generate anxiety. Then there is the reality of leaving one's homeland, family

and friends. This may create a feeling of loneliness and separation – an emotional deficit. The most obvious way of overcoming this is, firstly, to form friendships with others facing the same predicament – fellow workmates and those participating in the same occupational networks in the locality. But, secondly, for reasons already discussed, it is also likely that those to whom a person is most closely drawn are individuals experiencing a similar situation, namely, *other strangers or non-nationals* whose roots also lie outside the host society. In this context, the following remarks by an unmarried, British respondent (aged 40 years) who was working on a project in Malta, are especially revealing:

> I think you tend to make friends most ... with people who are in the same predicament as you. People who are perhaps working there and who are not from that area ... because they also have a need to socialise ... they haven't got a home environment to go back to either. The people I have met and get on with best are Australian and Croatian people ... Malta isn't really their home either. It's a bit like being a student, everybody is in the same boat. You need to make new friends and they do too ... and I think that people who are working overseas tend to stick together, it becomes a small community within a community ... though I do know some Maltese people as well ... but not many.

In addition, forming friends with people of nationalities different from one's own may generate a sense of achievement and exhilaration that is more profound than the relations developed with fellow nationals. Recalling his Malta experiences as well as earlier stints working abroad, the same respondent suggested:

> I think that my foreign experience I will always remember ... whereas when I worked in the UK it tends to all draw into one memory whereas the overseas, I will always remember. Those people are more prominent in the memory of my life because they are different. I remember what happened and the people more readily.

(IV) The life cycle stage. The emergence of transnational social relations also depended on the personal profile of the respondents. We have seen hints of this already. Particularly significant, were, first, the current stage they had reached in their life course especially whether or not they were in a permanent partnership or marriage, second, whether they had any children and, last, whether their partner was of the same or a different nationality. Here, age was a key factor and at the time of the interviews in 2000 the mean age of the sample was around 39 years. Approximately two fifths had children at the time of the interviews, however, with only one or two exceptions, none of the respondents had been parents during their periods of prolonged working overseas. Even large and reputable firms operating in the building design sector make little provision for family life abroad. Many had also been unattached during their period overseas though being involved in a long-term relationship is possible providing there are no children and the partner's work is not situated too far away. Notable also was the fact that of the twenty-five respondents who were involved in long term/permanent marriages or partnerships at the time of the interview, or who previously had been for some years, in sixteen

cases these partnerships had involved cross-nationality relationships (sixty four per cent of this group). In four cases these relationships had preceded the main period spent working overseas – and indeed helped to motivate the decision to seek overseas employment – but the remainder had established these partnerships following a period spent working abroad. Indeed, these appear to have been one of the main consequences of participation in transnational life. Such, mixed-nationality relationships, in turn, are likely to generate further reliance upon and exposure to transnational friendships and networking.

Social Class and Cultural Capital

The preceding section demonstrated that the cultural 'others' mostly encountered by the transnational professionals were people similar to themselves; youngish, educated, unattached individuals of several nationalities working on the same project or who circulated within a geographically and occupationally proximate milieu. Here, the 'culture' they shared was constructed out of a multiplicity of elements in addition to everyday work and a similar professional ethos. Probably chief among these is a middle class social status and background (Colic Peisker, 2002). This provided a cultural and personality tool kit conferring confidence and adaptability. Thus, most of the respondents – seventy one per cent of the sample – came from social backgrounds where fathers (and sometimes mothers too) had either been professionals or successful entrepreneurs. Only, twenty nine per cent (nine individuals) came from more lowly backgrounds with fathers who were artisans, shop salesmen, lorry drivers and so on. Clearly, most of this group came from relatively privileged backgrounds. But social class is also shaped by education and here, by definition, all respondents had attained higher educational qualifications. It seems likely that all university-trained (or its equivalent) individuals, irrespective of their nationality or parental background, share certain orientations: the ability to think analytically and the willingness to ask questions; an awareness of the limits to one's own knowledge but at the same time an ability to seek additional skills; an individualistic perspective or unit of identity which, in turn, creates a preference for a largely self reliant lifestyle and work experiences providing autonomy and creativity; and an openness and curiosity with respect to new experiences and ideas.

But, in addition, other common elements are readily to hand for aiding the construction of a shared transnational life space, especially where individuals belong to the same age, generational and life-cycle cohort. Here, we could include the following: an interest in local or international art, music, literature, travel and holidays; the sharing of stories about families and friends back home as well as personal life and work histories; pooled observations and gossip concerning local host society; a curiosity about comparing tastes and customs in the various home societies from which the members hail; and a range of possible leisure interests in sport, global popular music and films. The point about all these items is that they *largely transcend local and national cultural differences*. Moreover, it is exactly this quality that enables them to be brought readily into use for cementing multinational friendship networks capable of spanning time and space. At the same time, they exist over and beyond the ties already created through everyday work experiences.

In short, at least in terms of shared cultural capital, globalization is indeed helping to create a transnational middle class just as the observers mentioned at the beginning of this chapter have suggested. The members of this class generally find that what unite them is far more significant that those national and cultural differences that might have divided them in an earlier age. When living abroad such professionals may not be especially drawn towards the 'locals'. Rather they are searching out individuals from the host and other countries who are very similar to themselves and drawing upon a shared bank of transnational middle class orientations.

Having explored the experiences of these professionals working abroad we now consider two of the long term implications, evident from their case histories that point to an emergent global society: the formation of multinational friendship networks and the key role of women professionals in these processes.

The Formation of Multinational Friendship Networks

When working overseas the respondents had participated in various non-work friendship networks. A large proportion of the leisure time spent with these friends involved drinking in bars and discos, eating in restaurants or visiting late-night films and other cultural events. In most cases (seventy five per cent of the respondents) these sociability networks involved people of the same or similar professional interests whether these were work colleagues or professionals employed on similar projects but for different firms.[1] The minority (twenty-five *per cent*) who interacted more with people outside their occupational/professional community – mostly with locals rather than expatriates – mostly did so due to 'special' circumstances, for example, individuals who had lived abroad long enough to put down non-work family and friendship roots in their adopted city.

These non-work friendship networks demonstrated three salient characteristics. First, friends from the host society (locals) were much more likely than expatriates to be present in these networks. Of course, this is hardly surprising given the presence of locals in streets, shops and places of residence, and the likelihood that several, perhaps most, work colleagues will be locals along with suppliers, clients and sub-contractors.[2] Nevertheless, fellow-nationals living in the same location offer a highly congenial, uncomplicated mode of access to friendships and speak the same language. Indeed, formally, expatriate venues were often the 'natural' home towards which those living abroad would gravitate. Given these magnetic forces it was surprising to discover that in only seventeen out of the forty-nine overseas friendship situations in which the respondents had participated overall did expatriates figure at all. Moreover, only in four situations did they provide the *sole* source of non-work companionship and even here, as with five other situations involving at least some expatriates, those involved were 'untypical' fellow-nationals: either people in mixed-nationality marriages and/or individuals whose own friendship networks consisted of people from several different nationalities.

Second, far fewer of these friendship networks than might have been expected, given the ubiquity of locals everywhere in the host society, were *predominantly or entirely* built around relationships with nationals. Thus, there were only nine instances where host society friends were the *sole* source of network companions, eighteen *per cent* (though locals were highly likely to contribute at least *some* of the participants in friendship networks), and we have already considered the reasons why this should be so.

Thirdly, the most frequent component of these non-work friendship networks tended to be people of mixed nationalities. Thus, in thirty-two of these overseas situations (sixty five per cent of the total) friends from several or many nations other than the respondent's own, or the host, nation, provided a substantial, the main or the sole component. Consequently, these networks were partly sometimes completely multinational in composition,[3] and they demonstrated what Wittel (2001) calls 'network sociality' in that they consisted of clusters of individuals known to each other. They were *not* merely the worldwide friendships dependent upon and defined in relation to one single individual which Albrow (1997) has called 'sociospheres'.

Most of these multinational friendship networks had survived long after their members had dispersed. Thus, nearly two thirds of the sample had maintained contacts with some of their former overseas friends of different nationalities over the years (twenty-one individuals) through letters, Christmas cards, telephone conversations, emails or, more usually, a combination of these.[4] Moreover, twelve of these respondents (thirty-eight *per cent* of the sample) had engaged in mutual visiting often connected to holidays or a business trip. Sometimes theses visits involved entire families.

Women Professionals, Mixed-Nationality Marriages and Transnational Networks

The respondents' average age was around thirty-nine years. Those who had children had begun to establish their families only a few years prior to the interviews. The possibilities for coping with family life while working overseas are limited given the unwillingness of even the larger firms to provide the necessary resources. Accordingly, irrespective of their personal motivations for seeking work overseas, most had found that settling down with parental responsibilities was something that had to be postponed. Moreover, once family life was underway, the majority of respondents had confined their overseas work to making numerous very short visits to those foreign locations where their firms were engaged in supervising contracts. This was compatible with a reasonably satisfying family life though it was obviously not without problems. Thus, the period of prolonged overseas work experiences tends to coincide with life cycle stage.

Though the numbers involved are very small, the data from this study suggests that gender may play a significant role in the ability of professionals to construct a career trajectory which is ultimately compatible with having children. Thus, it was noticeable that all those respondents who had established a domestic life involving children were men. The time did not allow a detailed investigation of the circumstances involved but evidently they were able to establish a *modus operandi* with their respective partners whereby the latters' own careers had been placed partly on hold while their children were young. In contrast the seven women in the sample were all childless though five were involved in current long-term relationships and one of the other two had been married previously. In five of these seven cases, the partnerships involved mixed-nationalities. The average age of these seven women was thirty-seven years. What this suggests, perhaps, is that for many transnational professional women, career success and job satisfaction largely precludes rearing a family. Moreover, this may become even more difficult where a long term relationship involves mixed-nationalities since both may be involved in frequent traveling and the issue concerning to which country the individuals 'belong' and where they could put down mutually secure long term roots is far from straightforward.

It may be the case, therefore, that professional women with a transnational career profile find themselves involved in overseas experiences that propel them into long-term mixed-nationality partnerships and that force them to make a choice between a continuing successful career trajectory and having children – or which reinforces a previous decision not to have children. But such circumstances may mean that, unwittingly, such women are at the forefront of moves towards the evolution of a truly global society. This is because of their leading role in spearheading the construction of ever more complex and overlapping circuits of transnational networks, containing a decidedly multi-national mix of individuals, and on a more or less continuing basis. This is something which their male colleagues contribute towards so long as they remain unmarried or childless but from which they partly disengage when they adopt a more settled existence. Here, the following case study is especially revealing.

> Rachel was a thirty eight year old childless American national in a long-term relationship with a French partner. She had worked in the London office of an American company since 1989. In addition to living 'abroad' in Britain, her work had compelled her to make many short but regular visits to company sites in different parts of Europe (she made 34 such visits in 1999 alone). In London, many of her friends were from the office but few were English. Rather, most were foreign nationals who were often similarly involved in mixed partnerships. Though her work had not required her to take up residence in the European countries where most of her work was done, over the years she and her partner had become part of a network of friends across the UK, the USA and Europe consisting not just of a multinational group but also of couples involved in mixed marriages. These, in turn, were mainly involved in yet additional friendships with people living and working in similar circumstances – namely, overseas much of the time and in mixed partnerships. For example, some German members of her friendship network – originally met through clients and co-project workers – had invited her and her partner to join them on holidays.

Rachel's case is no doubt exceptional but it may point to an important reality. Thus, belonging to a pool of transnational friends – many of whom are also likely to be childless and involved in cross-national partnerships – becomes a way of life and a reference group. Such common experiences are especially likely to transcend strong feelings of nationhood. Eventually, as friends move onto to yet other countries and make friends with more like-minded individuals in the next host country, and because contacts are maintained, so new friends are added to the ever evolving and overlapping circuits of transnational social life.

Cosmopolitanism and Global Civil Society

Earlier we saw that many observers acknowledge the significance for the effective operation of the global economy of managers/professionals who can cope easily with cross border relationships and experiences. Yet, there is a often a parallel tendency to argue that the privileges and remoteness supposedly revealed by such groups leads to the equation of cosmopolitanism with social division and exclusiveness while far from taking a leading role in helping to build a strong global civil society these individuals – who are among those best equipped to do so – apparently demonstrate no such inclination. In this final section I want to try and unravel these arguments partly by drawing upon the data already presented but also by referring briefly to several other writers whose work on cosmopolitanism has been highly influential.

Hannerz's attempt (1990) to clarify the meaning of cosmopolitanism for those occupying contemporary transnational social spaces has been extremely useful. He defined cosmopolitanism as the willingness and ability to engage with the cultural 'other' mainly through face-to-face social interactions encountered in the "the round of everyday life in a community" (*ibid*: 240). He contrasted this sharply with other kinds of overseas experiences such as exile and tourism. A major criticism levelled against this rather aesthetic version of cosmopolitanism, however, is that it all too easily evokes and celebrates cultural elitism (for example, several of the contributors to Cheah's and Robbins's 1998 book). In contrast, Tomlinson's (1999) view of cosmopolitanism avoids such criticisms. He argues that the ultimate 'test' of cosmopolitanism is not just the willingness to interact with local cultural 'others' but the capacity to demonstrate a sense of ethical responsibility with regard to global problems (*ibid*: 183-86). Here, cosmopolitanism approximates to its original meaning, namely the idea of becoming a 'citizen of the world'. Yet, while we live morally and aesthetically within the wider world we remain embedded in the sphere of the local – a condition he describes, borrowing from Robertson's work (1995), as "ethical glocalism" (Tomlinson, 1999: 194).

This approach overlaps with but is perhaps a 'stronger' version of another recent perspective on cosmopolitanism explored by various recent commentators (Cheah and Robbins, 1998; Vertovec and Cohen, 2000). Thus, Cheah and Robbins (1998) suggest that many individuals and groups across the world display a capacity to think, feel and even act, at times, beyond their immediate local, ethnic, national or other ascriptive affiliations but this normally stops some way short of the capacity to identify with the whole of humanity. This actually existing, more grounded, everyday and even mundane version not only 'enables' far greater number of global citizens to be recognized as demonstrating some degree and kind of cosmopolitanism it also creates the possibility – once there is general recognition of its existence and value – of harnessing some of the energy currently embedded in primordial bonds to different kinds of projects for global justice. Such displays of everyday, probably spasmodic and inherently fragmented ethical/political orientation constitute, for Cheah and Robbins (1998), the much needed realm of 'cosmopolitics'.

Where, then, do the respondents included in the present study belong in these analyses of cosmopolitanism? Following Hannerz, I investigated whether the respondents had used their participation in the occupational culture provided by the building/design industry as a bridgehead for establishing deep attachments to the host society – for example, seeking non-work local friends or involvement in charities, churches, and so on. However, except for those who had become long term residents in the host country, most had failed to engage seriously in these ways with the host cultures. Similarly, there was little evidence of Tomlinson's cosmopolitans. While a few respondents claimed that working overseas had increased their knowledge of the particular societies in which they had lived and/or that they now felt much less tied to their own national culture, such awareness had not left them with a stronger ethical commitment towards solving world problems. Only two respondents insisted that their global understanding and actions had increased *because* of their transnational experiences, for example, becoming a permanent contributor to Oxfam. Most who claimed such orientations had held them before they first worked overseas.

While Hannerz's cultural engagement and Tomlinson's global ethical responsibility may apply to certain limited categories of people, such as some social scientists, connoisseurs or those seeking careers in international non-governmental organizations, there are several reasons why they may not be appropriate tests to apply to *everyone* who moves in transnational space including many professionals. Firstly, we have seen that there were many constraints deterring serious engagements with the cultural other. They included, long hours of work, absorption in the heavy demands of the project and the reality that many local colleagues are locked into separate, non-work social milieus and family ties. Secondly, as Friedman (1994), has suggested, in an age of endless global cultural flows there may be some difficulty in identifying the pure 'locals' whose culture remains largely intact and who are available for cultural intercourse with cosmopolitans. Then there is the question of the language barriers to such exchanges given that such 'true' locals area likely to be rooted in ancient traditions, probably live in rural locations or small towns, are tied to long-established occupations and such people may have little education. Accordingly, only non-locals with considerable linguistic competence may be able to navigate deep cultural engagements successfully.

Thirdly, Tomlinson's (1999) requirement of glocal ethicality as a mark of cosmopolitanism is also difficult to apply to many who live in transnational social space. For example, it may be unreasonable to expect people to cope with family and work while juggling identities, relationships and the management of a vast and ever-changing range of technical, social, cultural, linguistic and other skills – across transnational space – while simultaneously demonstrating a degree of ethical/political commitment towards solving world problems. Perhaps, Tomlinson is setting an impossibly demanding test for most individuals to meet including many transnational professionals. Fourthly, I suggest that the patterns of sociality demonstrated by the respondents in this study do qualify as constituting a valid kind of "actually existing cosmopolitanism" (Malcomson, 1998). While the latter mostly involves neither Hannerz's conscious engagement with the distant cultural other nor Tomlinson's ethical glocalism, it does demonstrate bridge-building activities which lead to the creation of new and viable commonalities between individuals from different national backgrounds. These multinational friendship networks also celebrate national cultural identities while simultaneously exploring the crossovers between cultures. The fact that shared middle class orientations obviously provide a pre-existing framework without which the construction of such social spaces would be much more difficult, detracts neither from the achievement of building viable multinational friendship networks nor from their importance in underpinning global economic life. Moreover, in a world where deep primordial divisions continue to flourish within and between countries, the commonalities that it seems *can* be constructed between the middle class professionals of many countries is surely to be valued notwithstanding the 'bourgeois' lifestyles they evince.

Fifthly, a number of respondents emphasized that their companies were strongly committed to implementing environmentally-responsible practices and this was what had partly attracted them to work for these companies. They regarded the operationalization of such green practices as a central part of their job responsibilities. At the same time, many were proud to be working for companies and with fellow professionals they regarded as leading exponents of innovative and exciting design models in international architecture many of whose projects were widely seen as offering path-breaking styles and working procedures – including in the environmental sphere. While we may not attach the same degree of cultural significance as these respondents did to some of the 'grand' and highly commercial projects with which they had been associated it is valid to point out that outside family life and for those fortunate to be in employment it is this immediate sphere of daily work where most of us can best hope to act out a responsible existence and demonstrate our desire to contribute to the common good. For the great majority of human beings, work and family life is where community, national and global affiliation has to begin and never more so if these tasks are approached with special pride, dedication and commitment.

Finally, in the age of the nation-state, civil society partly grew out of the pre-existing overlapping and dense networks of family, local community, occupational, regional, religious and ethnic affiliations, most of which initially had little direct 'political' significance. We also know that the growth of a capitalist mass market for knowledge through the spread of inventions such as the printing press, accompanied by a quickening of market exchanges across most economic regions and sectors associated with early industrialization and the expansion of cities, the intelligentsia, the emergence of public places, and so on – as Habermas, Anderson and others have explained so fruitfully – all helped massively to extend and deepen the power of national civil society by generating the technologies and spaces which made it easier and necessary for people to communicate effectively and the common interests spurring them to join forces. Presumably, if a truly effective global civil society is to emerge in future, an exactly parallel set of social and economic processes also need to unfold at the global level working alongside overt political activities as these spread out from their points of strongest origin at the national level and converge into international streams. If the construction of ever denser networks of sociality and economic interdependencies at the global level are essential in order to underpin and enrich a grass-roots global polity then the transnational professionals discussed in this paper certainly have their own important role to play.

Notes

[1] There are often strong inter-firm and/or inter-professional connections at work either because of sub-contracting arrangements between different companies or the existence of links with universities and private or government institutions.

[2] The reliance on locals for friendship was much more likely in the case of the minority group, of respondents whose most important networks were non-work related.

[3] In identifying the multinational composition of these networks I excluded overseas friends made as a result of brief working visits but not permanent stays, those formed in student life unless these involved a work component and the friendships of the UK nationals not formed while they were abroad. In all instances the data refers only to friendships carried over from work into non-work life. Other kinds of friendships, such as with neighbours or formed with locals where respondents eventually settled 'permanently', were excluded.

[4] Here, friendships with locals were included.

References

Albrow, M. (1997), 'Travelling beyond Local Cultures: Socioscapes in a Global City', in J. Eade (ed.), *Living the Global City: Globalization as a Local Process*, London, Routledge.

Basch, L., Schiller, N.G. and Blanc, C.S. (1994), *Nations Unbound: Transnational Projects, Postcolonial Predicaments and Deterritorialized Nation States*, New York, Gordon and Breach.

Bauman, Z. (1998), *Globalization: The Human Condition*, Cambridge, Polity Press.

Beaverstock, J.V., Smith, R.G. and Taylor, P.J. (1999), 'The Long Arm of the Law: London's Law Firms in a Globalizing World-Economy', *Environment and Planning A*, 31(10), pp. 1857-76.

Beaverstock, J.V., Smith, R.G. and Taylor, P.J. (2000), 'Geographies of Globalization: United States Law Firms in World Cities', *Urban Geography*, 21(2), pp. 95-120.

Boden, D. and Molotch, L. (1994), 'The Compulsions of Proximity', in R. Friedland and D. Boden (eds), *Space, Time and Modernity*, Berkeley, University of California Press.

Bourdieu, P. (1984), *Distinction: A Social Critique of the Judgement of Taste*, Cambridge, Mass:, Harvard University Press.
Boyd, M. (1989), 'Family and Personal Networks in International Migration: Recent Developments and New Agendas', *International Migration Review*, 23, pp. 638-70.
Burbach, R., Nunez, O. and Kagarlitsky, B. (1997), *Globalization and its Discontents: The Rise of Postmodern Socialisms*, London, Pluto.
Calhoun, C. (2002), 'The Class Consciousness of Frequent Travellers: Towards a Critique of Actually Existing Cosmopolitanism', in S. Vertovec and R. Cohen (eds), *Conceiving Cosmopolitanism: Theory, Context and Practice*, Oxford, Oxford University Press.
Carroll, W.K. and Carson, C. (2003), 'The Network of Global Corporations and Elite Policy Groups: A Structure for Transnational Capitalist Formation?', *Global Networks: A Journal of Transnational Affairs*, 3(1), pp. 29-58.
Castells, M. (1996), *The Rise of the Network Society*, Oxford, Blackwell.
Chan, K.B. (1997), 'A Family Affair: Migration, Dispersal, and the Emergent Identity of the Chinese Cosmopolitan', *Diaspora*, 6(2), pp. 195-213.
Cheah, P. and Robbins, B. (1998) (eds), *Cosmopolitics: Thinking and Feeling Beyond the Nation*, Minneapolis, University of Minneapolis Press.
Colic-Peisker, V. (2002), 'Migrant Communities and Class: Croatians in Western Australia', in P. Kennedy and V. Roudometof (eds), *Communities Across Borders: New Immigrants and Transnational Culture*, London, Routledge.
Contreras, O. and Kenney, M. (2002), 'Global Industries and Local Agents: Becoming a World-class Manager in the Mexico-USA Border Region', in P. Kennedy and V. Roudometof (eds), *Communities Across Borders: New Immigrants and Transnational Cultures*, London, Routledge.
Faist, T. (2000), *The Volume and Dynamics of International Migration and Transnational Society*, Oxford, Clarendon Press.
Featherstone, M. (1990), 'Global Culture: An Introduction', in M. Featherstone (ed.), *Global Culture: Nationalism, Globalization and Modernity*, London, Sage.
Friedman, J. (1994), *Cultural Identity and Global Process*, London, Sage.
Gouldner, A.W. (1989), 'Cosmopolitans and Locals: Towards an Analysis of Latent and Social Roles', in J. Steven (ed.), *Classic Readings in Organizational Behaviour*, Pacific Grove California, Brooks/Cole Publishers.
Hannerz, U. (1990), 'Cosmopolitans and Locals in World Culture', in M. Featherstone (ed.), *Global Culture: Nationalism, Globalization and Modernity*, London, Sage.
Hannerz, U. (2003), *Foreign News*, Chicago, University of Chicago Press.
Kennedy, P. (2004), 'Making Global Society: Friendship Networks among Transnational Professionals in the Building Design Industry', *Global Networks: A Journal of Transnational Affairs*, 4(2), pp. 157-79.
Malcomson, S.L. (1998), 'The Varieties of Cosmopolitan Experience', in P. Cheah and B. Robbins (eds), *Cosmopolitics: Thinking and Feeling Beyond the Nation*, Minneapolis, University of Minneapolis Press.
Merton, R. (1957), *Social Theory and Social Structure*, Glencoe, Ill, Free Press.
Micklethwaite, J. and Wooldridge, A. (2001), *A Future Perfect: The Challenge and Hidden Promise of Globalization*, London: Random House Publishing.
Mitchell, K. (1995), 'Flexible Circulation in the Pacific Rim: Capitalism in Cultural Context', *Economic Geography*, 71(4), pp. 364-82.
Nonini, D.M. (1997), 'Shifting Identities, Positional Imaginaries: Transnational Transversals and Reversals by Malaysian Chinese', in A. Ong and D.M. Nonini (eds), *Ungrounded Empires: The Cultural Politics of Modern Chinese Transnationalism*, New York, Routledge.

Nonini, D.M. and Ong, A, (1997), 'Chinese Transnationalism as an Alternative Modernity', in A. Ong and D.M. Nonini (eds), *Ungrounded Empires: The Cultural Politics of Modern Chinese Transnationalism*, New York, Routledge.

O'Riain, S. (2000), 'Net-working for a Living: Irish Software Developers in the Global Workplace', in M. Burawoy *et al.* (eds), *Global Ethnography*, Berkeley and Los Angeles, University of California Press.

Reich, R. (1991), *The Work of Nations: Preparing Ourselves for Twenty-First Century Capitalism*, New York, Simon and Schuster.

Robbins, B. (1998), 'Actually Existing Cosmopolitanism', in P. Cheah and B. Robbins (eds), *Cosmopolitics: Thinking and Feeling Beyond the Nation*, Minneapolis, University of Minneapolis Press.

Robertson, R. (1995), 'Glocalization: Time-Space and Homogeneity-Heterogeneity', in M. Featherstone, S. Lash and R. Robertson (eds), *Global Modernities*, London, Sage.

Sassen, S. (1991), *The Global City: New York, London, Tokyo*, Princeton, NJ, Princeton University Press.

Sassen, S. (2000), *Cities in a World Economy*, Thousand Oaks, Calif., Pine Forge.

Sassen, S. (2002), 'Introduction: Locating Cities on Global Circuits', in S. Sassen (ed.), *Global Networks: Linked Cities*, New York, Routledge.

Sklair, L. (2001), *The Transnational Capitalist Class*, London, Blackwell.

Storper, M. (1997), 'The City: Centre of Economic Reflexivity', *The Service Industries Journal*, **17**(1), pp. 1-27.

Tomlinson, J. (1999), *Globalization and Culture*, Cambridge, Polity Press.

Vertovec, S. and Cohen, R. (2002) (eds), *Conceiving Cosmopolitanism: Theory, Context and Practice*, Oxford, Oxford University Press.

Wittel, A. (2000), 'Towards a Network Sociality', *Theory, Culture and Society*, **18**(6), pp. 51-76.

Zhou, Y. and Tseng, Y-F. (2001), 'Regrounding the "Ungrounded Empires": Localization as the Geographical Catalyst for Transnationalism', *Global Networks: A Journal of Transnational Affairs*, **1**(2), pp. 131-54.

Chapter 8

The Global Compact: Corporate Citizenship in Action, but is it Enough?

Lisa Whitehouse

Introduction

The debate concerning the legitimization of the exercise of public power by private corporations, within both academic literature and managerial practice, has witnessed an apparently natural progression over the last seventy years. Beginning in the 1930s with the recognition of the separation of ownership and control, through the heyday of corporate social responsibility in the 1970s, it has more recently evolved into the modern concept of corporate citizenship. The claim, implicit in much of the corporate citizenship literature, is that corporate social responsibility has had its day and that a new approach to the regulation of corporate social power is needed.

This chapter seeks to examine this claim by questioning the extent to which corporate citizenship can serve as an effective tool in the regulation of private corporations. In undertaking this task, an examination of a model of corporate citizenship already in operation, namely, the United Nations Global Compact, will be undertaken. As a voluntary initiative, designed to encourage participating corporations to adopt and publicise examples of good corporate practice, the Global Compact exhibits characteristics consistent with a model of corporate citizenship and underscores, 'the rising importance of corporate citizenship' (Post and Berman, 2001: 66).

A review of the Global Compact, however, indicates that corporate citizenship, by itself, will prove ineffective in justifying the exercise of social power by corporations. The voluntary nature of the concept (Windsor, 2001: 46), with its assumption that society may expect but cannot demand that corporations exceed their minimum legal obligations, results in a situation in which corporate citizenship will fail to constrain those corporations most in need of regulation. It is essential, therefore, to look elsewhere for an effective method of regulating corporate social power. While this may involve the creation of new and innovative concepts, this chapter will argue that corporate social responsibility still holds sufficient potential to achieve this goal.

Despite the ambiguity which surrounds the concept, a distillation of its fundamental tenets results in a definition of corporate social responsibility as a duty, imposed upon corporations, to prevent or remedy any 'social costs' (Kapp,

1971) that arise out of corporate activity. Corporate social responsibility, in operating as a minimum legal obligation, leaves open the opportunity for corporations to undertake activities which exceed this and other legal duties and consequently, will allow them to be perceived as good corporate citizens. It is proposed, therefore, that in order to justify the exercise of public power by corporations, corporate citizenship must be viewed, not as a substitute for corporate social responsibility but as a complement to it.

Defining Terms – Corporate Social Responsibility

The debate concerning the regulation of the exercise of social power by corporations has undergone an evolutionary process which appears to make natural the assumption that corporate social responsibility has been superseded by the concept of corporate citizenship. The seeds of this evolutionary process were sown by Berle and Means (1936) who, in identifying and analysing the implications of the separation of ownership and control within large corporations, opened up the boundaries of managerial discretion. As Stokes (1986) indicates, "[o]nce the link between property ownership and control is severed there no longer seems to be any compelling reason why the shareholders should receive all the profits of the company or why corporate managers should run the company in their interests alone."

Despite the potential for managers to become "a purely neutral technocracy, balancing a variety of claims by various groups in the community and assigning to each a portion of the income stream on the basis of public policy rather than private cupidity" (Berle and Means, 1936: 356), the tradition within Anglo-American models of regulation has been to demand that directors prioritise the interests of shareholders above all others, constituted by the pursuit of profit maximization (see Parkinson, 1996; Roach, 2001; Wedderburn, 1985). The opportunity, offered by the work of Berle and Means (1936), to expand the range of interests capable of recognition within the decision-making processes of management may not have been taken up within legal doctrine (Stokes 1986: 168), but the position within academic debate and managerial practice has been markedly different.

Questions regarding the justification of the 'single-minded pursuit of profit' (Clarkson, 1995: 112) by company managers, were raised in the early 1930s (see Berle, 1931; Dodd, 1932) but it was during the 1970s that the debate flourished, resulting in the construction and detailed analysis of the concept of 'corporate social responsibility'. Although the concept lacks any universally accepted definition (Stone, 1975: 72), there is a unifying theme apparent within much of the corporate social responsibility literature, which is, a concern to make 'legitimate' (see Davis, 1973; Wood, 1991) the exercise of social power by private corporations.

The 'crisis of legitimacy of the business company' (Stokes, 1986: 159), which gave rise to the creation of the concept of corporate social responsibility, arose out of the convergence of a number of factors. The first and most obvious factor concerned the increase in size of some corporations and the extension of their reach into multinational and global markets. The implications of this increase in size have been noted by Galbraith (1973) and Donaldson (1982: 7), who states that "[w]ith size comes power. Large corporations are capable of influencing mainstream societal events and this power is not only economic, but social and political."

This ability, on the part of large corporations, to exercise what Parkinson (1996: 22) describes as 'social decision-making power', raises concerns for the reason that "companies are able to make choices which have important social consequences: they make private decisions which have public results" (Parkinson, 1996: 10). More significantly, this power is no longer being exercised with recourse to meaningful standards or regulation. The traditional sources of such regulation, namely, shareholders, market forces, consumer sovereignty and national and international regulatory systems, have been shown to fall short of legitimating the exercise of public power by private corporations (Galbraith, 1973; Jenkins, 2001; Parkinson, 1996; Sutton, 1993) which, as Stokes (1986: 156) indicates, is of particular concern for the reason that "power unless limited and controlled may threaten the liberty and the equality of the individual which are the two fundamental tenets of liberalism itself".

While there is a consensus among many academics that the power exercised by large corporations lacks justification, no agreement has been reached in respect of the means by which to achieve legitimacy. A review of the relevant literature reveals a multitude of different meanings ascribed to the concept of corporate social responsibility and a variety of different methods by which to achieve it. These methods range from the implementation by corporations of philanthropic ventures (see Blumberg, 1972; Henning, 1973; Sheikh, 1996), to an obligation "to take proper legal, moral-ethical, and philanthropic actions that will protect and improve the welfare of both society and business as a whole" (Anderson, 1989: 9).

The ambiguity apparent in the concept has provided those who may seek to criticize it with ample opportunity to raise concerns in respect of its potential impact. Levitt's (1958: 42) suggestion that the concept "echoes as a new tyranny of fad and fancy", was developed further by the most noted critic of corporate social responsibility, Friedman (1969: 133), who described it as a "fundamentally subversive doctrine" which undermined the one and only social responsibility of business, which is to maximize profit.

Despite attempts by many academics to define the concept and to counter such criticisms, corporate social responsibility remains, in its current form, an ambiguous concept incapable of practical implementation in any meaningful sense. It is, perhaps, for this reason that the debate concerning the imposition of checks and balances on the exercise of public power by private corporations has left corporate social responsibility behind and moved on, arguably, to more fertile ground in the form of corporate citizenship.

Corporate Citizenship

The transition from corporate social responsibility to corporate citizenship, apparent within both academic literature and managerial practice during the 1990s (Wood and Logsdon, 2001: 85), appears, at first instance, to be indicative of a shift in emphasis rather than any radical variation in the attempt to regulate corporate activity. The two concepts derive from a similar concern to legitimate the exercise of social power by private enterprises but, they differ in terms of their conception of the corporation. While corporate social responsibility views the corporation as a source of vast and 'unbridled power' (Stokes, 1986: 156), corporate citizenship chooses to view the corporation as a citizen, engendered with rights and responsibilities in much the same way as other citizens (Andriof and McIntosh, 2001: 14). Although it has been suggested (Windsor, 2001: 49-50), that more may be expected of the large and powerful corporate citizen, ultimately, the responsibilities are, "equivalent to those expected of an individual ordinary citizen".

While this may appear to be a subtle variation on a recurrent theme, the manner in which we conceive of the corporation alters dramatically the manner in which we may seek to regulate it. In viewing the corporation as a 'social enterprise' (Dahl, 1972) capable of exercising significant power which may affect greatly the welfare of individuals, communities and society generally, it would appear necessary, in an attempt to legitimate that power, to have recourse to external and democratically validated standards and processes, the most obvious examples being the law and the judicial system. Corporate social responsibility, therefore, recognizes the imbalance in the power relationship between corporations and those who may be affected by the corporation's activities and, as a result, compels corporations to abide by democratically determined standards of behaviour. This, at least, is the theory, which underpins corporate social responsibility, the reality is that such regulation has not been forthcoming.

Corporate citizenship, on the other hand, in viewing the corporation as an individual, demands that they abide by *existing* legal obligations coupled with the aspiration that they will exceed these minimum legal requirements by implementing behaviour which society will deem to be socially responsible, "just as individuals have citizenship-related responsibilities over and above obeying the law, so do corporations" (Van Buren, 2001: 56). The view that corporate citizenship offers a 'watered-down' version of corporate social responsibility is supported by Wood and Logsdon (2001: 86) who suggest that, "the obligatory aspects of corporate social responsibility are replaced by a weak legalistic obligation (pay taxes, obey the law) and a voluntaristic approach to community problems and opportunities".

The relatively subtle distinction between corporate social responsibility and corporate citizenship is evidenced by the recent proposals of the European Commission (2001) and the UK Department of Trade and Industry (2002). Despite referring consistently to the concept of corporate social responsibility, the recommendations put forward by the Commission and the DTI emphasize the need for corporations to exceed voluntarily their minimum legal obligations. To this extent, therefore, both the Commission and the DTI are asking corporations to behave like good corporate citizens rather than seeking to impose a model of corporate social responsibility.

It is, perhaps, the voluntary nature and narrow scope of corporate citizenship which makes it attractive as an alternative to the much broader concept of corporate social responsibility. The argument is that if corporate social responsibility was too radical an idea to be implemented by regulators then a concept, more agreeable to corporate managers, might offer a more effective starting point in the attempt to constrain corporate power. It has been suggested, in particular, that the narrowness of corporate citizenship means that it, "concerns a much smaller group of stakeholders and issues, making it easier to measure the concept and to evaluate company performance" (Wood and Logsdon, 2001: 85).

Although corporate citizenship may offer a more practical guide to corporate managers in their attempt to be perceived as good corporate citizens, the concept, like corporate social responsibility, suffers from what Preston and Post (1975: 53) have described as a 'fatal flaw', that is, "an absence of boundaries to the scope of managerial responsibility and an absence of criteria for appraising managerial performance, either with respect to the specified areas selected for concern or the decisions and actions taken". If corporate citizenship is intended to be used as a measure of the extent to which corporations are meeting the expectations of society in behaving as good corporate citizens then it is necessary to establish the criteria by which to judge that activity. While some activities, for example, may appear to be models of undeniably good practice, the behaviour of the corporation taken as a whole may be less than perfect. As McIntosh (2001: 4) indicates, "the company that is viable economically through its good use of financial, social and environmental resources may not be good for society. If the company then distributes some of its wealth through philanthropy, it does not necessarily make the company socially responsible".

It is necessary, therefore, to establish guiding principles which both corporate managers and those seeking to judge the behaviour of corporations can use to assess the extent to which such behaviour meets with the demands of corporate citizenship. Guidance on this issue is provided by Wood and Logsdon (2001), who offer at least three citizenship models, ranging from the minimalist theory of civic association to the universal human rights model. In reassigning his original definition of corporate social responsibility, Carroll (2001: 139) also identifies the 'four faces' of corporate citizenship as, economic, legal, ethical and philanthropic. While the identification of these various models may prove helpful in establishing the necessary criteria, it may prove to be of more assistance, at this early stage in the construction of a framework of corporate citizenship, to examine a model which is already being used in practice, namely, the United Nations Global Compact. The benefit to be gained in presenting an account of this initiative is that it offers an insight into the manner in which a model of corporate citizenship might operate in practice and it also serves as an established starting point from which to develop a more refined version of corporate citizenship.

The Global Compact

The creation and continued survival of the United Nations Global Compact, announced at the World Economic Forum in Davos, Switzerland, in January 1999 and implemented in July 2000, owes much to the commitment and enthusiasm of the United Nations Secretary-General, Kofi Annan. His personal quest to create a more responsible global economic community has led to the creation of the Global Compact which calls on participating companies to embrace nine universal principles within the area of human rights, labour standards and the environment.

A review of the Global Compact, however, raises questions regarding its underlying objective and in particular, whether it is being used as an example of good practice, designed to initiate change within national and international regulatory systems or, whether it is intended to be effective, in and of itself, as a means of curbing the excesses of global business. While it is difficult, at this stage, to evaluate the success of the Global Compact, it is clear that its fundamental aim of contributing to the emergence of "shared values and principles, which give a human face to the global market" (Global Compact Office, 2001: 1) is admirable.

Like much of the debate concerning corporate social responsibility and corporate citizenship, the United Nations Global Compact is value-based, specifying in detail the values it intends to promote and uphold. Its effectiveness, however, is not compromized by the traditional claims of cultural or ethical relativism, such as those made by Donaldson and Werhane (1988: 19-20), who suggest that, "all value judgments are relative to particular contexts". The claim, made by the United Nations, is that the Global Compact encompasses nine *universal* principles, drawn from the Universal Declaration of Human Rights and the International Labour Office's Fundamental Principles on Rights at Work, which corporations are expected to adopt within their own areas of business. To this extent, therefore, the Global Compact is consistent with the 'global integrated' approach towards international business, which, as Wood and Logsdon (2001: 95) explain, "encourages the corporation to maintain policies, processes and structures that are consistent with the company's expressed mission and values across all relevant cultures".

The ability of the United Nations to create such principles derives, in large part, from its unique position as "a central international forum capable of formalising relationships between governments, business and non-governmental organisations as well as bringing together leading experts to further the field as a whole" (Cohen, 2001: 186). The universal quality of the nine principles becomes apparent upon a reading of them:

Human rights

Businesses should:
1.   Support and respect the protection of internationally proclaimed human rights; and
2.   Make sure they are not complicit in human rights abuses.

Labour standards

Businesses should:
3.   Uphold the freedom of association and the effective recognition of the right
      to collective bargaining;
4.   Uphold the elimination of all forms of forced and compulsory labour;
5.   Uphold the effective abolition of child labour; and
6.   Eliminate discrimination in respect of employment and occupation.

Environment

Businesses should:
7.   Support a precautionary approach to environmental challenges;
8.   Undertake initiatives to promote greater environmental responsibility; and
9.   Encourage the development and diffusion of environmentally friendly
      technologies (Global Compact Office, 2001: 2).

A reading of the nine principles indicates the standard of behaviour
currently being undertaken by global corporations. If it is necessary to request that
corporations eliminate all forms of forced and compulsory labour, abolish child
labour and eliminate discrimination in respect of employment and occupation, then
it seems reasonable to assume that such activity is commonplace. If that is the case,
it is questionable whether the Global Compact will prevent such activity from
being undertaken now or in the future, particularly in light of the regulatory model
it adopts.

The introduction of the Global Compact is indicative of the changing
nature of societal expectations regarding the role of business and its relationship
with communities, on a local, national and global level. It is also, perhaps more
importantly, indicative of the shift away from the regulation of transnational
corporations (TNCs) by nation states and towards the use of voluntary codes of
conduct, as Jenkins (2001) suggests:

> ... the ideological shifts of the 1980s, and the globalization of economic activity,
> meant that nation states have been less willing and less able, to perform many of
> these regulatory functions in recent years. It is in this context that a new emphasis
> has been placed on self-regulation and the social responsibility of business.

In an attempt to encourage companies to adopt willingly the nine
universal principles, rather than compelling them to do so, the United Nations has
chosen to adopt a model of voluntary or self-regulation, with the Global Compact
operating as, "a voluntary initiative that seeks to provide a global framework to
promote sustainable growth and good citizenship through committed and creative
corporate leadership" (Global Compact Office, 2001: 1). To this extent, therefore,
it mirrors the international codes of conduct which emerged during the 1970s,
including the ILO's (1977) *Tripartite Declaration of Principles Concerning
Multinational Enterprises and Social Policy* and the OECD's (1976) *Declaration
on International Investment and Multinational Enterprise*. These codes have been
criticized by Jenkins (2001: 4) for their failure to impact significantly upon the

activities of TNCs. A result, which he claims, is due to their voluntary nature and the lack of effective sanction for non-compliance. While the Global Compact is similarly voluntary in nature, it has attempted to improve upon the performance of these international codes.

The United Nations, aware of the potential for abuse, is keen to prevent corporations publicising their commitment to the nine principles without adopting and providing evidence of positive action, "[t]he Global Compact is not a regulatory instrument, a legally binding code of conduct or a forum for policing management policies and practices. Nor is it a 'safe-harbour' allowing companies to sign-on without demonstrating real involvement and results" (Global Compact Office, 2001: 1).

The means by which participating companies are expected to demonstrate their 'real involvement and results' include the posting on the Global Compact's website, once a year, of a case-study indicating "progress made or a lesson learned in implementing the principles" (Global Compact Office, 2001: 2) and the publication by the company of its commitment to the nine principles in mission statements, annual reports and newsletters. Due to the voluntary nature of the Global Compact and the status of the United Nations, it is not willing to publicize the names of those companies, who fail to provide such information, or those who indicate a lack of effective commitment to the nine principles. As Cohen (2001: 196) makes clear, "the fundamental weakness of the UN's role as a global leader in corporate citizenship is that is does not possess any enforcement capability".

It may be assumed that the objective of the United Nations, in using encouragement rather than compulsion, is to achieve a gradual shift in the way managers exercise discretion from the inside out, so that ultimately, compliance with the nine principles becomes an integral and unquestioned element of the decision-making process. This approach has its advantages but, the underlying concern with self-regulation is that, "[s]ince adherence is voluntary it is not universal and those whose activities are most in need of regulation are least likely to subscribe to them" (Page, 1980: 28). By 2002, 100 major multinationals and 1000 other companies were engaged in the Global Compact (Global Compact Office, 2001: 2). While some of these corporations may have chosen to participate in the initiative so as to create a perception of compliance, thereby allowing the corporation to promote itself as a 'good corporate citizen', supported and endorsed by the United Nations, it is possible that the Global Compact will encourage these companies to adopt at least some examples of good practice, as Windsor (2001: 41) suggests, this is to be welcomed, for "even gross imperfection of motives should not be treated as the implacable enemy of at least some good outcomes". More worrying, however, is the likelihood that those most in need of regulation will not choose to participate in the Global Compact.

A Return to Corporate Social Responsibility?

The United Nations Global Compact may be commended as a bold attempt to change attitudes for the better within global corporations. The limited scope of its coverage, both in terms of the number of participants and the principles it espouses, and its reliance upon voluntary participation, however, serve to highlight the problems associated with it and in turn with corporate citizenship generally. In expecting, rather than demanding, that corporations abide by established values and principles, corporate citizenship may be guilty of failing to regulate those corporations that are most in need of it. Unlike the Global Compact, however, corporate citizenship is also guilty of failing to specify the principles or standards which should guide corporate managers in their attempt to be good corporate citizens.

In this respect, the Global Compact offers a starting point, indicating the type of principles that society should expect corporations to adhere to, over and above their existing legal obligations. Other than this, however, corporate citizenship conveys a vague sense of what it means to be a good corporate citizen. Waddock (2001: 28-29) in establishing the value-laden nature of corporate citizenship, suggests that the values guiding it must be 'constructive' or 'end values', that is, "deeply felt core values, which inspire the human spirit". Although Dion (2001: 119-123) and Waddock (2001: 29) offer some concrete examples taken from certain companies, reference to end values such as, "heroic customer service, worldwide reliability of services and encouragement of individual initiative" are sufficiently vague to prevent any meaningful evaluation of the company's success in achieving them. As Stone (1975: 72) suggests, however, it may well be this very degree of ambiguity that makes such terms popular with academics, practitioners and, in particular, politicians, "bad enough that the notion is fuzzy. Even worse, it is transparently this very fuzziness that accounts for its broad consensus of support". The inherent danger in failing to define or set the criteria for corporate citizenship, however, is that it becomes 'open to capture' by powerful or interested groups, as Van Buren (2001: 57) suggests, "the corporate citizenship concept, without an adequate normative grounding, may be used in such a variety of ways by different groups (companies, NGOs, academics), all of which have vested interests in particular definitions, that it fails to progress beyond being a metaphor".

The dangers apparent in relying upon corporate citizenship as the means of constraining corporate power have also been enhanced by the rejection of corporate social responsibility by regulators, academics and practitioners. Corporate citizenship, without corporate social responsibility, will prove ineffective in achieving consistent and broad based reform of corporate activity. The reason for this derives from the regulatory nature of the two concepts. Whereas corporate citizenship operates upon a voluntary basis with no sanctions imposed for non-compliance, corporate social responsibility can and should be viewed as a form of mandatory regulation.

If the underlying objective of reform is to make legitimate the exercise of social power by corporations then, as Mason (1959: 6) suggests, there is a potential answer – "[o]ne possible route [to legitimacy] leads through court decisions to a rule of law designed to make equitable and tolerable the actions of inevitable private power". The benefit of making use of the law as a means of regulating corporations is that the question as to whether a company is being socially responsible becomes not, "whether the decision violates any moral standards" (Velasquez, 1988: 13) but whether the decision violates particular legal standards. Corporate activity thereby becomes legitimate by reference to an external process validated through the normal constitutional procedures of a liberal democracy. If corporate social responsibility is to avoid the criticisms raised in respect of corporate citizenship, in terms of failing to offer specific guidelines, however, it is necessary to establish the content of those legal standards.

Stone (1975: 30) in questioning what we want the law to accomplish, identifies two interrelated goals. The first is 'distributive', to redistribute losses so that corporations pay or compensate for the damage they cause. The second is 'reductive', designed to deter such losses from being occasioned in the first place. These goals may be achieved in any number of ways but, it seems appropriate to make use of an existing and traditional legal tool, namely, the imposition of a duty upon managers which would oblige them to, "avoid creating social injury and to correct any past social injuries for which they can be held directly responsible" (Bagley and Page, 1999: 912).

Managers would, therefore, be under a duty to avoid or to remedy any social costs arising out of corporate activity, which would include "all those harmful consequences and damages which third persons or the community sustain as a result of the productive process, and for which private entrepreneurs are not easily held accountable" (Kapp, 1971: 14). The extension of liability to include new types of harm is not unusual, the best example of this being the creation, by the House of Lords in the case of *Donoghue v Stevenson* ([1932] AC 562), of a general duty of care in negligence. It is conceivable, therefore, that companies could owe a duty of care to parties with whom they have a sufficiently proximate relationship in respect of foreseeable social harm.

In practice, such a duty would oblige managers to consider the interests of those likely to be affected by their decision and would provide those affected with the opportunity of preventing foreseeable social harm or seeking redress for harm already occasioned. Such a duty would meet with the claims of Robertson and Nicholson (1996) and Wood (1991: 697) who suggests that, "[b]usinesses are not responsible for solving all social problems. They are, however, responsible for solving problems that they have caused, and they are responsible for helping to solve problems and social issues related to their business operations and interests".

In defining corporate social responsibility as a duty, imposed upon company managers, to avoid or remedy any foreseeable social harm, its relationship with corporate citizenship becomes apparent. Rather than having superseded corporate social responsibility as the 'concept of choice' (Wood and Logsdon, 2001: 86), corporate citizenship is the perfect complement to a regulatory regime founded upon the principles of corporate social responsibility, offering, as it does, the opportunity for corporations to exceed their minimum legal obligations and promote themselves as good corporate citizens. It is essential, however, if the exercise of social power by corporations is to be made legitimate, that corporate social responsibility be reinstated as the primary concept within academic debate, managerial practice and public policy.

Concluding Remarks

It is accepted within socio-political debate and even within managerial practice (Habisch, 2001) that corporations have to change the way that they do business. The increased concentration of social, political and economic power within these private institutions has not been matched by an increase in measures designed to make such power legitimate. In seeking to achieve such reform, there are two obvious choices: reliance is either placed upon corporations to initiate reform according to what they perceive to be the expectations of society, which is consistent with the underlying tenet of corporate citizenship or, society imposes such expectations upon corporations by means of mandatory regulation, consistent, according to this paper, with the fundamental principle of corporate social responsibility.

The evidence in support of the former option, offered by a review of the United Nations Global Compact, is not promising. While its aims are commendable, its potential to act as an effective means of legitimating corporate power is weakened by its voluntary nature and limited scope. While it may be unfair to criticize the Global Compact for failing to achieve a task it never set out to accomplish, it does serve to illustrate the potential weakness of a system founded upon the principles of corporate citizenship. Despite its frailties, the concept of corporate citizenship is worthy of further investigation and implementation. What this paper has sought to show, however, is that this task must be undertaken in conjunction with or as a task secondary to the revitalization of the concept of corporate social responsibility.

References

Anderson, J.W. (1989), *Corporate Social Responsibility: Guidelines for Top Management*, New York, Quorum Books.
Andriof, J. and McIntosh, M. (2001), 'Introduction', in J. Andriof and M. McIntosh (eds), *Perspectives on Corporate Citizenship*, Sheffield, Greenleaf Publishing.
Bagley, C.E. and Page, K.L. (1999), 'The Devil Made Me Do It: Replacing Corporate Directors' Veil of Secrecy with the Mantle of Stewardship', *San Diego Law Review*, **36**(1), pp. 897-910.
Berle, A. (1931), 'Corporate Powers as Powers in Trust', *Harvard Law Review*, **44**(7), pp. 1049-74.
Berle, A. and Means, C.G. (1936), *The Modern Corporation and Private Property*, New York, Macmillan.
Berle, A. (1993), 'Traditional Theory and the New Concept of the Corporation', in B. Sutton (ed.), *The Legitimate Corporation*, Oxford, Blackwell.
Blumberg, P.I. (1972), *Corporate Responsibility in a Changing Society*, Boston, Boston University Press.
Carroll, A.B. (2001), 'The Moral Leader: Essential for Successful Corporate Citizenship', in J. Andriof and M. McIntosh (eds), *Perspectives on Corporate Citizenship*, Sheffield, Greenleaf Publishing.
Clarkson, M.B.E. (1995), 'A Stakeholder Framework for Analyzing and Evaluating Corporate Social Performance', *Academy of Management Review*, **20**(1), pp. 92-117.

Clutterbuck, D. (1981), *How to be a Good Corporate Citizen*, London, McGraw-Hill.

Cohen, J. (2001), 'The World's Business: the United Nations and the Globalisation of Corporate Citizenship', in J. Andriof and M. McIntosh (eds), *Perspectives on Corporate Citizenship*, Sheffield, Greenleaf Publishing.

Dahl, R.A. (1972), 'A Prelude to Corporate Reform', *Business and Society Review*, 1, Spring, pp. 17-23.

Davis, K. (1973), 'The Case For and Against Business Assumption of Social Responsibilities', *Academy of Management Journal*, 16, pp. 312-22.

Department of Trade and Industry (2002), *Business and Society: Corporate Social Responsibility Report 2002*, London, DTI.

Dion, M. (2001), 'Corporate Citizenship as an Ethic of Care', in J. Andriof and M. McIntosh (eds), *Perspectives on Corporate Citizenship*, Sheffield, Greenleaf Publishing.

Dodd, E.M. (1932), 'For Whom are Corporate Managers Trustees?', *Harvard Law Review*, 45, pp. 1145-63.

Donaldson, T. (1982), *Corporations and Morality*, New Jersey, Prentice Hall.

Donaldson, T. and Werhane, P.H. (1988), *Ethical Issues in Business: A Philosophical Approach*, New Jersey, Prentice Hall.

European Commission (2001), *Promoting a European Framework for Corporate Social Responsibility*, Green Paper COM(2001)366, Brussels, Commission of the European Communities.

Friedman, M. (1969), *Capitalism and Freedom*, Chicago, University of Chicago Press.

Galbraith, J.K. (1952), *American Capitalism – The Concept of Countervailing Power*, Massachusetts, Riverside Press.

Global Compact Office (2001), *The Global Compact – Corporate Leadership in the World Economy*, New York, United Nations.

Habisch, A. (2001), 'Foreword', in J. Andriof and M. McIntosh (eds), *Perspectives on Corporate Citizenship*, Sheffield, Greenleaf Publishing.

Henning, J.F. (1973), 'Corporate Social Responsibility: Shell Game for the Seventies?', in R. Nader and M.J. Green (eds), *Corporate Power in America*, New York, Grossman.

Jenkins, R. (2001), *Corporate Codes of Conduct: Self-Regulation in a Global Economy*, Geneva, United Nations Research Institute for Social Development.

Kapp, K.W. (1971), *The Social Costs of Private Enterprise*, New York, Schocken Books.

Levitt, T. (1958), 'The Dangers of Social Responsibility', *Harvard Business Review*, 36, pp. 41-50.

Maignan, I. and Ferrell, O.C. (2000), 'Measuring Corporate Citizenship in Two Countries: The Case of the United States and France', *Journal of Business Ethics*, 23(3), pp. 283-97.

Mason, E.S. (1959), 'Introduction', in E.S. Mason (ed.), *The Corporation in Modern Society*, Massachusetts, Harvard University Press.

McClaughry, J. (1972), 'Milton Friedman Responds', *Business and Society Review*, 1, Spring, pp. 5-16.

McIntosh, M. (2001), 'Editorial', *Journal of Corporate Citizenship*, 3, Autumn, pp. 3-8.

Page, A.C. (1980), 'Self-Regulation and Codes of Practice', *Journal of Business Law*, 24, pp. 28-39.

Parkinson, J.E. (1996), *Corporate Power and Responsibility*, Oxford, Clarendon Press.

Post, J.E. and Berman, S.L. (2001), 'Global Corporate Citizenship in a Dot.Com World', in J. Andriof and M. McIntosh (eds), *Perspectives on Corporate Citizenship*, Sheffield, Greenleaf Publishing.

Preston, L.E. and Post, J.E. (1975), *Private Management and Public Policy*, New Jersey, Prentice Hall.

Roach, L. (2001), 'The Paradox of the Traditional Justifications for Exclusive Shareholder Governance Protection: Expanding the Pluralist Approach', *The Company Lawyer*, **22**(1), pp. 9-15.

Robertson, D.C. and Nicholson, N. (1996), 'Expressions of Corporate Social Responsibility in U.K. Firms', *Journal of Business Ethics*, **15**(10), pp. 1095-105.

Sheikh, S. (1996), *Corporate Social Responsibilities: Law and Practice*, London, Cavendish.

Stokes, M. (1986), 'Company Law and Legal Theory', in W. Twining (ed.), *Legal Theory and the Common Law*, Oxford, Oxford University Press.

Stone, C.D. (1975), *Where the Law Ends: The Social Control of Corporate Behaviour*, New York, Harper & Row.

Sutton, B. (1993), 'Introduction: The Legitimate Corporation', in B. Sutton (ed.), *The Legitimate Corporation*, Oxford, Blackwell.

Van Buren, H.J., III (2001), 'Corporate Citizenship and Obligations of Fairness', *Journal of Corporate Citizenship*, **3**, pp. 55-67.

Velasquez, M.G. (1988), *Business Ethics: Concepts and Cases*, New Jersey, Prentice Hall.

Waddock, S. (2001), 'Integrity and Mindfulness: Foundations of Corporate Citizenship', in J. Andriof and M. McIntosh (eds), *Perspectives on Corporate Citizenship*, Sheffield, Greenleaf Publishing.

Wedderburn, D. (1985), 'The Legal Development of Corporate Responsibility; For Whom Will Corporate Managers be Trustees?', in K.J. Hopt and G. Teubner (eds), *Corporate Governance and Directors' Liabilities*, Berlin, Walter De Gruyter.

Windsor, D. (2001), 'Corporate Citizenship: Evolution and Interpretation', in J. Andriof and M. McIntosh (eds), *Perspectives on Corporate Citizenship*, Sheffield, Greenleaf Publishing.

Wood, D.J. (1991), 'Corporate Social Performance Revisited', *Academy of Management Review*, **16**(4), pp. 691-718.

Wood, D.J. and Logsdon, J.M. (2001), 'Theorising Business Citizenship', in J. Andriof and M. McIntosh (eds), *Perspectives on Corporate Citizenship*, Sheffield, Greenleaf Publishing.

Acknowledgements

The author would like to thank the British Academy, the Economic and Social Research Council, the Nuffield Foundation, the Socio-Legal Studies Association and the University of Hull for financing this research.

Chapter 9

Transnational Corporations: Power, Influence and Responsibility

Sorcha MacLeod and Douglas Lewis

Introduction

The traditional Westphalian conception of international law being state centred is becoming increasingly inappropriate in a global society where non-state actors wield great power. This is true even outside a strict legal context as we are also seeing a "significant shift in international relations theory away from a state-centred 'balance of power' paradigm ... towards a 'transnational relations' analysis". (Muchlinski, 1999: 90).

The issue of corporate social responsibility is vexing. It sets at odds those who champion the 'business case' and advocate little or no corporate regulation, e.g. TNCs, and those who would impose compulsory regulatory mechanisms on corporations, e.g. NGOs. At the Sixty-Ninth Conference of the International Law Association in London, July 2000, René Van Rooij, Chief Legal Counsel for Shell posed the question "Hasn't the case for mandatory rules become more rather than less acute in the 21st century?" He continued:

> I am convinced that the answer is a firm 'no' for two reasons. First of all, the power of multinational companies is generally widely exaggerated. Secondly, the 21st century is the age of IT, of transparency, of globalisation. An age where speed will be of the essence. An era where the rigidity of mandatory rules of law would stifle activity, mute communications and create strife rather than prosperity. In short, *we have entered the age of self-regulation.*[1] [emphasis added]

Recent years have seen a proliferation of the type of self-regulatory measures advocated by Dr Van Rooij. TNCs as diverse as IKEA, Kmart, Philips, Levi Strauss and Shell itself have produced Codes of Conduct detailing workers' rights, environmental policies and ethical standards purportedly adhered to by the company wherever it operates.[2] NIKE, in addition, has appointed a Vice-President for Human Rights and recently the Board of Directors created a 'Corporate Responsibility Committee'.[3] The practice of social accounting has gained momentum and visibility.[4] Often these measures have been implemented in direct response to worldwide criticism of operational practices by non-governmental organisations (NGOs), consumers and citizens of the countries in which the corporations function. Such measures have been have rarely been implemented voluntarily by TNCs. More often they are a product of direct and indirect pressure.

It is interesting to note that many of these informal mechanisms utilize the language of international law and often reiterate the provisions of the International Labour Organization Conventions or the text and aims of international human rights documents such as the Universal Declaration of Human Rights. However, it is questionable whether such mechanisms are effective. Nonetheless, the arguments put forward in favour of self-regulation are countless. Numerous propositions are put forward as 'good' reasons for supporting self-regulation. It has been suggested the self-regulation results in financial savings while legislation stifles innovation and causes strife and judicial decisions cause uncertainty for commercial enterprises.[5] Opponents argue that self-regulation instruments are weak, unenforceable, non-consensual, inappropriate and subject to frequent flouting.[6]

The chapter examines some of the recent trends in the regulation of TNCs, in particular, international developments under the auspices of the Organisation for Economic Cooperation and Development (OECD) and the Global Compact, regional developments at the European Union (EU) and national developments in the UK. The role of NGOs and the Trade Union movement is considered throughout.

The International Level: 'The Global Economy needs Global Rules'[7]

In the OECD Guidelines On Multinational Enterprises: *A Common Blueprint For Action*,[8] it is argued that:

> ... now is a particularly promising time for global instruments to have a major impact on international business behaviour and to play a prominent role in the public debate about the respective roles of companies, governments and individuals in ensuring that a broad cross section of the world's people can enjoy improved economic, social and environmental welfare. (Gordon, 2001)[9]

Originally drafted in 1976, the OECD Guidelines for Multinational Enterprises ('the Guidelines') are recommendations addressed to multinational enterprises (MNEs) by adhering states which set out principles of acceptable behaviour for corporations in the social and environmental sphere globally.[10] It is indicative of the increasing importance of corporate governance that the Guidelines were revised in 2000, and 2001 saw the publication of the first Annual Report on their operation.[11]

The Guidelines form part of the OECD Declaration on International Investment and Multinational Enterprises, and adhering governments agree to promote their observance among MNEs.[12] Although the Guidelines are voluntary and non-binding for MNEs,[13] subsequent to the OECD Council Decision of June 2000 governments are obliged to set up National Contact Points (NCPs) in order to implement and promote the Guidelines among all corporations operating in or from their territory. This has been done with varying degrees of success.[14] Under the Guidelines individual states are given wide latitude in relation to NCP structural arrangements. Some NCPs are single departments within government ministries (e.g. the UK), others are 'multi-departmental' and operate across a range of ministries, (e.g. Korea) and a third group of NCPs are 'tripartite' incorporating commercial and trade union representatives as well as a number of Ministries (e.g. Sweden).[15] Finland's NCP is unique in being 'quadripartite', composed of business, trade unions, various ministries and significantly NGOs.[16] However, it is recognized that characterizing the NCPs in this way 'does not provide a full picture of the scope and breadth of consultation'.[17] Social partners and NGOs participate in the process formally and informally, so for example, in the USA they are consulted 'via the Advisory Council on International Economic Policy or individually on an *ad hoc* basis'.[18]

In relation to the legal effect of the Guidelines, it is made clear that they are not intended to supplant domestic laws, but are regarded as an 'add-on' to national legal provisions.[19] In terms of content, the Guidelines are broadly designed to facilitate and improve foreign investment by providing 'principles and standards of good practice' in relation to human rights, labour standards and the environment.[20] MNEs are encouraged to cooperate closely with local communities, uphold and apply 'good corporate governance principles' and 'develop and apply effective self-regulatory practices'.[21] In addition, there are relatively detailed provisions on disclosure matters which emphasize the need for full and accurate information to be made available in relation to structure, activities, financial situation,[22] performance, accounting, audit, environmental and social reporting ('where they exist') plus other basic information relating to ownership, objectives, affiliates, voting rights, etc.[23] Employment and Environmental matters are dealt with in separate provisions.[24] In relation to labour issues, the Guidelines concentrate on trade union rights, child labour, forced labour, discrimination, collective bargaining and health and safety. The environmental provisions address environmental management systems, disclosure of information, health and safety, technology, training, etc. Finally the Guidelines deal with Bribery, Consumers, Science and Technology, Competition and Taxation.[25]

Procedurally, in addition to the NCPs, the Guidelines fall within the remit of the Committee on International Investment and Multinational Enterprises (CIME), which is required to coordinate 'exchanges of views' on relevant matters.[26] Those to be consulted include the Business Industry Advisory Council (BIAC),[27] the Trade Union Advisory Council (TUAC),[28] as well as 'other non-governmental organisations'.[29] BIAC and TUAC are officially regarded as operating on an equal footing, with an emphasis being placed on 'strict parallelism of treatment'.[30] Whilst it would appear that the 'business case' carries most weight with adhering governments, further research will be necessary to determine the extent to which this is true. Another interesting anomaly is that while individual corporations are permitted to make representations to CIME about Guideline matters relating to their own interests, 'the Committee shall not reach conclusions on the conduct of individual enterprises'.[31] There is no institutional mechanism for ensuring compliance with the Guidelines.

The Business Industry Advisory Council (BIAC) stance on the Guidelines is unequivocal:

> The Guidelines must remain voluntary – not legally binding. They are not designed to replace national or international legislation or individual company or sectoral codes of conduct.[32]

Clearly and unsurprisingly BIAC vehemently supports the voluntary nature of the Guidelines and indeed goes further by condemning the Dutch government's proposals to oblige MNEs to adhere to the Guidelines as a prerequisite for obtaining export credit coverage and government subsidies.[33] It states: 'such an action would set a very negative precedent that should be avoided and in no way should be followed by other countries'.[34] Opposing any form of mandatory regulation is a recurring theme for big business in a variety of contexts. It can be seen, for example, in the individual corporate and collective industry responses to the EU's Green Paper on Corporate Social Responsibility.[35] It could appear to some that for BIAC the Guidelines represent a corporate marketing opportunity rather than an authentic opportunity to moderate corporate misbehaviour:

> For companies, the wide coverage of the Guidelines represents a blueprint for management systems and practice in today's world where companies are subject to wider scrutiny than ever before. Used positively, the Guidelines are a helpful tool for companies positioning themselves in the global economy.[36]

Predictably, BIAC focuses on and prioritizes one aspect of the Guidelines; that being the improvement of 'the climate for foreign direct investment'.[37] The social responsibility facet of the Guidelines appears to be secondary. Unsurprisingly, both the Trade Union and NGO position is different. NGOs are particularly frustrated by their 'formal exclusion' from the Guidelines' international implementation process.[38] This would appear to conflict with the more general global project of widening stakeholder participation in the whole process of Corporate Social Responsibility (CSR).[39] However, it should be noted that the Council's Decision of June 2000 does require that NGOs be permitted to make their views known. There is also NGO dissatisfaction with the lack of a system for monitoring the 'effectiveness of the ... Guidelines in achieving corporate sustainable behaviour'.[40] On the face of it, the NGOs are not lobbying for the Guidelines to be made binding on MNEs. However, they do stress the need for practical solutions by stating that they have 'no interest in an instrument that will not have an actual impact on the ground'.[41] In light of this, it is hardly surprising that the adhering states report that NGOs are reluctant to become involved at national level via the NCPs:

> Some NCP reports note that NGOs were not always enthusiastic about participating in Guidelines implementation. The Swedish report states that NGOs' expressions of interest in the Guidelines were 'limited' while the Canadian report notes that NGOs seem quite sceptical about the Guidelines' effectiveness.[42]

This may be connected to the weaknesses in the NCP system rather than an inherent unwillingness to participate on the part of the NGOs. TUAC asserts that 'too few NCPs have involved the social partners and NGOs in promoting the Guidelines'.[43] This leads to the conclusion that '[i]f governments do not take the Guidelines seriously it is unlikely that companies will do so'.[44]

A further point to note about the NGO position in relation to the nonbinding nature of the Guidelines is that it is very positive about the Dutch developments. The links between implementation of the Guidelines and 'financial instruments' are regarded as establishing 'policy coherence'.[45] They urge the Committee on International Investment and Multinational Enterprises (CIME) to support and expand such policy coherence in the future.[46] TUAC is also positive about this development (although not to the same extent as the NGOs) and argues that:

> ... the Guidelines should be used as a reference point for anticipated corporate good behaviour for those companies receiving voluntary state assistance, including export credits [sic] guarantees.[47]

It is also noted that in Germany there are references to the Guidelines on application forms for outward investment guarantees.[48] This is not referred to or opposed by BIAC, probably because there is no obligatory element.

Within the OECD, and specifically in relation to the Guidelines, trade unions are in an entirely different position from the NGOs as a consequence of the creation of TUAC and its formal recognition since 1962. In the Annual Report 2001 TUAC criticizes the poor performance of the National Contact Points (NCPs) since their inception.[49] It seems to suggest that many NCPs have failed to retain 'the confidence of the social partners' by falling short of the key criteria of 'visibility, accessibility, transparency and accountability'.[50]

The Annual Report highlights the continuing gulf between industry and NGOs. Unfortunately the familiar 'regulation v. no regulation' standoff is merely reproduced without offering solutions. Nevertheless, the solutions seem obvious: (1) regulation, (2) self-regulation or (3) some alternative hybrid or 'third way'. It would appear that so long as the BIAC viewpoint carries more weight than that of the NGOs and the TUAC within the context of the OECD, the Guidelines will remain voluntary and nonbinding, which is of course exactly what corporations desire. The influence of TNCs behind the scenes at both the international and national level is well documented.[51] There is also an established corporate view that 'these things take time' and therefore the effects of voluntary corporate initiatives, e.g. corporate codes of conduct, should be allowed to filter down. Moreover, those corporate leaders who contend that TNCs 'cannot be required to solve all the world's problems' are missing the point about the concept of Corporate Social Responsibility.[52] No one expects TNCs to 'solve the world's problems'. However, there *is* an expectation that TNCs do not add to them by, for example, polluting the environment or by being complicit in human rights abuses perpetrated by state actors. Furthermore, social philanthropy does not equate to social responsibility: 'it's about how you make your profits, not how much profit you give away'.[53] In a post-Enron world it is clear that the concept of Corporate Social Responsibility should not be defined and delimited by corporations themselves. Quite simply the conflict of interest is too great:

> the notion that the company has binding obligations beyond those to its shareholders – the heart of corporate citizenship – is, or should be a genuinely subversive doctrine, going to the heart of what a company is and does. To that extent the free market Neanderthals are dead right: social responsibility is indeed a constraint on the manager's sacred duty to pursue shareholder value by any means possible.[54]

Ultimately, the 'world's problems' can only be resolved through cooperative *and* regulatory measures that involve *all* stakeholders and operate at the global, regional and domestic level. At the global level, the recent United Nations Global Compact initiative goes some way to implement such a 'hybrid' approach.

United Nations Global Compact

Mary Robinson in her capacity as the UN High Commissioner for Human Rights has written:

> It's not a simple case of choosing between voluntary or regulatory systems to induce corporate responsibility ... Regulation is crucial to minimise abuses and to enforce compliance with minimum norms but it alone will not establish the business case for making the necessary changes. To do so we must provide incentives, so that doing the right thing also makes good business sense. (Robinson, 2002: 34)[55]

The recently created Global Compact (GC) attempts to steer the difficult course between these starkly opposing regulatory options.[56] Nine Principles relating to human rights, labour standards and the environment were laid down and corporations were asked voluntarily to "embrace, support and enact" internationally recognized standards in these three areas.[57] These core values are derived from the Universal Declaration of Human Rights,[58] the International Labour Organization's Declaration on Fundamental Principles and Rights at Work,[59] and the Rio Declaration on Environment and Development.[60] Much emphasis is placed upon the benefits of "socially responsible business" such as the "advantages of a good social reputation", "reduction of damaging criticism" as well as "being more in touch with markets, customers and consumers".[61] Companies committed to the GC further undertake to promote the Compact via corporate documentation, e.g. annual reports, mission statements, training programmes and press releases. Importantly, the GC harnesses UN "inter-agency cooperation", bringing together the ILO, UNEP, UNHCR and UNDP.[62] Although the GC is a voluntary initiative, it differs from the OECD's Guidelines in two important ways. Firstly, corporations subscribing to the Compact are required, as a condition of their participation, to submit on an annual basis concrete examples of measures taken to comply with the Nine Principles.[63] These are to be posted on the GC website to ensure that there is an element of transparency in the process. Unfortunately, of the 30 corporate submissions made during the 2001 pilot phase none were deemed 'worthy of publication'.[64] Several problems were identified ranging from "substantial degrees of organizational change" to "difficulties assessing the priority of corporate citizenship relative to profit-generating business activities".[65] In an attempt to resolve some of these problems, companies will now be required to formulate their submissions in accordance with a "concise template" in order to focus on the "strictly factual elements of company experience".[66] Companies must respond to four questions:

What is the issue being addressed? What actions has [sic] the company undertaken? Which of the nine principles have been addressed? What are the results of the company's efforts?[67]

This is a promising response to genuine stakeholder concerns, although, it remains to be seen whether or not it will have a positive impact on TNC behaviour. There is a risk that it will merely encourage TNCs to focus on the style, rather than the substance of their submissions.

Secondly, the GC Advisory Council was convened by the UN Secretary-General in January 2002. The Advisory Council comprises "senior business executives, international labour leaders, public policy experts and the heads of civil society organizations".[68] Notably, it is the 'first UN advisory body composed of both private and public sector leaders'.[69] Whilst the GC is "neither an instrument for monitoring companies nor a regulatory regime", the Advisory Council has a significant role to play.[70] It has four key priorities: (1) safeguarding the "integrity of the GC"; (2) serving as "advocates" of the GC; (3) providing "expertise"; and, (4) offering "advice on policy and strategy".[71] Again on a positive note, the Council has issued guidelines "regarding the official use of the Global Compact logo" after NGOs expressed concern about corporate abuse and exploitation.[72]

Other positive developments include the expansion of the GC Learning Forum to encompass a "global academic network" that will engage in relevant research and analysis.[73] There also seems to be a genuine desire to foster stakeholder participation in the process and recognition of the importance of 'high-level advocacy'.[74]

Nevertheless, the architects of the GC must strive to ensure that it does not become yet another global instrument which is commandeered by TNCs for marketing purposes.

The Regional Level: European Union

On a regional level, the European Union has been relatively slow to embrace the concept of CSR despite the long European tradition of 'socially responsible entrepreneurs'.[75] However, there have been several initiatives over the years that regulate corporations in the social sphere both within the EU and externally, e.g. the European Employment Strategy, EU-Ecolabels, the Eco-Management and Audit Scheme (EMAS) and the Cotonou Agreement.[76] In July 2001 the Commission published its Green Paper on Corporate Social Responsibility.[77] This initiative was designed to stimulate debate about CSR within the European context rather than 'making concrete proposals for action'.[78]

The Green Paper draws on the concept of the 'triple bottom line' and asks several key questions including: (1) What is the role of the EU in the development of CSR? (2) What is the role of CSR in corporate business strategies? (3) What is the role of other stakeholders? (4) How should CSR strategies be monitored and evaluated? (5) What mechanisms are most appropriate for developing CSR? And at what level?[79]

There were 261 responses to the Green Paper,[80] with only 9 Member States responding.[81] Of the 49 individual company responses more than half were from UK based corporations.[82] The trade union movement submitted 16 responses,[83] while NGOs submitted 35 responses.[84]

Unfortunately, the Green Paper constricts the debate by broadly relying on a very limited, and business oriented, definition of CSR describing it as:

> A concept whereby companies integrate social and environmental concerns in their business operations and in their interaction with their stakeholders on a voluntary basis.[85]

Unsurprisingly, this emphasis on the voluntary nature of CSR did not find favour with some of the NGOs responding to the Green Paper.[86] Likewise, the proposition that CSR is something that should be *integrated* into business operations as opposed to being the starting platform from which business is conducted was negatively received. The trade unions and the NGOs advocated a 'regulatory framework' that established 'minimum standards' and ensured 'a level playing field'.[87]

Another criticism levelled against the Green Paper is that that there was too much focus on the 'business case' as opposed to considering the interests of the wider constituency of stakeholders. It has also been said that the Commission's definition of CSR is flawed. In particular, it is not clear *what* the Commission is seeking to protect through the adoption of CSR. Much confusion has been caused by reference to a wide variety of international legal instruments e.g. the Universal Declaration on Human Rights, ILO Conventions and the UN Convention on the Rights of the Child. Again there is clear conflict between those who want regulation and those who do not.

It is interesting to note that in the responses to the Green Paper there is a remarkable homogeneity between individual corporate responses as well as the responses of industry representatives. There is a definite emphasis on self-regulation, a lack of enthusiasm for enforcement mechanisms, temporization of implementation requirements, the voluntary nature of CSR, good practice and a general abhorrence of a 'one-size fits all' approach to CSR.

Published in July 2002, the European Commission's response to the Green Paper is both disappointing and heartening in equal respects. Entitled the *Communication from the Commission concerning Corporate Social Responsibility: A Business Contribution to Sustainable Development*, it clearly adheres to the 'business case'. There are references to frameworks, promotion, assistance, awareness, support and good practice but no indication that formal regulation is a possibility. In addition the Commission has retained the flawed definition of CSR. On a more positive note, there is firm support for the OECD Guidelines that may impact upon the operation of the OECD NCPs and result in deeper cooperation. Further, convergence is encouraged between codes of conduct by utilizing the OECD Guidelines and ILO Conventions. On a practical level several proposals are made. Firstly, there is a proposal to create an EU Multi-Stakeholder forum on CSR with "the aim of promoting transparency and convergence of CSR practices and instruments".[88] Secondly there are concrete strategies proposed to integrate CSR into all EU policies including employment and social affairs policy, enterprise policy, environmental policy, consumer policy and public procurement policy.[89] The Commission Communication also specifically addresses external relations polices and advocates the promotion of CSR in line with the "Communications on the EU role in promoting human rights standards and democratisation in third countries".[90] This includes "the use of bilateral dialogue with Governments" and "trade incentives", as well as "engaging directly with multinational enterprises".[91] Within the context of general support for the OECD guidelines, however, it is interesting to note that the Commission suggests that access to subsidies and export credit insurance and access to public procurement could be made "conditional on adherence to and compliance with the guidelines". Finally, the Commission encourages public administrations, itself included, to "practice CSR principles".

The National Level: National Examples: Current CSR Developments in the United Kingdom and France

In recent years, the UK has been relatively proactive in promoting CSR. For example, it was the first state to appoint a Minister for Corporate Social Responsibility in 2000. The Cabinet Office publication, *Rights of Exchange: Social, Health, Environmental and Trade Objectives on the Global Stage*, sets out comprehensively the government's policies on sustainable growth and development.[92] Additionally, at the international level, the UK NCP has received praise for its progress in this area from TUAC, particularly for its promotional literature.[93] Despite its support for the OECD regime, the UK government seems to support the so-called 'third way' of regulation:

> CSR moves us on from old paradigms that see social benefit and economic successes as mutually exclusive, and either regulation or pure voluntary action as the only answers.[94]

This philosophy has not found favour among some politicians, as evidenced by the introduction of a Private Members Bill on Corporate Responsibility in June 2002.[95] It is apparent that many do feel that formal regulation is the only way forward. The Bill, if enacted as it stands, will apply to all UK registered companies and all companies operating within the UK with an annual turnover of more than £5m.[96] It is a wide-ranging and ambitious proposal which attempts to regulate TNCs in a fairly detailed manner. Section 3 of the Bill imposes an obligation to prepare and publish yearly reports on "any significant environmental, social, economic and financial impacts of any of its operations"[97] both in the preceding year and in the future. There is also a requirement to publish reports on corporate "employment policies and practice", the details of taxes or monies paid to "governments for any country of operation" and the particulars of all direct or indirect party political donations.[98] In addition, companies must "take reasonable steps" to ensure that any reports produced are made available to stakeholders,[99] relevant regulatory bodies and "any other person with an interest in the report". These provisions also apply to any subsidiary of a company covered by the Bill, "wherever registered".[100] Sections 7 and 8 deal with directors' duties and require directors to take into account environmental and social factors when reaching corporate decisions. Directors will be held personally liable for "significant adverse environmental or social impacts" arising from negligence or wilful misconduct.[101] Section 9 makes provision for the creation of a "Corporate Responsibility Board", which is to be responsible for issuing guidelines on the content of the various statutory reports. Amongst other things, it will also define the terms "significant" and "reasonable steps". The Board must include persons with relevant expertise and stakeholders.[102] Stakeholders are also granted remedies under the Bill.[103] For example, a stakeholder may request that a company amend an inaccurate report, although companies are not required to consider unmeritorious requests. Where a company refuses to amend a report, the stakeholder may appeal to the Board for redress. The Board may dismiss or uphold the application or suspend judgment on the application. Regardless of the outcome, the Board will be required to publish reasons for its decision. Penalties for breach of these provisions are dealt with in section 11. For individuals, a breach may result in imprisonment, a fine or disqualification from being a director. Additionally, a company may be prevented from trading on the stock exchange or required to cease operation altogether. It is suspected that this Bill may be a step too far and may never reach the statute books. However, it is significant that the drafters of the Bill chose to adopt a broad brushstroke approach rather than a more detailed legislative proposal.

The UK is not alone in attempting to impose more stringent reporting standards upon companies. In a wider European context, mandatory CSR reporting recently came into force in France. The amendments to the *Nouvelles Regulations Economique (NRE)* are an attempt to entrench the concept of the "triple bottom line" within French companies.[104] Corporations listed on the French Stock Exchange will be required to report on a variety of issues ranging from energy consumption and environmental emissions to employee working conditions and compliance with ILO standards. There is also an obligation to report on engagement with stakeholders including local communities and NGOs. While it is true that the NRE lay down *minimum* reporting standards, their mandatory imposition means that they are an important step forward in ensuring CSR. Clearly, other countries will be observing the outcome with interest.

Conclusion

The bottom line for constitutionalists and democrats generally, therefore, is to ask to what extent can global and regional organisations, national governments, NGOs and trade unions ensure accountability on the part of TNCs?

Within the international OECD framework the problem is clear. The Guidelines remain voluntary and non-binding. It seems also for the most part that the majority of governments are not taking their NCP obligations seriously. Undoubtedly, there has been an alienation of NGOs within the system and they at least feel that there is too much emphasis on and pandering to the 'business case'. There is a real perception that corporations may use the Guidelines as a mere marketing ploy. As things stand, it is almost impossible to measure the influence of the Guidelines on TNCs without an effective monitoring and compliance regime. The Global Compact initiative on the other hand appears to be engendering genuine stakeholder participation and dialogue with civil society actors. Additionally, it has widespread and influential support. Although the Compact remains voluntary, the creation of a broad-based Advisory Council seems to provide a level of monitoring. Certainly, corporate submissions are scrutinized for compliance and steps have been taken to try to ensure that the Compact logo and concept are not hijacked by industry marketing departments. However, the Compact is at an early stage of development and implementation. It will be some time before it can be determined whether it has overcome its initial teething problems. The latest UN initiative, the Draft Norms on the Responsibilities of Transnational Corporations and Other Business Enterprises with Regard to Human Rights, have received widespread and influential support particularly within the NGO sector and are the most detailed statement to date of the potential human rights obligations of TNCs.[105] These Draft Norms are designed to complement the Global Compact project and like the GC recognize that TNCs ought to comply with a variety of international human rights norms. Like the Global Compact, however, it remains to be seen whether the Draft Norms will be effective in influencing TNC behaviour while an implementation and monitoring mechanism has not yet been initiated. With a regulatory lacuna at the international level attention must be focused on the regional and domestic levels. It is at these levels that that the 'invisible' influence of TNCs through such organizations as the Trans-Atlantic Business Dialogue or indeed individual corporations could and should be tackled.[106]

At the regional level, the European Union has some valuable contributions to make to the implementation of CSR. A powerful player within the WTO and an influential role model for Association of Southeast Asian Nations (ASEAN) and others the EU has the opportunity to lay down a system of 'best practice' for corporate actors. It could be argued that publishing a Green Paper without including a framework proposal for legislation is an opportunity lost. However, the Commission has made several concrete proposals for practical implementation and integration of CSR within the EU. Notwithstanding, these proposals, there is a tendency for the Commission to champion the 'business case'. The European Union is in a position to make a difference and on the evidence of the Green Paper and the Commission's response there is a real hope that CSR will remain firmly at the top of the agenda.

Nationally, the OECD National Contact Points are not operating effectively and it is too soon to measure the effect of the Global Compact at this level. The NCPs must be strengthened and this can only be achieved if governments commit to the system and engage with the social partners. Individual states such as the UK are continuing to move the debate forward by actively supporting and implementing the global initiatives. The same can be said of some enlightened corporate actors. However, states can and ought also to implement CSR principles into the public sector supply chain. This may become easier if the EU's CSR conditionality measures become reality. In the meantime, it is open to governments throughout Europe and the rest of the world to follow the lead of France and introduce compulsory measures to ensure responsible corporate behaviour.

On present trends, TNCs are unlikely to regulate themselves voluntarily to generally accepted standards of behaviour. In a post-Enron world, socially responsible behaviour cannot merely be assumed. It is time for, at least, skeletal regulation. Corporate Social Responsibility rules should operate at the global, regional and national level in order to be effective, since global and regional regimes are ineffective without the support of national governments. Moreover, corporate regulation must be accompanied by incentives such as tax allowances. Ultimately, TNCs are extremely effective at putting across the 'business case' for self-regulation both behind the scenes and in public whereas other stakeholders have considerable hurdles to overcome. It is the responsibility of international, regional and national actors, governmental and non-governmental, to ensure economic development without sacrificing common values. Clearly the EU has a unique and crucial role to play in ensuring that corporate enterprises behave in a socially responsible manner, most effectively through European legislation.

Notes

[1] Text of a speech delivered to a plenary session entitled 'Foreign Investment, Human Rights and Development: Integration or Fragmentation?' at the Sixty-Ninth Conference of the International Law Association, London, July 2000 [on file with authors].

[2] The text of these Codes of Conduct and others are reproduced in Blanpain (2000: 329-86).

[3] Press Release, 10 September 2001, 'NIKE Board of Directors and CEO Philip H. Knight Create Corporate Responsibility Committee', http://www.nikebiz.com/media/n_crboard.shtml.

[4] Shell International recently won a social reporting award run by AccountAbility and the Association of Chartered Accountants. The "inclusion of negative information and opinions" was cited as a key reason for the award (see Adams, 2000).

[5] See individual corporate responses to the EU Green Paper 'Promoting a European Framework for Corporate Social Responsibility' COM (2001) 366 final, http://europa.eu.int/comm/employment_social/soc-dial/csr/csr_responses.htm (e.g. Abbey National, Agilent Technologies, Chiquita).

[6] E.g. November 2000, 'Adidas attacked for Asian 'sweatshops' in breach of its own Code of Conduct', *The Guardian* (23 November 2000); May 2000, Phil Knight withdraws donations and sponsorship from universities where students have campaigned against NIKE sweat shops, *The Guardian* (May 2000). See also NGO responses to the EU Green Paper (note 5).

[7] ICFTU (1999: 78).

[8] Witherell (2001).

[9] This Working Paper forms part of the Annual Report (OECD, 2001a: 57-69).

[10] For a general overview of the structure and workings of the Guidelines see OECD Guidelines for Multinational Enterprises, Revision 2000 particularly the Commentary; (for example see also Karl, 1999: 89-106).

[11] The OECD Guidelines for Multinational Enterprises, Revision 2000.

[12] OECD Declaration on International Investment and Multinational Enterprises, 27 June 2000.

[13] Guideline I(1) "Observance of the Guidelines is voluntary and not legally enforceable".

[14] See discussion infra.

[15] 'Summary Report of the Chair of the Meeting on the Activities of National Contact Points', Annual Report (OECD, 2001a: 12). See also Annex 1 'Structure of the National Contact Points' (OECD, 2001a: 20-24). Denmark, Norway, Sweden, France and Belgium have tripartite NCPs.

[16] See note 15.

[17] See note 15.

[18] See Annex 1, 'Structure of the National Contact Points' (OECD, 2001a: 24).

[19] The OECD Guidelines for Multinational Enterprises, Revision 2000, Commentary (OECD, 2000b: 41, para.2): "The Guidelines are not a substitute for nor should they be

considered to override local law and regulation. They represent supplementary principles and standards of behaviour of a non-legal character, particularly concerning the international operations of these enterprises".

[20] Guidelines I(1) and II(1) and (2).

[21] Guidelines II(3), (6) and (7).

[22] Ironic post-Enron et al.!

[23] Guideline III(1), (2), (3) and (4).

[24] Guidelines IV and V respectively.

[25] Guidelines VI, VII, VIII, IX and X respectively.

[26] Council Decision, June 2000 II(1).

[27] The BIAC is composed of industrial and employers' associations from OECD member states.

[28] The TUAC is composed of national trade union organisations from OECD member states. Both the TUAC and BIAC have secretariats are based in Paris and engage in formal and informal contact with the OECD itself. TUAC was deemed to be the organisation most representative of labour interests. See OECD (2001b) document 'Relations with BIAC and TUAC', 7 June 2001.

[29] OECD Council Decision, June 2000 II(1) and (2).

[30] See note 29.

[31] Council Decision, June 2000 II(4).

[32] 'Business Industry Advisory Council (BIAC) Statement', in OECD Guidelines for Multinational Enterprises: Global Instruments for Corporate Responsibility, Annual Report (OECD, 2001a: 35).

[33] OECD (2001a: 34). The BIAC continues: "The Guidelines and their related implementation procedures are unequivocal in underscoring their voluntary nature with regard to MNEs". To render an essential element of international financial competitiveness conditional upon "acceptance" and to pursue such acceptance with tools of "enforcement" – or in other words, negative "sanctions" – are abridgements of the terms and spirit of the Guidelines and of the premise upon which BIAC leadership submitted the Guidelines to members for their consideration.

[34] BIAC Statement (OECD, 2001a: 34).

[35] Commission of the European Communities, Green Paper 'Promoting a European Framework for Corporate Social Responsibility' COM (2001) 366 final, http://europa.eu.int/comm/employment_social/soc-dial/csr/csr_responses.htm (hereafter referred to as the 'Green Paper').

[36] BIAC Statement, Annual Report (OECD, 2001a: 35).

[37] OECD (2001a: 31).

[38] 'NGO Statement on the OECD Guidelines for Multinational Enterprises' in OECD Guidelines for Multinational Enterprises: Global Instruments for Corporate Responsibility, Annual Report (OECD, 2001a: 46): "The unconvincing explanation given is that the NGOs are not organised in a similar fashion as BIAC and TUAC."

[39] See for example the OECD Response to the EU Green Paper at http://europa.eu.int/comm/employment_social/soc-dial/csr/csr_responses.htm: "Each of the main actors involved in corporate responsibility programmes – business, trade unions, NGOs, governments and international organisations – offers a distinctive perspective and body of knowledge and expertise. The challenge is to bring these distinctive competencies together and to incorporate them into a shared way of seeing things and a common blueprint for action". See also the Global Compact references to "stakeholder participation".

[40] OECD Response to the EU Green Paper, p. 47 para.4.

[41] OECD Response to the EU Green Paper, p. 47 para.4.

[42] 'Summary Report of the Chair of the Meeting on the Activities of National Contact points' in OECD Guidelines for Multinational Enterprises: Global Instruments for Corporate Responsibility, Annual Report (OECD, 2001a: 13).

[43] 'TUAC Survey of the Functioning of National Contact Points', Annual Report (OECD, 2001a: 39; hereinafter 'TUAC Survey' [pp. 37-41]).

[44] TUAC Survey, p. 40. If this is indeed the case, it hardly surprising that NGOs remain apathetic.

[45] 'NGO Statement on the OECD Guidelines for Multinational Enterprises', in OECD Guidelines for Multinational Enterprises: *Global Instruments for Corporate Responsibility, Annual Report* (OECD, 2001a: 47).

[46] OECD (2001a).

[47] TUAC Survey, p. 39.

[48] The TUAC survey (p. 39) also singles out Finland because companies receiving export credits "are assumed to observe the Guidelines".

[49] TUAC Survey, p. 37.

[50] TUAC Survey, p. 38.

[51] See for example (Lewis, 2001: 245ff.) for a discussion of the influence of the Trans-Atlantic Business Dialogue (TABD) a powerful network of 100 European and American CEOs; (see also Lewis, 2002). For a discussion of TNC influence at the national level see (MacLeod, 1999).

[52] BIAC Statement (OECD, 2001a: 32).

[53] S. Hilton, Letter to *The Guardian* (11 June 2002). See also C. Caulkin, 'Good Thinking, Bad Practice', *The Observer* (7 April 2002); R. Reeves (2001) 'The Way We Work', *The Guardian* (17 July), accessed 12 July 2002, http://www.guardian.co.uk/Archive/0,4273,4222812,00.html; T. Macalister 'Corporate Ideals "Manipulated"', *The Guardian* (15 May 2002).

[54] Caulkin (2002).

[55] This would accord with the notion that the implementation of broad regulatory instruments eases the negotiation of regulatory detail.

[56] See Kell (2002: 4). "The Global Compact is an ambitious and unprecedented experiment to fill a void between regulatory regimes, at one end of the spectrum, and voluntary codes of industry conduct, at the other. It is a cooperative framework based on internationally established rights and principles."

[57] United Nations Global Compact, 'The Nine Principles', http://www.globalcompact.org.

[58] UN Doc.A/811 10th December 1948.

[59] ILO 86th Session, 18th June 1998.

[60] UN Doc. A/CONF.151/26 (Vol. I) 12th August 1992.

[61] 'The Global Compact and Human Rights', http://www.globalcompact.org.

[62] Global Compact Report (2002: 3).

[63] Global Compact Report (2002: 8).

[64] NGO Letter to Kofi Annan Recommending Redesign of Global Compact, 29th January 2002 at http://www.globalcompact.org (see also Global Compact Report, 2002: 18-19). 'According to a review conducted by an independent team of academics, none of the company submissions conformed to the guidelines suggested by the Global Compact Office, and 15 of the submissions did not directly address the implementation of the nine principles.'

[65] See note 64.

[66] NGO Letter to Kofi Annan, p. 19.

[67] NGO Letter to Kofi Annan, p. 19.

[68] NGO Letter to Kofi Annan, p. 7. See Appendix A, p. 31 for a list of current members. The Council has created two working groups: the Working Group on Company Participation and Civil Society Engagement and the Working Group on Compact Leadership.

[69] NGO Letter to Kofi Annan, p. 19.

[70] NGO Letter to Kofi Annan, p. 17.

[71] NGO Letter to Kofi Annan, p. 7.

[72] NGO Letter to Kofi Annan, pp. 7, 9. See also note 63. Daimler Chrysler is charged with appropriating the GC logo in its corporate literature.

[73] NGO Letter to Kofi Annan, p. 6. The report also notes that the GC is being taught increasingly on MBA courses "thus rooting the Global Compact in education".

[74] NGO Letter to Kofi Annan, pp. 13, 6. See, for example, *the Global Policy Dialogue on the Role of Business in Zones of Conflict*, p. 13.

[75] *Communication from the Commission concerning Corporate Social Responsibility: A Business Contribution to Sustainable Development*, Brussels 2nd July 2002, COM (2002) 347 final, p. 5.

[76] *Communication from the Commission concerning Corporate Social Responsibility: A Business Contribution to Sustainable Development*, pp. 13, 14, 19, 22.

[77] Commission of the European Communities, Green Paper, *Promoting a European Framework for Corporate Social Responsibility* COM (2001) 366 final, http://europa.eu.int/comm/employment_social/soc-dial/csr/greenpaper_en.pdf (Responses were invited from interested parties and submitted by 31 December 2001).

[78] Green Paper, p. 23, para.93.

[79] Green Paper, pp. 22, 23, para.92.

[80] Green Paper, n.12.

[81] Belgium, Germany, Finland, France, Ireland, Netherlands, Austria, Sweden, UK.

[82] Twenty-seven individual UK corporations responded. Another 32 responses were received from networks representing the corporate sector, e.g. International Chamber of Commerce, Law Centres Federation. A large number of UK based TNCs responded to the Green Paper. It may be that CSR has a high profile in the UK in the wake of, e.g., the RTZ asbestos litigation, and the BP Brent Spar fiasco. This could also explain the relatively large number of US firms responding e.g. NIKE, Levi Strauss. However, it is surprising that Shell did not submit a response in light of its experiences in Nigeria.

[83] Including the TUC.

[84] Including at the international level OXFAM, Amnesty International, Save the Children and WWF. UK NGOs submitting responses were Baby Milk Action IBFAN, Christian Aid, Friends of the Earth, New Economic Foundation (NEF) and the Solicitors Pro Bono Group.

[85] Green Paper, p. 6.

[86] See for example response from Amnesty International, p. 6. AI argues that CSR should not be an "add-on to core business activities" and states that the assumption that CSR should be viewed as voluntary is "flawed in that it fails to take account of the reality that voluntary approaches are generally implemented in response to consumer and community pressures, industry peer pressure, competitive pressure or the threat of new regulations or taxes", i.e. rarely voluntarily.

[87] Commission Communication, p. 4.

[88] Commission Communication, p. 17.

[89] So for example incorporating CSR into a new framework directive harmonizing the fairness of commercial practices and producing a handbook on 'green' public procurement. (Commission Communication, pp. 21, 22).

[90] COM (2001) 252 final.

[91] COM (2001) 252 final, n.77, pp. 22, 23.

[92] Published September 2000. A new report is due shortly.

[93] TUAC Survey, p. 39; Department of Trade and Industry, 'Business and Society: Corporate Social Responsibility Report 2002', DTI/Pub 6060/5k/05/02 NP, May 2002, p. 43.

[94] 'Business and Society: Corporate Social Responsibility Report 2002', p. 43.

[95] Corporate Responsibility Bill, Bill 145, 53/1, 12 June 2002. Australia has also attempted without success to introduce compulsory CSR. See the Corporate Code of Conduct Bill 2000, which proposed regulation of Australian corporations operating overseas. The Joint Statutory Committee on Corporations and Securities rejected it on 28 June 2001 on the basis that it was unnecessary and unworkable. In October 2000, USA Congresswoman Cynthia McKinney introduced, the TRUTH Act of 2000 (Transparency and Responsibility for US Trade Health) HR 5492. The bill sought to require US companies operating abroad to

disclose information about their operations e.g. the location and address of facilities, age and gender of employees, environmental performance, and labour practices.

[96] S.1(1)(a) and (b).

[97] S.3(1)(a) and (b).

[98] S.3(1)(c) and (d).

[99] S.(3)(3) defines "stakeholder" non-exhaustively as shareholders and investors, employees, communities and individuals.

[100] S.6.

[101] S.8(a), (b) and (c).

[102] S.9(7).

[103] S.10.

[104] Loi relative aux nouvelles regulations économiques, Loi 2001-420 du 15 Mai 2001.

[105] UN Doc. E/CN.4/Sub.2/2003/12 (2003). See, for example, the Amnesty International Public Statement, of 8 August 2003 at 'Human Rights Responsibilities of Transnational Corporations and Other Business Enterprises', 55th Session of the Sub-Commission on the Promotion and Protection of Human Rights (28 July–15 August 2003) AI Index: POL 30/012/2003 (Public).

[106] See Lewis, 2001: 245ff., 2002 for a discussion on the significant influence of the TABD particularly in relation to the EU and the WTO. For an example of an individual corporation's influence at the national level see the case of Texaco in Ecuador described in (MacLeod, 1999). For a discussion of regional CSR initiatives see (MacLeod, forthcoming 2004).

References

Adams, C. (2000), 'Help Firms to Open Up', *THES*, (3 November), p. 18.

Amnesty International Public Statement (2003), 'Human Rights Responsibilities of Transnational Corporations and Other Business Enterprises', paper presented at 55th Session of the Sub-Commission on the Promotion and Protection of Human Rights, 28 July–15 August. AI Index: POL 30/012/2003 (Public).

Blanpain, R. (ed.) (2000), *Multinational Enterprises and the Social Challenges of the XXIst Century*, London, Kluwer.

Caulkin, C. (2002), 'Good Thinking, Bad Practice', *The Observer* (7 April 2002).

Commission of the European Communities (2001), Green Paper 'Promoting a European Framework for Corporate Social Responsibility' COM (2001) 366 final, http://europa.eu.int/comm/employment_social/soc-dial/csr/csr_responses.htm.

Commission of the European Communities (2002), 'Communication from the Commission Concerning Corporate Social Responsibility: A Business Contribution to Sustainable Development', Brussels, 2 July 2002, COM (2002) 347 final.

Corporate Code of Conduct Bill 2000 (Australia).

Corporate Responsibility Bill, Bill 145, 53/1, 12 June 2002 (Australia).

Department of Trade and Industry (2002), 'Business and Society: Corporate Social Responsibility Report 2002', DTI/Pub 6060/5k/05/02 NP, May 2002 (UK).Draft Norms on the Responsibilities of Transnational Corporations and Other Business Enterprises with Regard to Human Rights, UN Doc. E/CN.4/Sub.2/2003/12 (2003).

Global Compact Report (2002), http://www.globalcompact.org.

Gordon, K. (2001), 'The OECD Guidelines and Other Corporate Responsibility Instruments: A Comparison', Working Papers on International Investment No. 2001/5, OECD Directorate for Financial, Fiscal and Enterprise Affairs.

Hilton, S. (2002), 'Letter', *The Guardian* (11 June 2002).

ICFTU (1999), *Building Workers' Human Rights in to the Global System*, Brussels: International Confederation of Free Trade Unions.

Individual Corporate Responses to the European Commission Green Paper, 'Promoting a European Framework for Corporate Social Responsibility' COM (2001) 366 final, http://europa.eu.int/comm/employment_social/socdial/csr/csr_responses.htm.

International Labor Organization (1998), 'Declaration on Fundamental Principles and Rights at Work', paper presented at ILO 86th Session, Geneva, 18 June.

Karl, J. (1999), 'The OECD Guidelines for Multinational Enterprises', in M.K. Addo (ed.), *Human Rights Standards and the Responsibility of Transnational Corporations*, London, Kluwer.

Kell, G. (2002), 'Introduction and Overview', in Global Compact Office (ed.), *The Global Compact: Report on Progress and Activities*, pp. 3-4, http://www.globalcompact.org.

Lewis, N.D. (2001), *Law and Governance: The Old Meets the New*, London, Cavendish.

Lewis, N.D. (2002), 'Law and Globalisation: An Opportunity for Europe, its Partners and for Legal Scholars', *European Public Law* 8(2), pp. 219-39.

Loi Relative aux Nouvelles Regulations Economiques, Loi 2001-420 du 15 Mai 2001 (France).

MacLeod, S. (1999), 'Maria Aguinda v. Texaco Inc.: Defining the Limits of Liability for Human Rights Violations Resulting from Environmental Degradation', *Contemporary Issues in Law*, 4(2), pp. 189-209.

MacLeod, S. (2004), 'Regional Regulatory Responses to Corporate Social (Ir)Responsibility', in S. MacLeod and J. Parkinson (eds), *Global Governance and the Search for Justice: Corporations and Corporate Governance*, Oxford, Hart Publishing.

Muchlinski, P.T. (1999), *Multinational Enterprises and the Law*, Oxford, Blackwell.

NGO Letter to Kofi Annan Recommending Redesign of Global Compact, 29 January 2002, http://www.globalcompact.org.

OECD (2000a), Declaration on International Investment and Multinational Enterprises, 27 June.

OECD (2000b), Guidelines for Multinational Enterprises, Revision 2000.

OECD (2001a), 'OECD Guidelines for Multinational Enterprises: Global Instruments for Corporate Responsibility', Annual Report 2001, Paris, OECD.

OECD (2001b), 'Relations with BIAC and TUAC', 7 June.

OECD Response to the European Commission Green Paper, http://europa.eu.int/comm/employment_social/soc-dial/csr/csr_responses.htm.

Press Release, 'NIKE Board of Directors and CEO Philip H. Knight Create Corporate Responsibility Committee', 10 September 2001, http://www.nikebiz.com/media/n_crboard.shtml.

Rio Declaration on Environment and Development UN Doc. A/CONF.151/26 (Vol. I), 12 August 1992.

Robinson, M. (2002), 'Beyond Good Intentions: Corporate Citizenship for a New Century', RSA World Leaders Lecture, *RSA Journal*, 3(6), pp. 34-6.

The Guardian (2000), 'Adidas Attacked for Asian "Sweatshops"', (23 November).

TRUTH Act of 2000 (Transparency and Responsibility for US Trade Health), HR 5492 (USA).

United Nations Global Compact, 'The Nine Principles', http://www.globalcompact.org.

United Nations, 'The Global Compact and Human Rights', http://www.globalcompact.org.

Universal Declaration on Human Rights UN Doc.A/811, 10 December 1948.

Van Rooij, R. (2000), Text of a speech delivered to a plenary session entitled 'Foreign Investment, Human Rights and Development: Integration or Fragmentation?' at the Sixty-Ninth Conference of the International Law Association, London, July 2000 [on file with authors].

Witherell, W.H. (2001), OECD Response to the EU Green Paper 13 December 2001, http://europa.eu.int/comm/employment_social/soc-dial/csr/csr_responses.htm.

Chapter 10

Global Civil Society and Spaces of Resistance

Ray Kiely

Introduction

Attempts to theorize the concept of global civil society, and related notions of global citizenship, solidarity, and globalization from below, are fraught with difficulties. These relate to the contested nature of the terms globalization and civil society, and the fact that there is considerable overlap in discussions concerning these terms. For example there is dispute over the extent to which globalization has eroded the power of the nation-state, which, in turn, relates to debates over whether the state is part of civil society. Such arguments are not just of academic significance – they are central to debates over strategies required to challenge the hegemony of both neo-liberalism (including its 'Third Way' variant) and capital. This will become clear in the discussion below.

The rest of this chapter will address the issue of global civil society in the following way. First, it will outline the idea that 'globalization' has ushered in a new, radical politics (potentially if not actually) located in global civil society. This is associated with Richard Falk's argument that globalization from above has led to the development of a counter-hegemonic globalization from below. In this argument, global civil society is above all located in the development of 'people-centred' transnational social movements and Non-Government Organizations (NGOs). Some of the strengths of this argument are then identified, and related to important theoretical attempts to develop notions of cosmopolitan and transnational democracy, associated with writers like Daniele Archibugi and David Held. However, there are also problems with this perspective, which will then be identified in the second section. In particular, there is a tendency to rigidly contrast 'postmodern', global politics on the one hand, and modern, national politics on the other. This is reflected, for example, in a tendency to downplay the role of the nation-state. These critical points are important in identifying the ways in which some states can and do promote 'globalization from above', but also in recognizing that contrasting global civil society to older forms of politics may underestimate the extent to which such states continue to be important sites of struggle, and which may be used to facilitate – in some respects at least – progressive reforms that can be considered part of the process of building a 'globalization from below'.

My discussion is not intended to promote a rigid dichotomy between reactionary globalization and progressive state, or indeed the opposite. It is instead an argument that progressive politics cannot be easily located at discrete 'levels' or 'spaces', be it national, international or global – or indeed, as we shall see, local. In making these abstract arguments I will illustrate through the use of concrete examples in the third section, relating them to debates within the global 'anti-capitalist movement'.

Global Civil Society as Globalization from Below

Defining global civil society is no easy task, and a survey of the literature shows a variety of attempts. Anheier *et al.* (2001: 17) define it 'the sphere of ideas, values, institutions, organizations, networks, and individuals located *between* the family, the state and the market and operating *beyond* the confines of national societies, polities and economies'. Edwards (2001: 2) defines it as 'the arena in which people come together to advance their interests they hold in common, not for profit or political power, but because they care enough about something to take collective action'. Richard Falk (2000a: 163) argues that global civil society 'refers to the field of action and thought occupied by individual and collective citizen initiatives of a voluntary, non-profit character both within states and transnationally'. Finally, Naidoo and Tandon (1999: 6-7) define it as 'the network of autonomous associations that rights-bearing and responsibility laden citizens voluntarily create to address common problems, advance shared interests and promote collective aspirations'. These definitions are all rather imprecise, but they appear to refer to a 'third sector' independent of state and market, and operating beyond the territorial boundaries of the nation state. Implicit in much of the literature (see Naidoo and Tandon, 1999, for instance) is a contrast between 'bad' state bureaucracy and market profiteering on the one hand, and 'good' global civil society on the other.

Falk utilizes a similar contrast in his analysis of globalization. His basic argument is that 'globalization-from-above' has led to the emergence of a 'globalization-from-below' (Falk 2000b). The former is associated with the growing power of corporate capital *vis-à-vis* countervailing forces, which is reflected in the dominance of transnational corporations, global finance, and the decline of the 'compassionate state' (Falk 2000b: 49). However, the changes associated with the transnationalization of capital – growing global interconnectedness and an increase in the speed of such interconnectedness – also facilitates the growth of a globalization from below, which is further reinforced by the decline of state sovereignty. This time-space compression means the rise of ongoing global political campaigns, new media (particularly the Internet), greater mobility, and the spread of global norms such as human rights and democracy. This is reflected in the enormous growth of membership of international Non-Government Organizations, which grew by 72 per cent from 1990 to 2000 (Anheier *et al*, 2001: 5-6), and the growing globalization of the concerns of such organizations, reflected in part in the growing number of international civil society summits (Pianta, 2001).

Central to many definitions of global civil society is the idea that there has been a transnationalization of NGOs and/or social movements. Distinguishing between NGOs and social movements is far from straightforward, but it is usually assumed that the latter is more overtly concerned with social transformation. However, this distinction is itself problematic as both social movement activists and analysts may differ over the meaning of social transformation. Radical political parties, particularly those influenced by Marxism, often understood social transformation to mean a wholesale transformation of the mode of production, and a transition from capitalism to socialism. According to most analysts of so-called 'new social movements', social transformation should be understood both more narrowly and widely than this conception. More narrowly, because it does not necessarily mean a change in the mode of production and/or state power, but more widely as the concerns of social movements entail a widening of the recognition of the sources of domination in modern societies.

Debate over the novelty of 'new social movements' should be seen in this light. In the Western world at least, it is argued that we have moved from a modern industrial society to a late- or post- modern, post-industrial society, in which the main arena of conflict is no longer over material, economic or distributional issues. Instead, conflict is mainly concerned with 'quality of life, equal rights, individual self-realization, participation and human rights' (Habermas, 1987: 392). The focus is thus said to be on 'life politics' (Giddens, 1991: 214), in which rationalization and commodification are resisted by social movements advocating autonomy. Unlike old labour movements, new social movements are 'not oriented toward the conquest of political power ... but rather toward the control of a field of autonomy or of interdependence *vis-à-vis* the system' (Melucci, 1980: 220). This emphasis on autonomy has also been applied to social movements in the developing world, where one would expect a continued focus on 'material' issues. The 'post-development' school, however, champion social movements that resist the rationalising and homogenising thrust of 'development' (Escobar, 1995). In this approach, poverty is not so much a reality as a construction of the development discourse, a problem to be solved by 'more development'. In resisting such a discourse, social movements are said to be preserving their autonomy and upholding a politics based on cultural difference (Escobar, 2000).

Such approaches therefore regard a key characteristic of social movements as that of having autonomy from states and markets. The globalization of social movement activity thus returns us to the definition of a global civil society, independent of states and markets, outlined above. In a moment I want to problematize some of the contentions made by theorists of 'new social movements', not least in relation to understanding the emergence of the global 'anti-capitalist' movement. First however, I want to suggest that there is some common ground between new social movement theory and one of the key principles of the anti-capitalist movement (though see Hardt and Negri's [2000: 275] useful, but sympathetic critique), and this can be located at the level of organization.

Roger Burbach, one of the most influential thinkers in the 'anti-capitalist' movement, argues that the most distinctive feature of the movement is its postmodern, decentred politics. He argues that the movement is:

> postmodern in the sense that it has no clear rationale or logic to its activities while it instinctively recognises that it cannot be effective by working through a 'modern' political party, or by taking state power. It functions from below as an almost permanent rebellion, placing continuous demands on all the powers that be. (Burbach, 2001: 11)

De Angelis (2001: 112) makes the related point that the politics of the movement are inseparable from its organizational forms. These constitute 'new forms of social cooperation beyond the capitalist market' (De Angelis, 2001: 115). A similar point is made by Melucci (1989: 60) in his analysis of new social movements, when he argues that 'the organizational forms of movements are not just 'instrumental' for their goals, they are a goal in themselves'.

Naomi Klein (2001: 147) argues that the emergence of this non-hierarchical form of organization was, in part, facilitated by the Internet. The world wide web allows for the rapid spread of information and allows mobilization to occur 'with sparse bureaucracy and minimal hierarchy; forced consensus and labored manifestos are fading into the background, replaced instead by a culture of constant, loosely structured and sometimes compulsive information swapping'. For these reasons it makes no sense to talk of a single movement or alternative; it is a movement of movements, with many alternatives. Michael Hardt (2002: 114-18) takes this argument a step further, arguing that the organizational form that movements take is inseparable from their position in relation to globalization. He contrasts movements that uphold the defence of national sovereignty with movements that propose an alternative globalization based on democracy. The former generally organize and mobilize in classically modern ways – that is, through political parties, or interest groups, which put pressure on nation-states to implement reform. The latter is based on a horizontal, network form that bypasses national institutions and which proposes 'the democratisation of globalising processes' against the decentred but hierarchical global order (Hardt and Negri, 2001: 102; also Hardt and Negri, 2000). Hardt and Negri (2000: 7) are actually critical of the idea of global civil society, and they rather one-sidedly identify transnational NGOs as being a constituent part of Empire. On the other hand, their notion of a transnational multitude as a radical counter-power to Empire is actually not so far removed from Falk's notion of global civil society representing a globalization from below, which is based on alternative forms of organizing and new networks of global solidarity.

I will argue below that some of these contentions should be questioned, and can be considered overly one-sided. Nevertheless, they also point to important changes in forms of resistance and solidarity. A growing global solidarity movement can be identified, and there are concrete cases of genuine solidarity that go beyond the spectacular protests at international summits (see Cohen and Rai, 2000; Edwards and Gaventa, 2001; Waterman and Wills, 2001). Despite the efforts of various sectarian Trotskyist organizations to dominate these movements, a distinctive solidarity politics has emerged. For instance, predictable Trotskyist 'anti-imperialist' dogma propagated in response to the war in Afghanistan was resisted on the grounds that some political forces in the developing world were reactionary and so were justifiably condemned *along with* the US war (Yuen, 2001). Attempts were therefore made to build genuine networks of solidarity with oppositional movements in West Asia and the Middle East, rather than one-sidedly denounce US imperialism (World Social Forum, 2002).

Their own criticisms of the global anti-capitalist movement notwithstanding (Held and Hirst, 2002; Archibugi, 2002), theorists of cosmopolitan democracy champion the cause of a global civil society on the grounds that it at least has the potential to establish 'new modes of holding transnational power systems to account – that is, they help open up the possibility of ... "cosmopolitan democracy"' (Held, 2000: 29). This perspective can be interpreted as a 'left-liberal' version of Hardt and Negri's more radical arguments, albeit with some sophisticated qualifications by the cosmopolitans (Held, for example, does not deny the continued importance of the state). But for all their differences, both perspectives share the view that global civil society has in some ways undermined the nation state. Moreover, both perspectives tend to welcome such a process.

The rise of a global civil society is undoubtedly important, and it does in some ways represent a distinctive, novel form of politics. Nevertheless, this point can be overstated, as I discuss below, with particular reference to the anti-capitalist movement.

Global Civil Society, Social Movements and Anti-Capitalism: A Reconceptualization

Without wishing to deny the increase in intensity of global social movement/international NGO activity, or the utility of the concept of global civil society, this section questions some of the contentions concerning global civil society. The key critical point is that some theorists tend to present a dichotomy between the (outmoded) nation-state on the one hand, and (cutting edge, postmodern) global civil society on the other. This is most clear in the work of Hardt and Negri, and Burbach, discussed above, but the state/civil society dualism is also present to some extent in the more nuanced views of Archibugi and Held. Such a binary opposition should be rejected for the following reasons. First, states have played a key role in the process of globalization. Contrary to much of the globalization literature, which appears to reject any clear notion of agency promoting globalising processes,[1] more grounded analyses rightly point to the role of states in promoting pro-globalization policies. This can be seen in the promotion of various free trade agreements, and states choosing to join the World Trade Organization. Successive United States governments have committed themselves to free trade (albeit highly selectively and hypocritically), in part as an attempt to restore declining shares in the world market, a clear example being that of attempts to (selectively) liberalize world food trade (see Goodman and Watts, 1997). Much has been made of communications technologies such as the Internet and satellite television, which have clearly compressed time and space. However, the development of such technologies is inseparable from business and state (particularly military) interests, even if (as will become clear) their social, cultural and political effects are not reducible to such interests (Castells, 1996). These points are not made to deny the reality of social change but they are made to question a simplistic account of politics, which suggests that we have moved from a nation-state/national movement politics to a global institutions/global civil society politics. Instead, I am suggesting that we are witnessing a reconfiguration of the relationship between nation states and global – or perhaps more accurately, still international – civil society (see also Colas, 2002).

My argument then is that a rigid separation of nation state and global civil society rests on too deep a divide between old and new politics. A similarly rigid division can also be found in the work of new social movement theory, which clearly influences some of the claims made for the existence of a completely novel global civil society. Such a perspective rigidly separated 'post-material' life or identity politics from material, distributional or economistic politics. While a distinction between the two may be made, an overly rigid demarcation is deeply problematic. Anti-racist politics for example, are rarely just about the politics of recognition or difference, and usually involve demands with material implications. Moreover, such demands are often or even usually made on the state, and are not just about organising independently of 'modern institutions'. Similarly, the politics of 'old' labour movements are not simply material or economistic. Strikes are not just about wage demands, and even when this is the main cause, they involve wider struggles, not least over culturally contested terms such as dignity and fairness. Such struggles also have wider social implications beyond the immediate demands of the workplace. Indeed, one of the most significant global developments in recent years has been the development of trade union movements that have explicitly made alliances with other social movements and trade unions beyond nation states (Waterman and Wills, 2001). New social movement theory has little to say about these developments.

The development of the global 'anti-capitalist' movement over the last few years also undermines such dichotomies. The bewildering variety of movements that protested at Seattle in 1999 for instance undermines any easy identification of such organizations as 'materialist' or 'post-materialist'. This point applies equally to social movements from the 'South', whose demands cannot be identified, *contra* Escobar (above) as 'anti-development'. The issue of social movements from the 'South' is discussed in more detail below, but an immediate point needs to be made, which is that not all movements are intrinsically progressive, and when they are, their principal concern is with alleviating the effects of the uneven development of capitalism rather than the (supposedly) homogenising discourse of development (Kiely, 1999, and below).

Before discussing these questions in more specific depth, some of the more general political implications of my critique of notions of global civil society need to be drawn out. In doing so, this will lead back to a discussion of the politics of social movements, and the question of progressive and reactionary movements.

One potentially fruitful way of discussing the politics of global civil society is Anheier *et al.*'s (2001: 7) formulation in terms of '*positions in relation to globalisation*'. This has the advantage of specifying the concrete and dynamic ways in which global civil society is contested. Four positions are identified (Anheier *et al.*, 2001: 7-10): supporters, rejectionists, reformists and alternatives. Supporters are identified as transnational business and their allies, who favour global capitalism and support moves towards free trade and free capital flows. They are also said to support 'just wars' against 'rogue states'. Rejectionists are identified as being a mixture of anti-capitalist social movements, authoritarian states, and nationalist and fundamentalist movements. The left reject global capitalism, while both right and left support the preservation of national sovereignty. Short of the overthrow of global capitalism (the left), national protection of markets and capital controls are favoured (both left and right). Armed intervention in other countries is rejected except when it is in the national interest (the right), or as imperialist (the left). Reformists are composed of most international NGOs, many working in international institutions and many social movements. These actors support the reform of global capitalism, including specific proposals like a Tobin Tax and debt relief. They also favour some kind of international policing and civil society intervention to enforce human rights. Finally, the 'alternatives' position is composed of grassroots groups and some social movements, who want to opt out of globalization and establish local alternative economies. This may include some intervention in conflicts but not the use of military force.

Such a division is in many ways useful, but some caution is also necessary. This is because these divisions tend to be too static and ignore the ways in which movements may adopt different positions on particular issues, a point recognized by Anheier's co-writer Glasius (2001) in a further, single authored article. The question then becomes not one of rejection or acceptance of globalisation, or the championing of national or local alternatives, but the ways in which each of these 'spaces' is used in concrete circumstances. This point is concretized below.

Political Implications: Spaces of Resistance

The key question then is not to champion the global, at the expense of the local, or the national at the expense of the global, but to forge a progressive politics at each of these 'levels', one that recognizes the relationships between them. This section makes some suggestive comments about each of these, with particular reference to their political implications.

(i) Global Civil Society

First then, is the position most clearly outlined above by Hardt and Negri, that global civil society represents a progressive alternative to (nation-)state based politics. To reiterate, the argument is first that the development of such a civil society constitutes the development of a global solidarity in opposition to nationalist particularisms. A similar, though less anti-statist, case is also made by the more liberal cosmopolitans such as Held (above). Hardt and Negri then make a second, related argument that the form of organisation – networks – is less hierarchical and therefore more democratic than the old politics of orthodox Marxism. This argument is quite close to new social movement theory, and some of the claims made by contemporary anti-capitalist thinkers (see De Angelis and Burbach, cited above). Added to this is the often-made claim that the Internet helps to facilitate such non-hierarchical organization across and beyond national boundaries.

However there are strong grounds for challenging such claims, which relate to the issues of politics, representation, and inequalities within global civil society. First, the network form of organization does not in itself guarantee a progressive politics. Sections of international capital organize through networks, as do reactionary political movements such as al Qaeda (Castells, 1996, 1997). An exaggerated emphasis on forms of organization can also lead to an underestimation of the potential (in-)effectiveness of social movements. Certainly some activists in the anti-capitalist movement appear to believe that direct action is itself *the* politics, rather than one *part* of a wider movement for political change (see McKay, 1998) – a position close to the 'alternatives' perspective outlined by Anheier *et al* (above). One potential result of this approach to politics is that resistance through spectacle 'may offer no more than the experience of managed spectatorship' (Scott and Street, 2001: 50). The anti-capitalist movement has itself recognized and debated this problem, with some prominent thinkers advocating a move beyond 'summit stalking' (Klein, 2001: 152; also Brecher and Costello, 2000: 86-8). Certainly there is a fine line between advocating social transformation and retreating from mainstream society, and Hardt and Negri (2000: 274) are at times guilty of stepping over it, for instance in their rather uncritical endorsement of the 1960s hippy counter-culture. A similar point can be made regarding global networking through the Internet, which 'is not a substitute for traditional political activity and participation' (Smith and Smythe, 2001: 204). The Net is an important mobilising tool and it does facilitate genuine participatory dialogue among its participants, but cyberspace is no substitute for reality.[2] In other words, the organizational politics of cyberspace must be grounded in a politics based on place. Global civil society does not replace (or 'displace') national or local politics, even if it does change their form.

A simplistic advocacy of a global civil society also evades difficult questions of the representative nature of social movements and NGOs. Mats Karlsson (cited in Edwards, 2000: 3), the Vice President for External Affairs at the World Bank, has attacked NGOs for their 'weak accountability', 'shallow democracy' and 'precarious legitimacy'. One does not have to respect the democratic credentials of the World Bank and other multilateral institutions, or ignore the severe limitations of liberal democracies, to still accept the point that international social movements and NGOs do not possess 'the requisite degree of legitimacy and accountability to be considered as democratic representatives in a globalized political community' (Colas, 2002: 163). NGOs and social movements are themselves acutely aware of this problem, and have attempted to bridge the gap between global scaling up and accountability to the grassroots (Fox and Brown, 1998).

This issue of representation is not one of simply establishing accountable structures within particular movements. It also relates to the questions of 'who speaks for whom?' Clearly, global movements make the claim that they are representing the interests of people beyond their immediate members, but there is then the question of how they do so. This is a problem made all the more difficult by the massive inequalities in the global order, which may undermine the basis for alliances. Certainly reference to 'the multitude' (Hardt and Negri, 2000) is too vague a basis for alliance building, as is Burbach's (2001: ch.2) contention that globalization leads (to some extent at least) to a convergence between countries based on a levelling down process. The defensive power of organized labour in 'advanced' capitalist countries has declined in recent years, and this is reflected in the decline in value of real wages, but there has been an increasing divergence between countries (and classes) over the last thirty years, reflected in growing inequalities in trade, investment and income shares (Kiely, 2003). These facts make alliance building a far more difficult task than Burbach, Hardt and Negri contend. For example, anti-sweat-shop campaigns in the 'First World' claims to represent, or speak for, oppressed workers in the developing world. However, there is the obvious danger that such campaigns can easily become protectionist, in that they may call for trade boycotts or import controls, which lead to factory closure in the developing world and protect jobs in the 'First World'. In making this point, I am not implying that anti-sweat campaigns ignore these problems. I am however suggesting that building a progressive politics based on 'global civil society' or 'the multitude', is more problematic than some advocates imply. Similar points could be made concerning different perspectives on debt cancellation for instance, or indeed the extent to which social movements support development (see Collins *et al*, 2001; Clark, 2001).

None of these critical comments imply wholesale rejection of the concept of global civil society, or the necessity or desirability of building genuine global solidarities. For all its limitations, the Internet is a useful mobilising tool and one that allows for genuine dialogue among participants. A cosmopolitan solidarity perspective is one that deserves support, not least because it rejects the effective indifference of a politics that uncritically supports state sovereignty in the context of genocide. What does need emphasising, however, is that given the continued power of the nation state, a politics that simplistically champions global civil society at the expense of, rather than in addition to, the former is highly problematic. It is to the nation state that I now turn my attention.

(ii) The Nation State

Hardt and Negri are not the only writers who rigidly contrast progressive global to backward national politics. Advocates of a global 'Third Way' make a similar contrast, albeit with radically different political implications. Thus, Peter Hain (2002) and Anthony Giddens (2000) have both contrasted the third way as the truly progressive global politics against left isolationists who want to defend state sovereignty. Hain for example denounces the 'rejectionist left' for being 'stuck in a timewarp', as it rejects both humanitarian intervention based on the promotion of global human rights (as in Kosovo and Afghanistan), and global trade based on economic growth and development. This approach is contrasted to the 'progressive internationalism' of Third Way social democrats.

This contrast of Third Way/progressive globalists with isolationist anti-globalizers is close to Anheier *et al.*'s characterization of the anti-capitalist movement as 'rejectionist' (see above). John Lloyd (2001) has similarly argued that a progressive global politics means embracing – but humanizing – globalization, as opposed to the rejectionists of the Far Left and nationalist right. Certainly there are reactionary opponents of globalization such as Pat Buchanan and elements of the AFL-CIO in the US, Fascist parties in Europe, and militant right wing nationalists in parts of the developing world (for discussions, see Hensman, 2001; Kessi, 2001; Krebbers and Schoenmaker, 2001). Much of the right-wing critique of globalization is based on a defence of 'national sovereignty' and 'cultural tradition'. It could even be argued that some elements of the anti-capitalist movement have (perhaps unwittingly) repeated such arguments (see some of the chapters in Goldsmith and Mander, 2001).

However, quite apart from the Third Way advocates' characterization of the anti-capitalist movement as isolationist (I have suggested that influential thinkers like Hardt and Negri are if anything *too globalist*), the basic problem with this dichotomy is once again one that is based on the notion of 'global good, local bad'. The Third Way commitment to global free trade ignores the fact that such a trading system would automatically benefit those locations with strong and highly established production facilities (Kiely, 2002a). Also, it is highly selective and based on increasing pressure on the developing world to open their economies while the 'First World' continues to protect areas where the former may have some advantages such as clothing and agriculture. The Third Way's modified free trade strategy of 'progressive competitiveness', in which capital and labour embark on a social partnership to protect 'their' company and 'their' jobs, also fails the test of progressive globalism. In this approach competitiveness is maintained by the development of high skilled, high value work, which is more competitive than cheaper labour elsewhere. This strategy is nationalist in that it effectively exports unemployment to less competitive areas, and is self-defeating as 'the whole point to this strategy is to increase exports and limit imports, (and) if all states were to follow this, there must be a general tendency towards competitive austerity' (Panitch, 2001: 14). Perhaps above all, the limitations of the Third Way's claim to represent a progressive global politics can be seen in the case of immigration, where advocates of free trade such as Anthony Giddens (2002) have called for strong immigration controls, which clearly restrict the free movement of labour. The global Third Way is thus selective about its internationalism, and ignores the fact that there are many ways to engage with the global beyond advocacy of global free trade or humanitarian war (see Kiely, 2002b).

These examples clearly show the fallacy of a rigid dichotomy between progressive global and reactionary national. The key issue for a progressive national politics is how the nation-state is used and who benefits from such policies. This can be seen in the case of national capital controls – a policy advocated by many on the far right as well as progressive left. The key point about such controls however is that they need not be reactionary so long as they are used for progressive purposes. They could be used to promote egalitarian policies both *within* and *beyond* the nation-state. Such a policy could include increased aid from 'advanced' to 'underdeveloped' countries, in terms of both quantity and quality – that is, aid not necessarily targeted at governments in the South, but rather at social movements committed to progressive social change (a case of state support to civil society). This strategy could also be applied to trade with sectors where there is evidence of a levelling up process among producers – a strategic trade policy based on genuine cosmopolitan principles.

Such policies could go hand in hand with more progressive international policies that more effectively challenged global inequalities than the rather timid third way. At Bretton Woods in 1944, Keynes envisaged the creation of an international institution that would be supplied with large amounts of credit, mainly from the advanced capitalist countries. This strongly interventionist institution would have the potential to massively transfer resources from the richer to the poorer countries, using the savings of those who did not wish to spend their money for the benefit of those who did – for long-term development (Brett, 1985: 47-51). This approach effectively amounted to a proposal that the main surplus countries (at this time, only the US), should put a substantial proportion of its resources at the disposal of the rest of the world. This proposal was successfully resisted by the United States, which provided the IMF with low levels of finance so that only short-term financing of balance of payments deficits was possible. Some provision was also made for long-term development through the World Bank, but this was nowhere near the amount that Keynes envisaged for a long-term redistribution of resources from rich to poor countries. Keynes's vision of a global policy of strong public interventionism and redistribution is far from being implemented to this day. It would probably take a massive transformation of global power relations for it to occur – and at the very least would entail the defeat of neo-liberal ideas – but it is clearly a policy that combines a politics based both on nation states and global civil society.

(iii) The Politics of the 'Local'

There is a growing academic literature, and a clear political tendency in the global anti-capitalist movement, to propose a 'localized' alternative to globalization (Hines, 2000; Goldsmith and Mander, 2001). Sometimes this can take a particularly reactionary form, as in David Korten's ecological populism, which asserts that 3.3 billion people living in 'sustainable societies', live a life based on meeting basic needs but which simultaneously rejects the over-consumption of affluent societies. Korten (1995: 280) argues that 'although their lifestyles do not correspond to our vision of consumer affluence, neither is it a vision of hardship'. Actually, these sustainable societies (with per capita incomes of US $700 to $7 500) are better characterized as having overcrowded roads, low life expectancy, low female literacy rates, high infant mortality rates, and massive inequalities. They also have very high rates of population growth – in part, a response to inequality and poverty (including gender) – but the fact of which is highly problematic for Korten, who combines a romanticization of poverty with a neo-Malthusian perspective on population (Korten, 1985: 34-5).

A slightly amended form of localism also pervades the work of post-development theory. Much is made in this work of autonomous spaces that evade the homogenising discourse of development (Esteva, 1992). Without wishing to downplay the ingenious ways in which the marginalized find ways of making a livelihood, the fact remains that marginalization also entails greater vulnerability. Social movements seeking to carry out progressive social change are not therefore concerned with rejecting modernity, but with greater access to (an admittedly radically transformed) modernity. Moreover, not all social movements have progressive politics, and post-development theory tends to romanticize resistance, providing little grounds for discriminating between the politics of specific social movements (Kiely, 1999; Parfitt, 2002). Friedman (1992: vii-viii) is surely right to state that, 'local action is severely constrained by global economic forces, structures of unequal wealth, and hostile class alliances. Unless these are changed as well, alternative development can never be more than a holding action to keep the poor from even greater misery'.

This is not to say that local initiatives are irrelevant (see below), but a politics based on a celebration of falsely homogenized local cultures is one that easily feeds into reactionary politics. In asking the question 'whose local culture?', one is forced to confront the fact that 'local communities' are often exclusive in terms of their relations to outsiders, and highly exploitative and oppressive in terms of class and gender relations (Kiely, 1999). A politics based on autonomy must address the question of what such autonomy means for different people (Jordan, 1994: 50). Post-development theory therefore over-emphasizes autonomy – be it from globalization, 'the West', or the development discourse – at the expense of social relations within localities.

While these comments suggest that an emphasis on the local is far from being intrinsically progressive, it does not mean, *contra* some extreme globalization theorists, that local places are either irrelevant or intrinsically reactionary. Indeed, globalization has not so much transcended as reinforced the importance of local place. Capital – financial as well as productive – does not exist in some hyper-mobile, post-social reality (Cox, 1997; Clark and O'Connor, 1997). It continues to locate – and concentrate – in specific locations. Thus, post-Fordist practices mean that final producers (or retailers) rely on a network of nearby suppliers to ensure that their inputs arrive 'just in time' for final assembly or sales (Kiely, 1998). The continued importance of location goes deeper than this however, because local places are not just functional to capital(ists), but are contested spaces. For example, Herod (2001) argues that a post-Fordist network of suppliers can actually give labour some strategic power, in that one particularly strategic supplier has the potential to undermine production for the whole company – a weak link in the network chain. This may then lead to important strategic question of how such withdrawals of labour link up to wider strategies of resistance, but they also clearly show the continued importance of the local.

Conclusion: Global Civil Society and Progressive Politics

This article has challenged the notion that global civil society represents a 'third sector', independent of both states and markets. It has argued that insofar as global civil society exists, it is part of a wider process of restructuring of the relationship between states and markets. Thus I agree with Colas' (2002: 43) characterization as civil society as 'a domain where the class antagonisms inherent in the structural power of both state and market play themselves out, chiefly through the medium of social movements'. Recent 'globalising' tendencies have not displaced the state; rather than theorising a zero sum game between state and civil society (or indeed markets), we need to theorize globalizing tendencies in the context of changing relations between state and civil society.

This point has enormous political implications. First, the notion that global civil society automatically represents a progressive 'globalization from below' must be questioned. This means that, for all the undoubted theoretical advances made in their different ways by (among others) Hardt and Negri, Held, and Falk, their assumptions concerning a progressive 'global sphere' working above and beyond a (reactionary?) 'national sphere' must be questioned. Politics based on demands placed on nation states *may* be reactionary, but they are not necessarily so. This point applies equally to the embrace of a 'global' or 'local' politics. Such stark separations are actually difficult to make, though contrary to some writers, it is still necessary to make them. What is true however, is that it a progressive politics is not one that falsely contrasts local, national or global politics as though these were not interlinked and as though there were not different political options both within and between these spaces. Thus, the 'Third Way' argument that it is progressive because it is explicitly global entirely ignores the choices that must be made in forging a progressive global politics (Kiely, 2002b). A similar argument can be made in relation to crude 'localizers' who oppose globalization in the name of 'the local'. In the case of the third way, the question must be 'whose global'; in the case of localisation, the question must be 'whose local'? Both analyses betray a 'spatial fetishism' (Massey, 2000), which ignores the social and political forces that operate within and between each sphere. My final point is that this discussion of global civil society and contemporary politics has far wider implications, for it should now be clear that contrary to the claims of some 'global' theorists (Giddens, 1994), we have not moved beyond the traditional politics of left and right.

Notes

[1] See, for example, Anthony Giddens (1991), who reifies globalization as a 'consequence of modernity', a description that is breathtaking for its lack of clarity and its confusion of

concept and social agency. For a carefully argued and devastating critique, see Rosenberg (2000).

[2] A similar point applies to theorists who exaggerate the speed of global interconnectedness to the point where meaning ceases to exist (Baudrillard, 1983), or where local places are irrelevant in the face of the 'space of flows' (Castells, 1989, 1996). Both approaches are in danger of reifying the global and ignoring the social agency involved in constructing – and resisting – (globalized) locations.

References

Anheier, H., Glasius, M. and Kaldor, M. (eds) (2001), *Global Civil Society 2001*, Oxford, Oxford University Press.

Archibugi, D. (2002), 'Demos and Cosmopolis', *New Left Review*, **13**, pp. 24-38.

Archibugi, D. and Held, D. (1995), 'Editors' Introduction', in D. Archibugi and D. Held (eds), *Cosmopolitan Democracy*, Cambridge, Polity Press.

Baudrillard, J. (1983), *In the Shadow of the Silent Majorities*, New York, Semiotext.

Brecher, J., Costello, T. and Smith. B. (2000), *Globalization from Below*, Cambridge, Mass., South End Press.

Brett, E. (1985), *The World Economy since the War*, London, Macmillan.

Burbach, R. (2001), *Globalization and Postmodern Politics*, London, Pluto.

Castells, M. (1989), *The Informational City*, Oxford, Blackwell.

Castells, M. (1996), *The Rise of the Network Society*, Oxford, Blackwell.

Castells, M. 1997), *The Power of Identity*, Oxford, Blackwell.

Clark, J. (2001), 'Ethical Globalization: The Dilemmas and Challenges of Internationalizing Civil Society', in M. Edwards and J. Gaventa (eds), *Global Citizen Action*, London, Earthscan.

Clark, G. and O'Connor, K. (1997), 'The Informational Content of Financial Products and the Spatial Structure of the Global Finance Industry', in K. Cox (ed.), *Spaces of Globalization*, New York, Guilford Press.

Cohen, R. and Rai, S. (eds) (2000), *Global Social Movements*, London, Athlone.

Colas, A. (2002), *International Civil Society*, Cambridge, Polity Press.

Collins, C., Gariyo, Z. and Burdon, T. (2001), 'Jubilee 2000: Citizen Action Across the North-South Divide', in M. Edwards and J. Gaventa (eds), *Global Citizen Action*, London, Earthscan.

Cox, K. (ed.) (1997), *Spaces of Globalization*, New York, Guilford Press.

De Angelis, M. (2001), 'From Movement to Society', in *On Fire*, London, One Off Press.

Edwards, M. (2000), *NGO Rights and Responsibilities*, London, Foreign Policy Centre.

Edwards, M. (2001), 'Introduction', in M. Edwards and J. Gaventa (eds), *Global Citizen Action*, London, Earthscan.

Escobar, A. (1995), *Encountering Development*, Princeton, Princeton University Press.

Escobar, A. (2001), 'A brief response to Ray Kiely's "Reply to Escobar"', *Development*, **43**(4) online, http://www.sidint.org/journal/online/Escobar434.htm.

Esteva, G. (1992), 'Development', in W. Sachs (ed.), *The Development Dictionary*, London, Zed Books.

Esteva, G. and Prakash, M. (1997), 'From Global Thinking to Local Thinking', in M. Rahnema and V. Bawtree (eds), *The Post-Development Reader*, London, Zed Books.

Falk, R. (1998), 'Global Civil Society: Perspectives, Initiatives and Movements', *Oxford Development Studies*, **26**, pp. 99-110.

Falk, R. (2000), 'Global Civil Society and the Democratic Prospect', in B. Holden (ed.), *Global Democracy*, London, Routledge.

Falk, R. (2000), 'Resisting "Globalization from Above" through "Globalization from Below"', in B. Gills (ed.), *Globalization and the Politics of Resistance*, London, Macmillan.

Fox, J. and Brown, L. (1998), *The Struggle for Accountability*, Cambridge, Mass., MIT Press.

Friedman, J. (1992), *Empowerment: The Politics of Alternative Development*, Oxford, Blackwell.

Giddens, A. (1991), *The Consequences of Modernity*, Cambridge, Polity Press.

Giddens, A. (1994), *Beyond Left and Right*, Cambridge, Polity Press.

Giddens, A. (2000), *The Third Way and its Critics*, Cambridge, Polity Press.

Giddens, A. (2002), 'The Third Way Can Beat the Far Right', *The Guardian*, May 3.

Glasius, M. (2001), 'Global Civil Society Comes of Age', at http://www.opendemocracy.net.

Goldsmith, E. and J. Mander (eds) (2001), *The Case Against the Global Economy*, London, Earthscan.

Goodman, D. and Watts, M. (eds) (1997), *Globalising Food*, London, Routledge.

Habermas, J. (1987), *The Theory of Communicative Action: System and Lifeworld*, Cambridge, Polity Press.

Hain, P. (2002), 'Embrace Global Action', at http://www.guardian.co.uk/Archive/Article.

Hardt, M. (2002), 'Today's Bandung', *New Left Review*, **14**, pp. 112-18.

Hardt, M. and Negri, A. (2000), *Empire*, Harvard, Harvard University Press.

Hardt, M. and Negri, A. (2001), 'What the Protestors in Genoa Want', in *On Fire*, London, One Off Press.

Held, D. (1995), *Democracy and the Global Order*, Cambridge, Polity Press.

Held, D. (1998), 'The Timid Tendency', *Marxism Today*, Nov/Dec special issue, pp. 24-7.

Held, D. (2000), 'The Changing Contours of Political Community: Rethinking Democracy in the Context of Globalisation', in B. Holden (ed.), *Global Democracy: Key Debates*, London, Routledge.

Held, D. and Hirst, P. (2002), 'Globalisation after 11 September', at http://www.opendemocracy.net.

Hensman, R. (2001), 'World Trade and Workers' Rights: In Search of an Internationalist Position', in P. Waterman and J. Wills (eds), *Space, Place and the New Labour Internationalisms*, Oxford, Blackwell.

Herod, A. (2001), 'Labour Internationalism and the Contradictions of Globalization: Or, Why the Local is Still Important in a Global Economy', in P. Waterman and J. Wills (eds), *Space, Place and the New Labour Internationalisms*, Oxford, Blackwell.

International Forum on Globalization (2002), *A Better World is Possible*, San Francisco, International Forum on Globalization.

Kessi, A. (2001), 'Millennium Round of the WTO under Fire from Both the Left and Right', in E. Yuen *et al.* (eds), *The Battle of Seattle*, New York, Soft Skull Press.

Kiely, R. (1998), 'Globalisation, Post-Fordism and the Contemporary Context of Development', *International Sociology*, **13**(1), pp. 95-114.

Kiely, R. (1999), 'The Last Refuge of the Noble Savage? A Critical Account of Post-Development', *European Journal of Development Research*, **11**(1), pp. 30-55.

Kiely, R. (2002a), 'Actually Existing Globalisation, Deglobalisation and the Political Economy of Anti-Capitalist Protest', *Historical Materialism*, **10**(1), pp. 93-121.

Kiely, R. (2002b), 'The Global Third Way versus Progressive Globalism', *Contemporary Politics*, **8**(3), pp. 167-84.

Kiely, R. (2003), 'The Race to the Bottom, and International Labour Solidarity', *Review: Journal of the Fernand Brudel Center*, **26**(1), pp. 67-88.

Klein, N. (2001), 'The Vision Thing: Are the Protests Unfocused or Are Critics Missing the Point?', in K. Danaher (ed.), *Democratizing the Global Economy*, Monroe, Common Courage Press.

Korten, D. (1995), *When Corporations Rule the World*, London, Earthscan.

Krebbers, E. and Schoenmaker, M. (2001), 'Seattle 1999: Wedding Party of the Left and Right?', in E. Yuen *et al.* (eds), *The Battle of Seattle*, New York, Soft Skull Press.

Lloyd, J. (2001), *The Protest Ethic*, London, Demos.

Massey, D. (2000), 'The Geography of Power', in B. Gunnell and D. Timms (eds), *After Seattle*, London, Catalyst.

McKay, G. (ed.) (1998), *DIY Culture*, London, Verso.

Melucci, A. (1980), 'The New Social Movements: A Theoretical Approach', *Social Science Information*, **19**(2), pp. 199-226.

Melucci, A. (1989), *Nomads of the Present: Social Movements and Individual Needs in Contemporary Society*, Philadelphia, Temple University Press.

Naidoo, K. and Tandon, R. (1999), *Civil Society at the Millennium*, West Hartford, Civicus.

Panitch, L. (with M. Shaw and P. Gowan) (2001), 'The State, Globalisation and the New Imperialism', *Historical Materialism*, **9**, pp. 3-38.

Parfitt, T. (2002), *The End of Development*, London, Pluto Press.

Pianta, M. (2001), 'Parallel Summits of Global Civil Society', in H. Anheier *et al.* (eds), *Global Civil Society*, Oxford, Oxford University Press.

Rosenberg, J. (2000), *The Follies of Globalisation Theory*, London, Verso.

Scott, A. and Street, J. (2001), 'From Media Politics to E-Protest? The Use of Popular Culture and New Media in Parties and Social Movements', in F. Webster (ed.), *Culture and Politics in the Information Age*, London, Routledge.

Smith, P. and Smythe, E. (2001), 'Globalisation, Citizenship and Technology: The Multilateral Agreement on Investment Meets the Internet', in F. Webster (ed.), *Culture and Politics in the Information Age*, London, Routledge.

Waterman, P. and Wills, J. (eds) (2001), *Place, Space and the New Labour Internationalisms*, Oxford, Blackwell.

World Social Forum (2002), 'Call of Social Movements' at http://www.forumsocialmundial. org/br/eng/portoalegrefinalenglis.asp.

Yuen, E. (2001), 'Introduction', in E. Yuen, G. Katsiaficas and D. Rose (eds), *The Battle of Seattle*, New York, Soft Skull Press.

Chapter 11

Global Citizenship, Globalization and Citizenship – An Unholy Trio?

Nigel Dower

Introduction

The purpose of this chapter is to defend the idea of global citizenship via an examination of the question: what are the relationships between global citizenship, globalization and citizenship? At first sight it may appear that there is an outright conflict between all three of them, but I shall argue for a broadly complementary account of the three key ideas – an intellectual *ménage à trois* with tensions!

Global Citizenship, Globalization and Citizenship: Some Arguments for Conflict

(i) Global Citizenship versus Globalization

It may be thought that globalization is primarily a process of global economic integration dominated by transnational corporations etc., and thus a remorseless juggernaut. This challenges the relevance of global citizenship in two ways:

First, the significant influence of globally concerned individuals is seen as marginalized. Insofar as agents are trying to pursue or promote certain kinds of ethically informed agendas such alleviating world poverty, addressing human rights violations, protecting the environment or responding to violence, these efforts are likely to come to very little because of the pervasive economic forces within the globalized economy. If they are addressed, it is only because they are consistent with the economic imperative of the market – and thus not addressed as global citizens would want them to be addressed.

Thus the normative underpinning of global citizenship is undermined, which brings us to the second point. If we accept the philosophical adage (derived from Kantian ethics) that 'ought implies can', then ethical pronouncements about what one should do, what everyone should do or what should be done only make sense on the assumption that it is possible for this to be done. If then the determinism implicit in globalization means things cannot be otherwise than they broadly are/will be, then global 'oughts' are irrelevant. Perhaps individuals can still make private judgments about what *they* should do e.g. to distance themselves from the world or to do their bit to make a few others better off, but broad prescriptions addressed to others generally or for changes in public policy flounder on the rocks of impossibility. But it is precisely the commitment of individuals to try and change the world according to their moral visions of a realizable 'better world' that marks the engagement typical of a self-styled global citizen.

(ii) Global Citizenship versus Citizenship

We can see tensions between global citizenship and citizenship both in ethical terms and in institutional terms. The idea of global citizenship has at least two elements to it, an affirmation of a certain kind of global ethic which includes emphasis upon global responsibility i.e. significant responsibility that is transnational, and a claim about some form of institutional embodiment – i.e. what the 'citizenship' bit is all about.

Ethically then global citizenship implies a cosmopolitan ethic and this challenges the ethical assumption behind citizenship both in its theoretical roots and in its prioritization of duties within states. Citizenship, it may be thought, is based on some form of communitarianism – that ethical norms and the scope of obligations arise within the historical traditions of particular societies or political communities. In a strong form, the approach may simply deny what global citizenship asserts, the existence of a cosmopolitan ethic or universal values and transnational obligations. But at the very least, in a weaker form, this idea at least suggests that even if there are some global obligations, they are weak compared with the duties of citizens within their own communities. So there is a conflict over the relative priorities to be given to society-based obligations and global obligations.

Institutionally citizenship of a global political order/community would undermine the status of citizenship in a state. If 'citizenship' is to have any real significance it must refer to either membership of a world state with a world government or at least of some formal political institutions in which individuals have a political role not mediated by the international system of states e.g. some form of global democracy. Insofar as those who in calling themselves (aspirationally) global citizens want us to move to such new global political arrangements, then what they want conflicts with and undermines the idea of citizenship within the state which depends upon the continuation of separate autonomous 'sovereign' states. We can already see this kind of conflict when we look at the idea of EU citizenship which for many is inconsistent with the citizenship of member states as we have known it.

(iii) Citizenship versus Globalization

If we turn to the third pairing of our three ideas, we can also see a *prima facie* case for seeing oppositions between the two ideas.

First, globalization undermines the capacity of citizens to control their own fate within their own borders. This does not of course formally stop them being citizens of their own country, but it does undermine one of the traditional assumptions about what it means to be a citizen of a state, particularly a republican state, namely collective control over the life-conditions enjoyed within that state. This undermining can be seen both in respect to socio-economic rights and in respect to political rights. With regard to the former we see for example many examples of jobs lost within a country because of cheaper imports or because firms disinvest in a country and engage in foreign investment with cheaper work forces. With regard to the latter we have what is called the 'democratic deficit', less and less control through the democratic processes within a country to determine the broad economic, social and legal framework of that country – because of the wider geo-political trends in the world, increasingly significant international law, or for some countries which are in the EU increasingly regulation by distant bureaucracy.

Citizenship loyalties/identities are also weakened because of the influences of cultural globalization. So far I have focused on economic globalization but we also have to recognize the influence of the globalization of communication which is creating new kinds of communities and identities – what Scholte calls the 'deterritorialization' of social space (Scholte, 2000). Insofar as citizenship depends not merely on formal institutions but also on certain kinds of mind-sets, the impact of globalization is to weaken or change those mind-sets, so that eventually the mental core of citizenship may become seriously eroded. This it may be thought is partly brought about by idea of global citizenship (itself as we shall see later being an aspect of globalization), but also through the development of many kinds of trans-societal identities, many of them highly 'particularist' i.e. focused on some particular concerns such as indigenous peoples or gay rights. These are what Scholte calls particularist communities and solidarities (Scholte, 2000).

I now turn to the second main task of the chapter which is to reconsider these pairs with a view to seeing how far they can be accommodated with each other. It is not part of my intention to argue that there are no tensions between them, even as I am going to interpret them, even less to deny that, as interpreted by some thinkers, there are serious antagonisms between them. Since each of these concepts is contestable, it is not surprising that on some views, conflicts abound. But at least there are plausible interpretations of them which, I suggest, lessen the conflict and make much of the common ground between them.

Globalization and Global Citizenship

My strategy in this part of the chapter is to show that first we should understand globalization as providing the 'space' within which global citizenship is *possible*; second that in fact certain aspects of globalization are *necessary* for global citizenship; and third, that those aspects of globalization can be regarded as *sufficient* for us to be able to talk of global citizenship as applicable in the modern world.

(i) The Possibility of Choice within a Multi-Faceted Process

It is important to see globalization as a multi-faceted process within which there are various possibilities for future developments, and therefore as not undermining the possibility of the kinds of 'oughts' which global citizens are likely to come up with. This kind of picture emerges very clearly if we recognize the many dimensions to globalization. For instance, Scholte (2000) identifies four key areas of production, governance, community and knowledge. If we recognize that there is nothing inevitable about the directions globalization takes, then there is as it were a social space of possibilities for ethical agency to engage. This does not, of course, mean that globalization *will* proceed as global citizens or globally oriented citizens want it to (indeed not all global citizens would agree about the direction they want anyway), merely that it *could*, or at least there are areas in which the way it goes may well be influenced by the collective actions of agents who have certain ethical agendas and work for them.

One of the key issues is over the relative power of the "prince, merchant, citizen" (Nerfin, 1987), that is nation-states, multinational companies of global civil society. This is not a foregone conclusion – much depends on how citizens themselves conceive of themselves. Recently Mary Robinson is reported to have said "there are two superpowers in the world today – the USA and global civil society!" This may seem a little exaggerated but it makes the important point that the potential for global influence of ordinary people networking is considerable.

The influence of the 'citizen' can be seen in at least two ways. First, there is the influence that can be exerted within the state through active participation in governance, and also on companies through the exercise of ethical consumer/investor power. That is, individuals with global concerns can write letters to parliamentarians, join organizations that lobby, or actually join political parties and work to change priorities within them. Additionally, it is well recognized that one way of creating global change is through the patterns of buying and investing. One may vote every now and then but one buys thing regularly, so the potential for change if enough consumers wished to signal new priorities or enough investors influenced the companies they invested in is great.

Second, there is the influence as a third force globally in 'global civil society', whether this is through formally constituted Non Governmental Organizations, more informal global social movements, informal networking on individuals with shared concerns (e.g. through the internet).

(ii) Globalization as a Precondition of Global Citizenship

If we look at global citizenship as essentially an *ethical* commitment, it may seem at first sight that globalization is not a precondition of global citizenship. Ethically globalization is certainly at one level irrelevant. Clearly cosmopolitanism predates globalization, and as an ethical position does not presuppose general acceptance/social embodiment etc. That is, the cosmopolitan ethical vision of the equality of human beings in one moral community goes back to the ancient Stoics and is in any case a vision that can be accepted by a thinker (thinking for herself as a global citizen) without any reference to globalization at all, without reference to what consensuses have emerged or what other people actually believe (Heater, 2002; Dower, 2003).

Yet, at another level globalization is very relevant to global citizenship. The argument has been made that *global* citizenship is distinct from earlier forms of *world* citizenship precisely because contemporary globalization makes possible new forms of identity (O'Byrne, 2003). This argument applies even at the ethical level. The *kind* of global ethic which is now accepted and which accepts a *significant* dimension of responsibility as global in scope (not just the acceptance of a *universal* framework) is partly a function of increased transnational knowledge and capacity. Nor it is an accident that when we speak of a global ethic we are not merely speaking of the ethical position of a particular individual thinker but of *shared* values – not shared in the minimal sense of 'happening to be the same' but shared in the sense of 'being recognized by people as the same as what is accepted by other people from all over the world?' And for this latter form of a global ethic the processes of globalization are actually highly significant.

If we look at global citizenship institutionally, first we can see that the communications/technology revolution has facilitated the development of global civil society. These institutions which exist in global public space/sphere are part of the *embodiment* of global citizenship. Second, the development of international institutions (e.g. the United Nations) and international law has created a global framework for more formal elements of global citizenship to because established – primarily (at the moment) the human rights framework, but incipiently the development of global duties of individuals. The latter is illustrated by the recent development of the International Criminal Court which established that individuals can be brought before the court for crimes against humanity.

(iii) Are Developments in Global Civil Society and International Law Sufficient for Global Citizenship (Beyond a Purely Ethical Interpretation)?

It may be thought that whilst globalization is a sufficiently open-textured process to *allow for* the possibility of the appropriate institutions of global citizenship to develop, and that current developments in global civil society and in international law certainly provide effective avenues through which *ethical* agendas of global citizenship can be promoted, nevertheless globalization has not provided the development of the right institutions for global citizenship in a full institutional sense to exist. This takes us to the heart of some of the more controversial aspects of the global citizenship debate, and I merely scratch the surface of this issue in what I remark below (see O'Byrne, 2003; Heater, 2002; Dower, 2000; Cohen, 1996).

The arguments against the claim that we are now global citizens may come in two forms, one form from those who oppose the idea altogether as inappropriate both now and in the future, and another from those who like the idea, welcome its future development, but deny its current existence. One of those in the former category is David Miller who argues that "citizenship in the full sense requires a political community" (Miller, 1999). This does not exist at the global level and its development is neither desirable nor in a sense possible since what is distinctive of and valuable about citizenship would be lost if it was not a feature of a 'bounded' community. On the other hand, those who favour its development may favour world government or the idea of world federalism or, alternatively, something less than world government but still a new kind of formal political order like cosmopolitan democracy (Archibugi and Held, 1995). Active engagement in global civil society is not sufficient. The human rights framework is inadequate both because it fails to capture the 'active participation' element essential to citizenship and because of its lack of enforceability. Only with formal political institutions would we have *global democracy* and real participation in *global governance*.

This line needs resisting because it relies on too formal an account of citizenship, democracy and governance, and underestimates the importance of the 'rights' dimension to citizenship (see also Dower, 2000).

Global governance may be defined as "the sum of the many ways individuals and institutions, public and private, manage their common affairs" at the global level (Commission on Global Governance, 1995: 2). Democracy may be seen as "prevailing when the members of a polity determine – collectively, equally and without arbitrarily imposed constraints – the policies that shape their destinies" (Scholte, 2000: 262). Given these two ways of thinking about global governance and democracy, it is plausible to see what globally oriented agents currently do through NGOs and available political processes as contribution to global governance and as exercising their democratic rights.

Thus on this view citizenship is participation in public affairs via whatever organs of expression are available. If as often happens, experts in NGOs contribute at international conferences to the shaping of international law, these individuals and these NGOs are contributing to governance and seeking in legitimate ways to influence global processes; the laws may be formally the agreements of states in the international society of states, but substantively, the shape and contents of laws and policies bears their influence. Likewise, the kinds of pressures of ordinary people protesting at meetings like Genoa 2001 indicate another kind of pressure which can be exerted – though we should note that there are many other ways of exercising influence in the world, either via political processes or in quite other ways. With the example of Genoa in mind it is easy to ask the question: was influence like this democratic? One may reply: "Why not?", if formal democratic mechanisms are absent and if, as is generally accepted, similar influence in domestic politics (writing letters, lobbying etc. i.e. exerting an influence out of proportion to one's voting strength) is generally regarded as democratic.

I now turn to the 'rights' element of citizenship. Although some see this as unimportant when compared with the active participation element (e.g. Miller, 1999), its significance should not be understated. One key point is the influential analysis given by T.H. Marshall (1973), which stresses the importance to citizenship of the bearing of formal rights, not least the socio-economic rights to receive benefits. If this is a significant part of 'being a citizen' within a state, it is entirely appropriate to point to the parallel in Human Rights law, which, even if not enforceable in the way domestic law is enforceable, provides a framework for appeals, a certain status, and consequently for many a certain empowerment to stand up for the interests of themselves and their group. The latter point reminds us that emphasizing rights does not mean emphasizing a 'passive' side to citizenship – defending one's rights may be as active an expression of citizenship as promoting the public good.

Citizenship and Global Citizenship

(i) Institutional Issues

Would citizenship of the state somehow be undermined if we became global citizens in an institutional sense? As already indicated in the previous section, the answer somewhat depends on whether one thinks that the institutional embodiment of global citizenship needs to involve something like a world state, or some form of supra-national political institutions in which citizens participated in decision-making at this supra-national level, or whether the institutional element is to be understood in a more modest way to involve participation in global civil society and/or the bearing of international legal rights and duties. If it is the latter, there is no formal conflict between the status of citizenship and that of global citizenship. Even if it is the former, there is only a conflict if one takes the meaning of citizenship within a state to be premised on sovereignty and precisely the absence of political participation at levels higher than the state which undermines that sovereignty. But such an interpretation of the value and meaning of citizenship is hardly necessary since there is no reason in principle why we cannot be citizens at different levels. That is precisely what we have with European citizenship alongside citizenship of the various member states.

(ii) Theoretical Ethical Issues

As we noted earlier citizenship involves membership of political community which confers special rights of members and duties to fellow members far in excess of any global commitments. This conflicts with cosmopolitanism because the latter asserts (i) the equal status of all human beings in that the interests of someone in another country are in principle of the same importance of those in one own country; (ii) an *a priori* theoretical grounding according to which the basic moral status of human beings is understood in terms of the universal characteristics of humanity or rationality, rather than in terms of what is established in any particular community. However this is an over-simple contrast. In a number of respects we can see, even at the theoretical level, grounds for denying this stark standoff.

There would, first of all, be a problem if cosmopolitanism were asserted as a set of first order principles for all actual decision-making; that is, every decision one makes has to take into the account the effects on any human beings, their interests or their rights. This is however counterintuitive and not generally how it is presented. It is better to see cosmopolitanism as supplying second order justifying principle for the development of rules, rights, institutions including institutions like political communities as best able to advance universal goals (see also Dower, 1998). This can be seen more clearly in the case of other types of relations like personal relations (e.g. the commitments we have to family or friends). It is not inconsistent with asserting the equality of all human beings to devote more of one attention to one's son's interest than to one's neighbour's son's interests. Furthermore most people reasonably devote much of their time promoting or protecting their own well being and believe they have a right to do so whilst fully accepting that one is no more important ethically than any other person. Likewise then the recognition that one has special relations and obligations towards members of one's own community or state is not in itself to deny the cosmopolitan perspective – though as a matter of fact most people probably put too much emphasis upon these special obligations (on which, see the next section).

One way of seeing the relationship between cosmopolitanism and the value of citizenship is to see the value of the latter as either derivative or constitutive or both – derivative in the sense just indicated as providing a way in which universal values are being promoted and protected, but also constitutive in the sense that amongst the cosmopolitan values which may be recognized may well be, and arguably should be, the universal value of both active participation in the communities of which one is part and the enjoyment of rights protected by laws and conventions. These are the values constitutive of citizenship. So the value of citizenship on this view need not be linked to any kind of communitarianism which denies or marginalizes universal values.

What however if the value of citizenship in political community seen as derived from a communitarian basis *and not derived from cosmopolitan foundation* as suggested above? Would we then have the contrast I indicated above? Even if this is accepted, it is still possible to have a cosmopolitan framework *in addition to* the communitarian position.

First, ethics may be at different levels: that is, our ethical thought derives from at least two sources, first a universal ethical framework in which all human beings have a certain status and second, a more specific set of ethical norms derived from a particular ethical tradition within an established community. It is possible to see Locke's ideas of ethical relations between human beings *as such* who are not in political community like a Swiss meeting an Indian in the woods as presupposing a basic universal ethic, whatever more complex moral framework may develop as a result of political association (Locke, 1960: 277).

Second, cosmopolitanism does not have to be seen as providing a *complete* ethical theory, rather a framework of basic goods/rights to be promoted or protected, beyond and above which other values are a matter of social variation and construction.

Third, in any case it is possible to see cosmopolitanism as derived from actual developments in *global community*. In other words, there may not be a deep conflict between communitarianism and cosmopolitanism if it is recognized that at least in the late 20th century and now there have developed sufficiently robust relationships, connections and shared practices and norms across the world for the idea of world community or at least world communities to have some social reality to it, rather than merely being an ideal in the minds of idealists. I say 'world community' or at least 'world communities' because it must be recognized that we are a long way off having a single world community of shared practices and values. There is however no doubt that *real* communities are no longer limited to certain geographical areas, whether local communities or nation-states. Whatever else globalization has done, it has certainly contributed to the development of these trans-boundary communities. So if one takes the view (which I personally judge to be one-sided) that all justification derives from communitarian premises, there is no reason in principle to deny that we may have both the community of citizenship and global community – this is no more of a problem than accepting alongside each other the community of citizenship and the community of one's town or neighbourhood.

Although relativists may remain sceptical about this, one can point to a number of developments in the modern world that point to the growing convergence of values shared by people who see themselves belonging to global communities. A powerful example of this is the development of human rights legislation ever since the Universal Declaration of Human Rights of 1948. It is not merely the development of human rights law that it important, it is the development of a moral culture in which the basic entitlements of human beings are increasingly accepted. More recent examples might be the Declaration Toward a Global Ethic in 1993 by the Parliament of the World's Religions (Küng and Kuschel, 1993) or the promulgation of the Earth Charter ever since its official launch in March 2000.

I have above outlined a number of different ways in which the value in cosmopolitanism and the value of citizenship can be cashed out. A full evaluation of these options and their critical comparison has not been attempted here and would take us away from the main point of this chapter. This is that on any of these views about the relationship, there is no reason in principle why the value of citizenship cannot be asserted alongside the value of cosmopolitanism. The *idea* of citizenship does not rule out the *idea* of cosmopolitanism or vice versa. Of course the relative importance of each may vary according to the different theories. So in practice those who stress the values of citizenship may see themselves as in conflict with those who make moral claims about what we should do from the cosmopolitan point of view.

(iii) Practice

In practice then there are issues to do with relative priorities amongst those who accept that there are specific obligations arising from membership of a particular political community and also accept some kind of global ethic and hence some degrees or kinds of trans-national obligations. Those calling themselves global citizens or advocating cosmopolitanism will press for stronger obligations with a global reach, whether for individuals, for government policy or for the ground rules of international trade and investment, those who resist global citizenship discourse and 'cosmopolitanism' arguing for some such obligations but on a rather smaller scale. Wherever one draws the lines, there will also always be internal conflicts (i.e. internal to each person's thinking) over the allocation of time, effort and resources. More money spent on Oxfam may mean less money spent on Shelter, more energy spent and advocated for energizing domestic politics may mean less energy spent or advocated for supporting the work of international NGOs and so on. The relative importance of 'national' obligations and other particularist agent-relative obligations as against the pull of cosmopolitan obligations is subject to constant negotiation/contestation. The debate in *For Love of Country* (Cohen, 1996) responding to Martha Nussbaum's lead article 'Cosmopolitanism and Patriotism' illustrates well the issues involved (Nussbaum, 1996). Each thinker will have her preferred priorities depending on the extent to which she accepts cosmopolitanism and how she understands its demands.

However, conflicts at this level should not be exaggerated. They certainly do not show a deep conflict between citizenship and global citizenship. Indeed a rather more fundamental issue centres on the relative amount of time, effort and resources people feel obliged to devote to 'public' causes whether in their own country or further afield *taken together* compared with what they feel obligated to devote to their close circle of friends and relatives and more particularly to exercising their right to pursue their own interests and projects. The issue is not peculiar to cosmopolitan ethics, but at the heart of ethics as such.

So far as the supposed conflict between the pull of citizenship and the pull of global citizenship goes, there may be a complementarity, since amongst the concerns that activate citizens these days are precisely global concerns. Pursuing global concerns may be seen as an expression of citizenship, whether through influencing or working within political parties or through joining NGOs that seek to influence national policies.

This leads to the point that the practice of governments is in part a function of an electorate's preferences, which may become increasingly cosmopolitan in orientation. This point is partly descriptive and partly normative. Descriptively it is unrealistic to suppose that governments will pursue foreign polices which are seriously out of line with what their electorates want – governments may lead or drag their feet, but the leash is so to speak only so long either way. So if we expect governments to pursue more globally oriented policies this is at least partly a function of what their citizens actually accept or promote. (It is of course partly a function of pressures from other states in the 'society of states', too.) Normatively, there is a limit to what governments 'ought' to do if the do not have a mandate from their people. Of course at one level we can say and indeed need to say that a government ought to do something (for example, for a believer in nuclear disarmament, to get rid of nuclear weapons), but that cannot be the whole story ethically since the relation which a government has with its people (and other countries) sets limits to what is ethically possible. So the tendency for people to become global citizens or at least, whether they use the terminology of global citizenship or not, to advocate globally oriented policies is crucial to creating the domain of political possibility within which a government is able to act. In many ways the re-ordering of domestic politics may the best hope for cosmopolitan agendas.

Citizenship and Globalization

The above analysis has established that as between global citizenship and globalization and between global citizenship and citizenship, there is no basis for any deep or inevitable conflict. Insofar as people accept the reality of globalization and continue to accept the values of citizenship, they have no reason to resist the acceptance of global citizenship. Indeed in the course of the analysis various positive argument for global citizenship have emerged. But the above analysis has also provided the materials for claiming a more positive relation between citizenship and globalization as well. Whilst a rapprochement between these two is not my main concern here, I conclude with a brief indication of how it goes, especially as this confirms several of the theses about global citizenship I have put forward.

If there is a democratic deficit in connection with citizenship and the kind of collective control or autonomy which citizenship was meant to confer on citizens, then the best hope may well be to strengthen the 'third force' through global citizenship and global civil society – and for these to occur globalization needs to occur. That is, one kind of globalization is needed to help counter the effects of other kinds of globalization. But the effect on citizenship of that form of globalization, which underpins global citizenship and global civil society, is more direct or intimate that this way putting it suggests. The effect is not that of a separate set of processes acting as an outside 'ally'. As we noted in the previous section, globally oriented agency may actually be channeled through domestic political processes, i.e. through *reoriented* national politics and the influence of national NGOs on domestic politics.

Global issues require at the very least 'globally oriented citizens' most of whom only become so because of the globalization of communication and community in the world. This, as Parekh has argued, may be an appropriate interpretation in the current world of what it means now to be a global citizen (Parekh, 2002) – especially if one thinks the *institutional* component for global citizenship is not yet present in the world). It will be apparent from what I have said earlier that I do think an institutional interpretation in terms of informal institutions and legal human rights is appropriate. But the point remains that, whether one stresses global citizenship as 'globally oriented citizens' or as something more than this, in neither sense is global citizenship as embodied in the processes of globalization hostile to citizenship. Indeed quite the reverse in providing resources through which the proper status of citizenship can be defended in the face of other less acceptable aspects of globalization. This is not to deny that insofar as citizenship is tied to the nation-state, then to the extent that the nation-state is itself subject to pressures from globalization, then citizenship as we have known it is too. But if citizenship is understood more broadly as membership of political communities which are in significant ways subject to the will of its members, then the future of citizenship is not necessarily under threat. Part of its being secure depends upon its linkages with not antagonisms with its cosmopolitan cousin – global citizenship.

References

Archibugi, D. and Held, D. (eds) (1995), *Cosmopolitan Democracy: An Agenda for a New World Order*, Cambridge, Polity Press.

Cohen J. (ed.) (1996), *For Love of Country: Debating the Limits of Patriotism*, Boston, Beacon Books.

Commission on Global Governance (1995), *Our Global Neighbourhood*, Oxford, Oxford University Press.

Dower, N. (1998), *World Ethics – The New Agenda*, Edinburgh, Edinburgh University Press.

Dower, N. (2000), 'The Idea of Global Citizenship – A Sympathetic Assessment', *Global Society*, **14**(4).

Dower, N. (2003), *Introduction to Global Citizenship*, Edinburgh, Edinburgh University Press.

Heater, D. (2002), *World Citizenship*, London, Continuum.

Küng, H. and Kuschel, K.J. (1993), *A Global Ethic: The Declaration of the Parliament of the World's Religions*, London, SCM Press.

Locke, J. (1960; original 1689), *Second Treatise of Government*, in P. Laslett (ed.), Cambridge, Cambridge University Press.

Marshall, T.H. (1973), *Class, Citizenship and Social Development*, Westport CN, Greenwood Press.

Miller, D. (1999), 'Bounded Citizenship', in K. Hutchings and R. Dannreuther (eds), *Cosmopolitan Citizenship*, Basingstoke, Macmillan.

Nerfin, M. (1987), 'Neither Prince nor Merchant: Citizen', *Development Dialogue*, 1.

Nussbaum, M. (1996), 'Cosmopolitanism and Patriotism', in J. Cohen (ed.), *For Love of Country: Debating the Limits of Patriotism*, Boston, Beacon Press.

O'Byrne, D.J. (2003), *The Dimensions of Global Citizenship: Political Identity beyond the Nation-State*, London, Frank Cass.

Parekh, B. (2002), 'Cosmopolitanism and Global Citizenship', *Review of International Studies*, **31**(2).

Scholte, J.A. (2000), *Globalization: A Critical Introduction*, Basingstoke, Palgrave.

Chapter 12

Concluding Remarks: Global and Local, Migration and Morality

John Eade

I have decided to contribute some concluding remarks rather than a conclusion because the chapters clearly indicate the diversity of approach and interpretation which people take on the issue of global ethics and civil society. Given the range of views expressed here, I feel justified in drawing on my own theoretical and substantive experience to elaborate briefly on some of the themes which these and other chapters explore.

Global and Local

Several contributors point to the intimate relationship between the global and the local. Against widespread popular assumptions that global forces were threatening to crush local institutions, academics have pointed out for some time now the ways in which global and local interact and how local social, cultural and political actors can exploit the global means of communication to link up with other local actors around the globe. Local actors can also reconstruct local traditions in active resistance to global forces, leading *inter alia* to ethnic revivalisms and retraditionalization (see, for example, Robertson, 1992; Hall; 1992; Nederveen Pieterse, 1995; Appadurai, 1996; Smith, 2001). The nation-state can be seen as part of this local resistance and reworking, so that some prefer to focus on transnationalism rather than globalisation. The journal, *Global Networks*, tries to have the best of both worlds by adding the sub-title *A Journal of Transnational Affairs*!

London vividly illustrates the intimate relationship between global and local. Its inhabitants and neighbourhoods have long been influenced by trading networks stretching around the globe. Indeed, London's position as a world or global city (see King, 1990; Sassen, 1991; Hall,2004), which acts as a prime site for global flows of capital and people, cannot be adequately understood outside the historical context of nineteenth and twentieth century colonial dominance and continuing neo-colonial economic, social and political links (see Eade, 1997, 2000).

The intertwining of global and local, empire and post-empire can be seen across the metropolis but here I will focus on my research interest – the East End. During the nineteenth century this area of London rapidly expanded with the growth of the docks, associated industries and manufacturing. In popular mythology the East End was seen as the dangerous Other to respectable London stretching westwards from the City of London and the West End. Here a restless working class struggled with poverty, insecure employment and wretched housing conditions. To this volatile mix were added the divisions of ethnicity and race through the settlement of Irish Catholics and East European Jews, for example (see Fishman, 1997).

The break-up of this industrial economic and social order overlapped with the unravelling of empire. The process had already begun before the Second World War but accelerated after 1945 through a vigorous rehousing programme, the creation of New Towns outside London which recruited skilled East End workers, and from the 1960s the gradual closing of the docks and associated industries. Yet while the empire unravelled, so migration from Britain's (ex)colonies rapidly expanded. In the East End migrant workers from East Pakistan, which became Bangladesh in 1971, settled north of the docks and revived the garment industry. As they spread across the western wards of Tower Hamlets during the 1980s, the dock localities were radically transformed by another migrant influx. White middle class settlers occupied the new housing generated by the redevelopment of the redundant docks as an extension of the City of London – the city's global finance and business heartland.

This part of the East End has undergone dramatic economic and social changes during the last fifty years, therefore, which vividly illustrate the power of global forces. At the same time people's understanding of those global forces have been expressed through a varied reinterpretation of what locality means to them. Here I want to focus on what the global and local has meant for Bangladeshis and the relevance of their diverse understandings to global ethics and civil society.

Reinterpreting Locality in a New Society: Some Bangladeshi Views

Much has been made of the ways in which the global flows of people, information and goods have impacted on localities during the late 20th and early 21st centuries. However, recent migration has frequently built on links forged during colonial rule and Bangladeshi settlement in London's East End is an example of these long established ties. Bangladeshi *lascars* (seamen) had been visiting the East End since at least the early 19th century and many among the first generation of Bangladeshi settlers built on these ties (see Visram, 1986; Adams, 1987; Gardner, 1995). The key difference between them, of course, lay in their exposure to the East End. The Bangladeshi migrants of the 1960s and 1970s usually saw their stay as temporary but many ended up staying and their children and grandchildren have put down even deeper roots in the metropolis (see Gardner, 2002). As a result, there has been an important change in what is transmitted through the transnational networks between these 'London' Bangladeshis and their relatives in Bangladesh and other parts of the globe, such as the Gulf states and N. America. The flow of information, for example, still concerns what is going on 'back home' but it also revolves around what is happening in the new home. Community debates are shaped by the experience of settling in London and carving out a distinctively

British Bangladeshi future in an ethnically and racially different society (see Eade, Fremeaux and Garbin, 2002).

These debates revolve around the issue of identity (personal and collective) and how to live out certain key identities based on national background, language, religion, gender, sexuality, generation and occupation. The debates in the public realm tended to become polarized between secularist and Islamist positions, although closer inspection revealed considerable similarities between these outwardly opposing views (see Eade and Garbin, 2002). Morality was a persistent theme in these debates, i.e. how could one live as a Bangladeshi Muslim in a predominantly secular western society? Although the question of morality focussed on local contexts, there was also an awareness of the ways in which local contexts were globally linked. Discussions about the future of 'arranged marriage' in the British context, for example, acknowledged the issue's wider ramifications given the transnational links between Bangladeshis in Britain, N. America, the Middle East and Bangladesh itself (see Samad and Eade, 2003). Local marriage customs were compared with Muslim practices elsewhere and with the moral codes which bound together members of the global Muslim community (*umma*).

This local discussion was clearly shaped by the global flow of information between relatives and friends and by the media. However, it raised the question which others have addressed in this volume – how can people look beyond globally interconnected communities to a global civil society? Migration to London had encouraged Bangladeshi settlers to make a number of new comparisons – between localities, genders, religions, classes, nations, for example. For some people there was an emerging sense of being part of a global Muslim community. However, few were prepared to locate the *umma* within a global civil society, because this would relativize Islam and appear to lead towards a predominantly secular vision of the globe.

What are the implications of this particular case study for the discussion of global ethics and civil society developed in this volume? There is much evidence of the cultural diversity which Bhikhu Parekh highlights as one of the principles of a global ethic (see p. 30 above). Bangladeshis Muslim settlement in London also illustrates the ways in which transnational networks have long been sustained across territorial boundaries, thereby encouraging greater integration between people around the globe. However, the growing strength of Islamist ideas among Bangladeshis and other British Muslims militates against Parekh's assertion that '[n]o culture has the monopoly of truth' (p. 30). While there is a degree of dialogue between community leaders and non-Muslims at local and national level, the belief that Islam provides the only true guide to life in a predominantly secular and, in various ways, hostile western society appears to have wide appeal. For many young Bangladeshis in particular, who are coping with the exigencies of everyday life in an area of the global city typified by deep social and economic inequality, identification with a morally superior Muslim community has great emotional and psychological advantages. We are closer to the world of passion and heat described by Kate Nash in her contribution than the cool cosmopolitanism which leads to cultural relativism and, of course, to my own academic disciplines!

References

Adams, C. (1987), *Across Seven Seas and Thirteen Rivers: Life Stories of Sylhetti Settlers in Britain*, London, THAP Books.

Appadurai, A. (1996), *Modernity At Large: Dimensions of Globalization*, Minneapolis, University of Minnesota Press.

Eade, J. (1989), *The Politics of Community: The Bangladeshi Community in East London*, Aldershot, Avebury.

Eade, J. (1992), 'Quests for Belonging: Bangladeshis in Tower Hamlets' in A. Cambridge et al., *Where You Belong: Government and Black Culture*, Aldershot, Avebury.

Eade, J. (1996), 'Nationalism, Community and the Islamization of Urban Space', in B. Metcalf (ed.), *Making Muslim Spaces in North America and Europe*, Berkeley, University of California Press.

Eade, J. (ed.) (1997), *Living the Global City: Globalization as Local Process*, London and New York, Routledge.

Eade, J. (2000), *Placing London: From Imperial Capital to Global City*, Oxford, Berghahn Books.

Eade, J. and Garbin, D. (2002), 'Changing Narratives of Violence, Struggle and Resistance: Bangladeshi and the Competition for Resources in the Global City', *Oxford Development Studies*, **30**(2), pp. 137-49.

Eade, J., Fremeaux, I. and Garbin, D. (2002), 'The Political Construction of Diasporic Communities in the Global City', in P. Gilbert (ed.), *Imagined Londons*, Albany, State University of New York Press.

Fishman, W. (1997), 'Allies in the Promised Land: Reflections on the Irish and the Jews in the East End', in A. Kershen (ed.), *The Promised land? The Migrant Experience in a Capital City*, Aldershot, Avebury.

Gardner, K. (1995), *Global Migrants, Local Lives: Travel and Transformation in Rural Bangladesh*, Oxford, Clarendon Press.

Gardner, K. (2002), *Age, Narrative and Migration: The Life Course and Life Histories of Bengali Elders in London*, Oxford, Berg.

Hall, P. (2004), 'European Cities in a Global World', in F. Eckardt and D. Hassenpflug (eds), *The European City in Transition*, Frankfurt, P. Lang.

Hall, S. (1992), 'The Question of Cultural Identity', in S. Hall, D. Held and A. McGrew (eds), *Modernity and Its Futures*, Cambridge, Polity, and Oxford, Blackwell.

King, A. (1990), *Global Cities: Post-Imperialism and the Internationalization of London*, London, Routledge.

Nederveen Pieterse, J. (1995), 'Globalization as Hybridization', in M. Featherstone et al. (eds), *Global Modernities*, London, Sage.

Robertson, R. (1992), *Globalization*, London, Sage.

Samad, Y. and Eade, J. (2003), *Community Perceptions of Forced Marriage*, London, Foreign and Commonwealth Office.

Sassen, S. (1991), *The Global City*, Princeton, NJ, Princeton University Press.

Smith, M.P. (2001), *Transnational Urbanism: Locating Globalization*, Oxford, Blackwell.

Visram, R. (1986), *Ayahs, Lascars and Princes: Indians in Britain 1700-1947*, London, Pluto Press.

Index

Locke, John 161
Logsdon, J.M. 111, 112, 113
London 166–7

McIntosh, M. 112
MacIntyre, A. 77
Mackey, J.P. 75
Macklin, Ruth 87n14
MacLeod, Sorcha 11, 12, 121–37
Marchetti, Raffaele 9, 57–73
market order 49, 50
Marshall, T.H. 159–60
Marx, Karl 3, 5, 9, 52, 55
Marxism 140, 145
Mason, E.S. 116
Means, C.G. 109
media 18, 42, 43
medical ethics 76, 77
Melucci, A. 140, 141
Merton, R. 95
Micklethwaite, J. 90
migrants 94–5, 167
Mill, J.S. 48, 49
Miller, David 158–9
minorities 10, 80–1, 82
Mitchell, K. 92
MNCs *see* multinational
    corporations
modernity 4, 6, 50, 149
Molotch, L. 92
moral agency 9, 65
moral philosophy 22–3, 48–9, 75–6
morality
    Bangladeshi community 168
    consequentialist
    cosmopolitanism 59
    dualistic concept of 49, 51
    erosion of moral authority 77
    intersubjectivity 55
    liberation philosophy 54
    market order 50
    Marx 52
    modern Western philosophy
        48–9
    norms 15
    ongoing human conduct 55

standards 46, 47, 55
universal 16, 17–18, 19, 20, 22–
    4, 26–7
    see also ethics; global ethic
Mouffe, C. 5
Muchlinski, P.T. 121
multiculturalism 6–7, 74, 78–9, 80,
    81
multinational corporations (MNCs)
    9, 18, 64, 67, 115, 121–37
    see also corporate citizenship;
    transnational corporations
Murdoch, I. 76
Murphy, John W. 8–9, 10, 11, 46–56
Muslims 26, 168
    see also Islam

Naidoo, K. 139
Nash, Kate 7–8, 9, 34–45, 168
nation 34–5, 37
nation-state model 1
    see also state
National Contact Points (NCPs)
    122–3, 124, 125, 129, 130,
    131
nationalism 7–8, 29, 34–6, 37–42,
    43, 145, 147
natural law 8, 16, 17, 21, 47, 48, 49
natural rights 17
NCPs *see* National Contact Points
Negri, A. 141, 142, 144–5, 146, 147,
    150
neo-colonialism 84, 166
neo-functionalism 5
neo-Kantianism 7, 34, 36, 43
neo-liberalism 6, 49–50, 89, 92, 138,
    148
neo-Marxism 6
networks
    Bangladeshi community 167, 168
    business 92
    friendship 4, 10–11, 93, 95, 96–
        102, 104
    global civil society 141, 145, 157
    suppliers 149
    see also sociality